ifications

Grammar, Structure, & Style

A Practical Guide to Advanced Level English Language

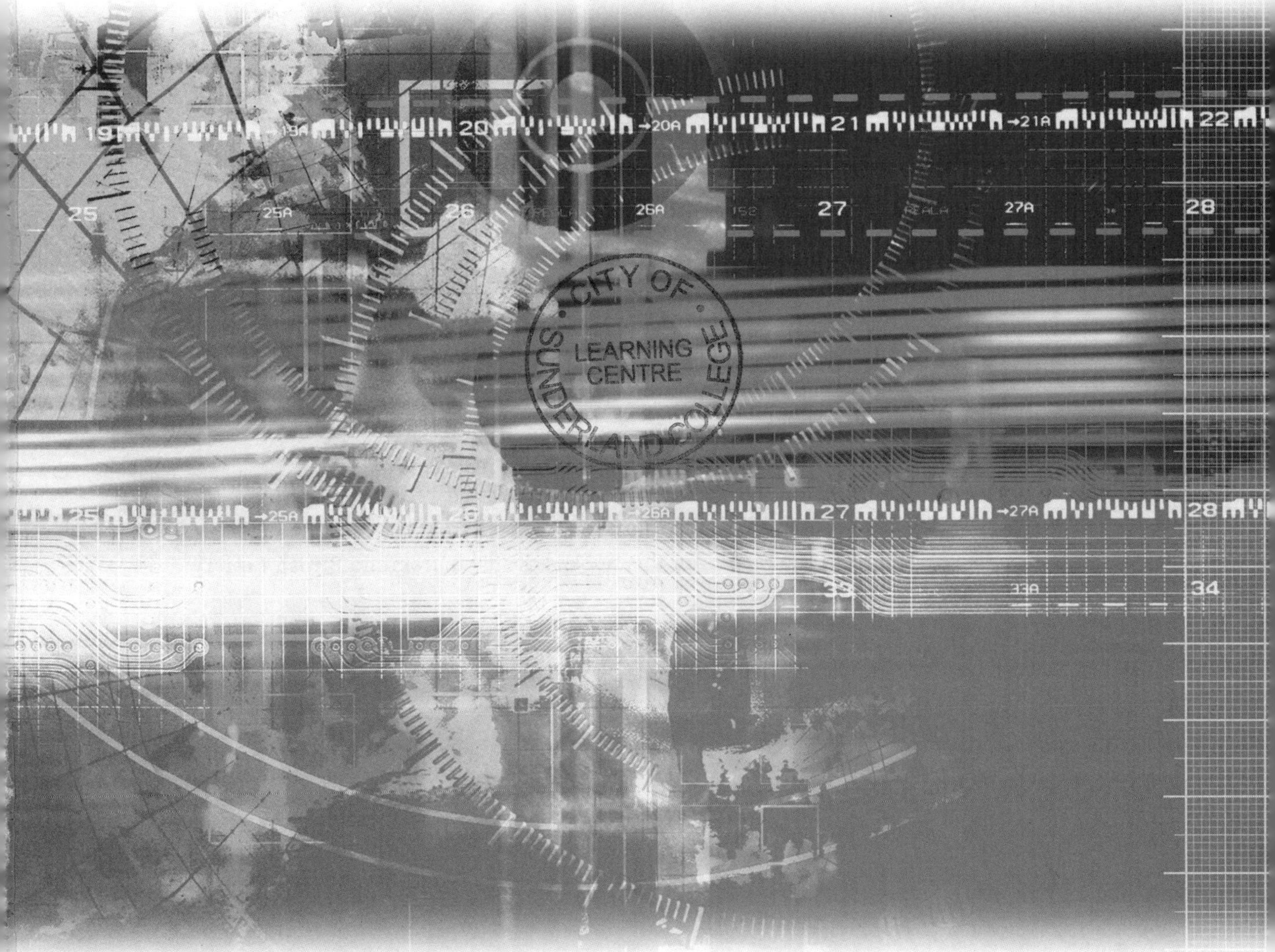

Shirley Russell

OXFORD

OXFORD
UNIVERSITY PRESS

Great Clarendon Street, Oxford OX2 6DP

Oxford University Press is a department of the University of Oxford. It furthers the University's objective of excellence in research, scholarship, and education by publishing worldwide in

Oxford New York
Auckland Cape Town Dar es Salaam Hong Kong Karachi
Kuala Lumpur Madrid Melbourne Mexico City Nairobi
New Delhi Shanghai Taipei Toronto

With offices in
Argentina Austria Brazil Chile Czech Republic France Greece
Guatemala Hungary Italy Japan Poland Portugal Singapore
South Korea Switzerland Thailand Turkey Ukraine Vietnam

Oxford is a registered trade mark of Oxford University Press in the UK and in certain other countries

First published 1993
Revised Edition published 2001
10 9 8

A CIP catalogue record for this book is available from the British Library

ISBN 978 0 19 831478 3

Typeset by AFS Image Setters Ltd, Glasgow

Printed in Great Britain by Bell & Bain Ltd, Glasgow

Contents

Acknowledgements	**iv**
Section A: The Structures of English	**1**
1 Language and Speech	**3**
Spoken English	3
Suprasegmental features of spoken English	21
The acquisition of language	30
Accent and dialect	47
2 Language and Grammar	**77**
The vocabulary of English	77
Grammar and syntax	95
Semantics	148
Section B: Language and the Social Context	**159**
3 Language and Society	**161**
The language of gender	161
The language of the media	168
The language of literature	195
4 Language Development	**219**
Historical change in language use	219
Current trends in language use	230
Section C: Analysis and Evaluation of Prose	**241**
5 Frameworks: Guidelines for the Analysis and Evaluation of Prose	**243**
6 Directed Writing	**251**
Approaching the tasks	251
Practice material	255
Directed writing practice	259
Index	**277**

Acknowledgements

The author and publisher are grateful to the following for permission to reprint copyright material:

Kingsley Amis: extract from *One Fat Englishman* (Victor Gollancz), reprinted by permission of The Orion Publishing Group Ltd.
Jason Barlow: extract from 'Porsche Majeure', first published in *GQ*, June 2000, © GQ/The Condé Nast Publications Ltd, reprinted by permission of The Condé Nast Publications Ltd.
Roland Barthes: extract from *Roland Barthes: Selected Writings* edited by Susan Sontag (Fontana, 1983), reprinted by permission of HarperCollins Publishers Ltd.
Albert Baugh and Thomas Cable: extracts from *A History of the English Language* (4e, 1993), copyright © 1993, reprinted by permission of Prentice-Hall, Inc, Upper Saddle River, NJ.
Steve Bell: 'If . . .' cartoon strip #1156 'Queen's Lecture on Population' first published in *The Guardian* (1985), copyright © Steve Bell, reprinted by permission of Steve Bell. All rights reserved.
Enid Blyton: extract from *The Castle of Adventure* (Macmillan Children's Books, 1994), reprinted by permission of the publishers.
Frank Bodmer: tables from *The Loom of Language* (George Allen & Unwin, an imprint of HarperCollins Publishers Ltd, 1987), reprinted by permission of the publishers.
David Burnley: extracts from *The History of the English Language* (Longman, 1992), copyright © Longman Group Ltd, reprinted by permission of Pearson Education Ltd.
Mary Byrne: prefix chart from *Eureka* (David & Charles, 1987), reprinted by permission of the publishers.
Wendy Cope: 'Men and Their Boring Arguments' from *Serious Concerns* (Faber, 1992), reprinted by permission of the publisher.
David Crystal: extracts from *Cambridge Encyclopedia of Language* (1987) and from *English Today* (1987/88), reprinted by permission of the publisher, Cambridge University Press; extracts from *Listen To Your Child: A Parent's Guide to Children's Language* (Penguin, 1986), copyright © David Crystal 1986, reprinted by permission of Penguin Books Ltd.
Roald Dahl: extract from *Charlie and the Chocolate Factory* (Penguin Books), copyright © Roald Dahl 1964, reprinted by permission of David Higham Associates.
Viv Edwards: extracts from *Language in a Black Community* (1986), reprinted by permission of the publishers, Multilingual Matters Ltd.
Helen Fielding: extract from *Bridget Jones's Diary* (Picador, 1996), reprinted by permission of Macmillan Publishers Ltd.
Ian Fleming: extract from *Doctor No* (Jonathan Cape, 1958), copyright © Glidrose Productions Ltd, 1958, reprinted by permission of Ian Fleming (Glidrose) Publications Ltd.
Alastair Forbes: extract from a review first published in *The Spectator*, reprinted by permission of the author.
Dennis Freeborn: extracts from *Old English to Standard English* (Macmillan, 1998), reprinted by permission of the author.
Richard Grant: extract from article first published in *Arena*, June 2000, reprinted by permission of *Arena*.
Ed Halliwell: extract from profile of Paul Smith first published in *FHM Collections*, Spring/Summer 2000, reprinted by permission of the author.
Martyn Harris: extract from 'The Story of English' first published in *New Society*, copyright © New Statesman 2000, reprinted by permission of New Statesman Ltd.
Russell Hoban: extract from *Riddley Walker* (Jonathan Cape), reprinted by permission of David Higham Associates Ltd.
Ted Hughes: 'Thistles' from *Wodwo* (Faber); 'The Thought Fox' and lines from 'Wind' from *The Hawk in the Rain* (Faber), reprinted by permission of the publisher.
Anthony Jones and Jeremy Mulford: extracts from *Children Using Language* (1971), copyright © National Association for Teaching of English (NATE) 1971, reprinted by permission of Oxford University Press.
T. W. Knight: table from *A Comprehensive English Course* (University of London Press, 1962), reprinted by permission of the RNIB, in accordance with the bequest of the author.
Tom Leonard: 'Unrelated Incidents – No. 3' from *Intimate Voices* (Galloping Dog Press), reprinted by permission of the author.
David Lodge: extract from *Nice Work* (originally published by Secker & Warburg, 1988) copyright © David Lodge 1988, reprinted by permission of The Random House Group Ltd.
George Orwell: extract from *Nineteen Eighty-Four* (Secker & Warburg, 1949), copyright © George Orwell 1949, reprinted by permission of A. M. Heath & Co Ltd on behalf of Bill Hamilton as the Literary Executor of the Estate of the late Sonia Brownell Orwell.
Samuel Pepys: extracts from *The Diary of Samuel Pepys* edited by Robert Latham and William Matthews, reprinted by permission of PFD on behalf of the Estates of Robert Latham and William Matthews and the Master, Fellows, and Scholars of Magdalene College, Cambridge.
Harold Pinter: extract from *The Dwarves* (Faber) and extract from 'The Dumb Waiter' from *Plays One* (Faber, 1999), reprinted by permission of the publisher.
John Price: 'Jason Prong meets the objectives' first published in *The Times Educational Supplement* (1985), reprinted by permission of the author.
Randolph Quirk: extract from *Use of English* (Longman, 1962), copyright © Longman Group Ltd, reprinted by permission of Pearson Education Ltd.
J. K. Rowling: extract from *Harry Potter and the Prisoner of Azkaban* (Bloomsbury, 1999), copyright © J. K. Rowling 1999, reprinted by permission of Christopher Little Literary Agency on behalf of the author.
Anthony Sampson: extract from 'London Hotels' first published in *The Observer*, reprinted by permission of PFD on behalf of Anthony Sampson.
Tom Stoppard: extract from *Professional Foul* (Faber, 1978), reprinted by permission of the publisher.
J. R. R. Tolkien: extract from *The Two Towers: Lord of the Rings* (HarperCollins Publishers Ltd, 1993), reprinted by permission of the publishers.
Robert L. Trask: extract from *Key Concepts In Language and Linguistics* (Routledge, 1999), reprinted by permission of ITPS Ltd.
Martyn Wakelin: extracts from *The Archaeology of English* (Batsford, 1988), reprinted by permission of the Chrysalis Picture Library.
Evelyn Waugh: extract from *Brideshead Revisited*, copyright © Evelyn Waugh 1945, reprinted by permission of PFD on behalf of the Estate of Evelyn Waugh.
David C. Webb: extract from a letter to *The Guardian*, reprinted by permission of the author.
John Wells: extract from 'Why Proper English is No Longer a Shore Thing' first published in *The Times*, 10.10.98, reprinted by permission of the author. The results of the survey have now been published in John Wells: *Longman Pronunciation Dictionary* (Pearson Education, 2000).
Sir Peregrine Worsthorne: extract from article first published in *The Spectator*, reprinted by permission of the author.
and also to:
Atlantic Syndication Partners for extracts from articles: 'Is E-mail Killing Literacy?' by Monica Porter, *The Daily Mail*, 26.10.99; and 'The Word-Wise Web' by Dermot Purgavie, 'Night & Day' magazine, *The Mail on Sunday*, 16.4.00.
Channel Four Television and **ENDEMOL Entertainment UK** for transcribed extract from *Big Brother*. Big Brother series produced by Bazal based on an original format by John de Mol Produkties and licensed by ENDEMOL Entertainment International.
Emap Elan Network for extracts from 'Editor's Letter' by Sally Brampton; from 'A Woman's Place is in the Wrong' by Suzanne Moore; and from 'Happy Eaters?' by Andrew Purvis; all from *Red*, June 2000.
General Domestic Applicances Limited for advertisement for Hotpoint Dishwasher.
The Guardian for extracts from articles: 'Sound Bites' first published in *Weekend Guardian*, 31.8.88, © The Guardian 1988; Third Leader, *The Guardian*, 16.9.80, © The Guardian 1980; 'The Quiet American Tiptoes Through' by Frank Keating, *The Guardian*, 27.6.00, © The Guardian 2000; 'The Joys of Text' by Richard Benson, first published in *The Guardian*, 3.6.00, © Richard Benson 2000; and 'Should We Simplify Spelling?' by Bill Keaney and Bill Lucas first published in Education Section, *The Guardian*, 20.10.92, © Bill Keaney & Bill Lucas, 1992.
Interbrew and Lowe Lintas Ltd for 'Bristol Bigheads' advertisement for Whitbread Trophy Bitter.
IPC Syndication for extract from 'Editor's Letter' by Terry Tavner from *Woman's Own*, 8.5.00, © Terry Tavner/Woman's Own/IPC Syndication.
Mirror Syndication International for extracts from articles: 'Pistol Pete's Whipping up a Storm' by John Cross, *The Daily Mirror*, 27.6.00; Editorial: 'Drive 'em down . . .', *The Daily Mirror*, 11.4.00; and Editorial: 'The Human Genome Project', *The Daily Mirror*, 30.6.00.
The National Magazine Company Ltd, courtesy of *Cosmopolitan* magazine for extract from 'Editor's Letter' by Mandi Norwood from *Cosmopolitan*, June 2000, © National Magazine Company 2000, and courtesy of *She* magazine for extract from 'Beauty Turns Over a New Leaf' by Nicola Moulton, *She*, June 2000, © National Magazine Company 2000.
News International Syndication for extracts from articles from *The Times*: 'On This Day, July 14 1837', *The Times*, 14.7.00: Editorial: 'Grace and Favour', *The Times*, 12.7.00; 'The Death of Liberalism' by Mary Ann Sieghart, *The Times*, 16.6.00; profile of Burt Bacharach, by Alan Jackson, *The Times Magazine*, 17.6.00; Editorial: 'Mapping the Genome', *The Times*, 23.6.00; 'The Genome General' by Ben MacIntyre, *The Times*, 23.6.00; 'You Are What You Smoke' by Jasper Gerard, *The Times*, 20.6.00; 'No Place for Hard Work' by Adam Sherwin, *The Times*, 7.6.00 – all items © Times Newspapers Ltd 2000; article on English language by Magnus Linklater, *The Times*, 3.8.00, © Magnus Linklater/Times Newspapers Ltd 2000; review of Gangster 1 by James Christopher, *The Times*, 8.6.00, © James Christopher/Times Newspapers Ltd 2000; leader, *Times Education Supplement*, 15.12.61, © Times Newspapers Ltd 1961; and cartoon 'Land of Hope and Gloree' by John Minnion, *The Times*, 18.7.00, © John Minnion/Times Newspapers Ltd 2000. For extracts from *The Sunday Times*: 'The Dwarfs are Off . . .' by Maurice Chittenden & Sue Reid, *The Sunday Times*, 18.6.00, © Times Newspapers Ltd 2000; and review of Gangster 1 by Brian Appleyard, *The Sunday Times*, 'Culture' section, 11.6.00, © Times Newspapers Ltd 2000; and for extract from *The Sun*: 'Booze is the Ruin of Britain' by Michael Lee, 11.5.00, © News International Newspapers Ltd 2000.
Telegraph Group Ltd for extract from Mandrake Column, *The Sunday Telegraph*, 14.7.85 and extract from 'Harry Potter and the Dyslexics' by Patience Thompson, *Daily Telegraph*, 22.9.99.
Volkswagen UK for advertisement for Volkswagen 'Golf'.
We have tried to trace and contact all copyright holders before publication. If notified the publishers will be pleased to rectify any errors or omissions at the earliest opportunity.

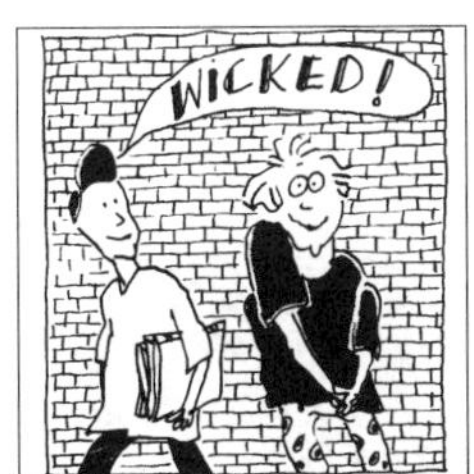

Section A:
The Structures of English

1 Language and Speech

Spoken English

Written versus spoken English

In educational circles, speech has always been considered less important than writing. The probable reasons for this include the following:

1. Teachers don't have to teach children to speak; they do have to teach them how to write, however, and so writing seems more valuable and more prestigious.
2. Higher education is largely delivered via textbooks, and its social importance adds prestige to the written language.
3. Great literature reaches most people in the form of books and lends its dignity and value to the written language.
4. Most spoken English is uttered 'off the cuff', spontaneously, and so it is less formal, less tidy, and grammatically less well structured than writing – and teachers in higher education dislike work that is untidy, disjointed, and ungrammatical.

This last reason for disparaging speech appeared only in the 1950s, when the introduction of the tape-recorder into academic life alerted us to what conversation really sounds like. As Hughes and Trudgill put it:

> When even highly educated people are chatting together with friends, their speech is very different from textbook conversations. They begin a sentence, then change their mind; they hesitate, then start again, differently; they muddle one grammatical structure with another. They omit various words, forget others, replacing them with *thingy* or *whatsit*; if necessary they will invent words just for the occasion. In a relaxed atmosphere they do not feel constrained to speak carefully, to plan what they are going to say . . .
>
> Hughes and Trudgill, *English Accents and Dialects*

This point is illustrated by the three-way conversation about the writing of dialogue that follows. The symbol (.) is used to indicate a micropause, where speakers pause very briefly.

> **T.D.** When writers try to err any good dramatist sets out to show how um people talk in ordinary in real life but it's interesting to see how they usually clean up the messy err aspects of talk when they start to actually um write it down (.) all the ums and errs the missing verbs and bits of bad grammar they all get tidied up and turned into correct English because as soon as you see them on paper they look terrible (.) they sound fine

because that's how we talk when we speak but they look terrible (.) we know the-the-the listeners would understand it but it um doesn't look (.) comprehensible in um writing just because it's um err-err it doesn't look well organized so writers always try to clean it up (.) or have done till recently anyway.

R.P. (*to* T.P) Do you do that?

T.P. Err well (.) the problem with writing um dialogue is (.) when (.) when I (.) first (.) start to write dialogue I err well I don't write it (.) that's the point I hear it at-at-at first in my head (.) and err (.) but then (.) the thing is that um you've got to err you've got to have it in a form (.) you've got to convey it to (.) it's got to be spoken by actors (.) and um (.) and you um if you gave actors something they couldn't read they wouldn't have anything (.) and err (.) most plays anyway are err are err published if you don't write it down an a if you don't tidy it up the publisher is err will do um (.) so what err (.) that's-that's what-what um what the what the playwright does is to um (.) is to write it down in a err (.) correctly if you like and err when the err (.) when the (.) what the cast (.) that's what actors are for they err they put all the speech err mannerisms back on into the um dialogue otherwise we wouldn't bother going to the theatre we'd just read the play instead if you see what I mean . . .

Activity

1 Clarify what T.P. has said by translating the speech into written English.

2 Explain what major difficulty you encountered in translating the speech into writing.

3 Discuss the differences between the sentence structures in the transcript and your written version of it. (The list of features of spoken English given in question 5, below, may help you to do this.)

4 Make your own recording of a spontaneous conversation between two or three people (it doesn't matter what it's about). Play it back a couple of times to get the general drift, then write it out *just as it is*. Use the following markers:

- **a** (.)(micropause), (1.0) (one-second pause), (2.0) (two-second pause), etc., to show where and for how long a speaker pauses;
- **b** a row of dots at the end of unfinished utterances to show they are incomplete;
- **c** *err* and *um* to indicate where speakers utter these filler sounds to give themselves time to think;
- **d** dashes to indicate repeated words or sounds, e.g. *err-err-err that-that.*

5 Look carefully at your transcript and see if it contains any of the following features:

- **a** unfinished sentences left to dangle in the air, e.g. *so I didn't . . . It was just that . . .*
- **b** interrupted constructions (sentences that are dropped half-way through in favour of another). e.g. *So I think that perhaps it's . . . What I'm trying to say is I think it's wrong.*

- **c** non-standard uses of grammar, e.g. *We was playing records; He done that riff I showed you.*
- **d** omissions (the leaving out of part of the sentence construction), e.g. *I'm trying to say I think it's wrong*, where the written construction would be *I'm trying to say* ***that*** *I think it's wrong.*
- **e** contractions, e.g. *don't, won't, can't, haven't, she's, they've, we'd.*
- **f** hesitation indicators such as *err* and *um*; repetitions of words, or filler sounds, e.g. *a-a-a-; the-the-the.*
- **g** informal language, e.g. the colloquial *bloke, guy, booze, great, stuff like that*, or slang such as *heavy, wicked, safe.*
- **h** fillers such as *sort of, you know, I mean.*

Talking point

Below are two passages of speech. One is an educated person reflecting on his academic experience, the other is spoken by the character Len in Harold Pinter's play *The Dwarves*. Read both extracts, then discuss how close Pinter's dialogue is to ordinary speech.

A He (.) seemed of course he had that kind of n err I-I'm err I-I err I-I err-err are you northern by any chance I was going to say that kind of northern (1.0) err (.) scepticism or at least questioning mind (1.0) which err (.) but of course he would mislead you with that he err he gave you the impression that he only err you know he gave you the impression that he was (.) sceptical and at times sceptical and nothing else (2.0) but I think he err (1.0) I think he appreciated the course there you know (.) from one or two things he said when I bumped into him.

B What you are, or appear to me to be, or appear to be to you, changes so quickly, so horrifyingly. I certainly can't keep up with it and I'm damn sure you can't either. But who you are I can't even begin to recognize, and sometimes I recognize it so wholly, so forcibly, I can't look, and how can I be certain of what I see? You have no number. Where am I to look, where am I to look, what is there to locate, so as to have some surety, to have some rest from this bloody racket? You're the sum of so many reflections. How many reflections? Is that what you consist of?

The Pinter extract is clearly more organized and rhythmic than ordinary speech. It has to be, for the sake of the audience. Would you want to sit through a play in which the characters expressed themselves like the speaker in A? As T.S. Eliot remarked, '. . . an identical spoken and written language would be practically intolerable. If we spoke as we write we should find no one to listen: and if we wrote as we speak we should find no one to read, The spoken and written language must not be too near together, as they must not be too far apart.'

In spite of appearances, then, spoken English is not just a looser, messier version of the written language. It is a different medium, with rules and conventions of its own – rules that speakers follow unconsciously, unaware of what they are doing. The most important of these are discussed below.

Activity

Read the passage below, adapted from Henry Sweet's *The Practical Study of Languages* in *The History of the English Language* by D. Burnley, then use it as the basis for a letter to the *Times Educational Supplement*, arguing that children should not be allowed to read the literature of a foreign language until they are masters of its speech.

> . . . most grammarians tacitly assume that the spoken is a mere corruption of the literary language. But the exact contrary is the case: it is the spoken which is the real source of the literary language. We may pick out the most far-fetched literary words and forms we can think of, but we shall always find they are derived from the colloquial speech of an earlier period. Even such forms as *thou hast, he hath,* were ordinary colloquialisms a few centuries ago, though they now survive only as fossil, dead colloquialisms, side by side with the living colloquialisms *you have, he has.* Every literary language is, in fact, a mixture of colloquialisms of different periods.
>
> Accordingly, it is now an axiom . . . of philology generally, that the real life of language is better seen in dialects and colloquial forms of speech than in highly developed literary languages . . .
>
> Important as this principle is from a scientific point of view, it is still more so from a practical one, and for the following reasons:
>
> If we compare the written and spoken language of a given period, we shall find that the literary language is full of superfluous words and phrases, which the spoken language nearly always gets rid of. Thus in the English spoken language the idea *sky* is expressed by this word only, while in the literary language it may also be expressed by *heaven, heavens, firmament* and *welkin.* So also the form *hath* was still used in literary prose in the last century in such phrases as *the author hath* . . . and it is still used in poetry and in the liturgical language of the Bible and Prayer-book, while in the spoken language the only form used is *has.* Again, nothing is more difficult than to give definite grammatical rules for the use of the subjunctive mood in literary English; in the spoken language the subjunctive is not used at all except in a few perfectly definite constructions, such as *if it were.*
>
> Again, in literature the context is often [so] vague [as to give no indication of the precise meaning of a word.] . . . In simple colloquial prose, on the other hand, the meaning of a word is generally quite clear from the context. The spoken language, too, is far stricter in its use of epithets: it hardly ever introduces an adjective or other qualifier except to convey some definite information . . . The spoken language also prefers a simple paratactic arrangement of sentences. The complicated periods of literary prose would, indeed, often be unintelligible in speech.
>
> We see then, that the advantage as regards clearness and definiteness is on the side of the spoken language: by starting from the spoken language we have less to learn, and we learn it accurately. Everything therefore points to the conclusion that in learning foreign languages we should follow the natural order in which we learn our own language: that is, that we should begin with learning the spoken language thoroughly, and then go on to the literary language.

Unconscious rules governing spoken English

Spoken English is often criticized for its disjointed and incomplete sentence constructions, and for its repeated use of 'filler' words such as *like, sort of, I mean, you know*, and *know what I mean*? Research, however, shows that speakers use both of these features in a highly patterned and rule-bound way.

Sentence structures peculiar to speech

How can disjointed sentence structures make meaning clearer for listeners, when in written English they have exactly the opposite effect? Consider the following pair:

a I'm very interested in irony – how to read it without becoming confused.
b I'm very interested in how to read irony without becoming confused.

Sentence (a) is clearly a disjointed sentence if measured against conventional written structures.

1 The second half of the sentence does not fit logically on to the first half: *how to read it* shows that the speaker is not interested in irony itself – only in the process of learning how to read it.
2 It does not fit grammatically, either. The first half of the sentence finishes with a noun, *irony*, and to be in proper apposition to it (that is, to match it in construction), the second half of the sentence should begin with another noun such as *technique*, not with the noun clause *how to read it*, e.g.:

I'm very interested in irony – a technique I find rather confusing.

According to Randolph Quirk, people use sentence structures like these a lot, both in real life and in plays that try to represent real conversation. He calls the technique of breaking apart the two halves of the sentence 'disjuncture', and points out that it has a very useful purpose: it foregrounds or draws attention to a certain item or items of information that readers might find hard to grasp in a longer, more conventionally flowing sentence. In a sentence like (a) above, *how to read it* stands out more clearly and makes a greater impact on the mind than it does in (b).

Quirk's research supports this idea. Students reading for English degrees at University College, London, were asked to assess which of the following versions of the same information they found easier to understand:

a He's doing research on the mineral resources of various parts of the Commonwealth – the procedures for assessing, the methods of surveying and the techniques for exploiting them.
b He's doing research on the procedures for assessing, the methods of surveying and the techniques for exploiting the mineral resources of various parts of the Commonwealth.

Interestingly, the group that were given sentence (a) absorbed on average sixty per cent of the information; the group given sentence (b) absorbed on average only forty per cent.

Speakers also use incomplete structures to foreground the most important items of information. Like the senders of telegrams (see the comments on 'glue' or structure words, page 137), they leave out any words that are not necessary for understanding and so concentrate listeners' attention on the ones that are. Writers of telegrams generally leave out prepositions, however: little grammatical words like *to*, *from*, *up*, *down*, *over*, *behind*, *across*, *on*, *in* and so on. *Send money Monaco Hotel Athens*, they write, not *Send money* ***to*** *me* ***at*** *the Monaco Hotel, Athens.*

Sports commentators in contrast use prepositions all the time, because they have to tell their listeners where people and things are in relation to one another:

Agassi ***to*** *Rafter*
the ball goes ***into*** *touch*
a good pass ***from*** *Beckham to Owen.*

They have to use adverbs also, to make their listeners see:

Davenport ***low*** *over the net.*

What we seldom find is subordinate adverbial clauses beginning with conjunctions like *when*, *where*, *because*, *unless*, etc. If commentators took the time to use lengthy subordinate clauses the next piece of action would be over before they could begin to describe it. And subordinate clauses would *sound* wrong in a sporting context, too: too *literary* as well as too leisurely. Raw physical effort is what commentators try to communicate, a world away from conventional written style. We do find a lot of phrases, however – both prepositional and adverbial.

A construction like *Beckham forward to Owen* shows perhaps the most common technique for shortening constructions – the leaving out of the verb. In conventional written English, *Beckham forward to Owen* would be written *Beckham* ***passes*** *forward to Owen.*

Speaking to interested and knowledgeable listeners drinking in every word, the commentator can foreground just the important items – player (*Beckham*), direction (*to*), and receiver (*Owen*). He doesn't have to mention passing because everybody understands that that is what's going on. Sometimes the adverb is left out too and we get the even simpler construction *Beckham to Fowler, Fowler to Owen . . .*

Verbs that commentators leave out very frequently are the *is* and *are* forms of the verb *to be*:

a as main verbs (*he is/they are*)
Fowler on the right wing now (instead of *Fowler* **is** *on the right wing now*)
b as auxiliaries helping to form the present continuous tense of another verb (*is/are moving*):
Ince moving towards goal now (instead of *Ince* **is** *moving towards goal now*).

The impersonal method of introducing a subject with the verb *to be* – *There is/are/was/will be*, etc. – is also ignored by commentators. They bring things into existence by simply mentioning them: *A tie-break of course if Henman evens the score with this one* (instead of **There will be** *a tie-break . . .*).

On the other hand, the verb *to be*, in the impersonal construction *it is*, (shortened to *it's*), is often used instead of the longer constructions used in writing: *It's Southgate now for England* rather than *Southgate* **is about to/is getting ready to take the penalty** *for England.*

Sometimes commentators leave out whole phrases and clauses by using prepositions in a way peculiar to themselves. In *Pip's Pride is showing good speed* ***from*** *Petardia* for example, *from* takes the place of a phrase such as *Pip's Pride is showing good speed* **in beating** *Petardia* or a clause such as *Pip's Pride is showing good speed* ***and is ahead of*** *Petardia.*

Even nouns, those vital content words, are sometimes dropped for the sake of speed: *There are still two to play* (instead of *There are still two* **holes** *to play*).

So are pronouns, together with linking *ands*: *Waqar comes in . . . bowls him!* Written conventionally, this would be *Waqar comes in,* **and he** *bowls him!*

Activity

1 Record two minutes of racing commentary from Radio 5. Make a written transcript of it.

2 Give examples of any of the following features you have found in your transcript.
- Use of present rather than past tense (to add drama, life, excitement)
- Heavy use of prepositions and adverbs (particularly the adverb *now*)
- Frequent use of prepositional and adverbial phrases
- Omission of verbs (particularly forms of the verb *to be*)
- Omission of pronouns
- Infrequent use of subordinate clauses
- Infrequent use of conjunctions such as *and.*

The role of fillers in speech

Fillers have a two-fold use in spoken English:

a They forge a friendly link between speakers and listeners. Quirk's students disliked the use of *you know* and *you see* from the style point of view, but found it *friendlier, more informal*, and so to be preferred in contexts where style was not important.

b They have several specific functions in a sentence; as David Crystal points out:

> they have a grammar of their own, being inserted at different places in the sentence according to the nature of the job they have to do.
>
> Thus, *you know* is often used:
>
> **1** at the beginning of a sentence, to soften the force of a statement: compare the abrupt *You should be more careful* with the more sympathetic *Y'know, you should be more careful.*
>
> **2** in the middle of a sentence, to introduce an explanation or illustration

of what has just been said: *He's just got a new BMX – you know, one of those tough little bikes . . .*
3 at the end of a sentence, as a kind of tag question to check that the listener has understood what is being said: *He's bought a BMX – you know?*
4 to mark the boundary between one topic and another: *you know, I've been thinking about that.*

Crystal, *English Today* magazine

Talking point Discuss the use of *you know* in the following two sentences.
John's bringing his – you know – flatmate.
She's left that bloke she was living with – you know.

You see and *I mean* are two other important fillers with specific speech functions, as Britt Erman has shown in her book *Pragmatic Expressions in English*. Her research reveals that English speakers use *you see*:

1 after a summarizing remark, or at the end of an explanation:
. . . and that's how the monkey got its tail, you see;
2 when someone is justifying a previous claim:
. . . so that's why I left, you see.

They use *I mean*, amongst other things, to clarify or justify something previously said: *I mean, how else could she have known?*

Where the prescriptive grammarian is irritated by such phrases, Crystal values them as 'facilitating mechanisms': for him they are:

> . . . the oil which helps us perform the complex task of spontaneous speech production and interaction smoothly and efficiently. They give the speaker an opportunity to check back, to plan ahead, and to obtain listener reaction, They give the listener an opportunity to keep up and to react.
>
> Crystal, *English Today* magazine

Conversation, or discourse interaction

 **Key words**
Speech-act: a unit of purposeful speech in a social context.
Discourse: a longer period of speech made up of individual speech-acts.

Principles underlying conversation

The kind of discourse we call conversation is paradoxical: it seems spontaneous and natural, yet it is governed by unspoken rules and conventions. Two main authorities have formulated these rules for our inspection, Grice and Lakoff.

Grice's rules of conversation

1 Quantity: Be as informative as required.
Be no more informative than required.
2 Quality: Say only what you believe to be true.
3 Relevance: Be relevant.
4 Manner: Be perspicuous.
Don't be ambiguous.
Don't be obscure.
Be succinct.

(quoted in Lakoff, *Papers from the 9th Regional Meeting of the Chicago Linguistic Society*, 1973)

Lakoff finds faults with these rules on three counts:

1 their difficulty of definition: what seems relevant, brief and clear to one speaker may strike another as obscure, verbose and off the point;
2 their promotion of boredom: if every speaker in every context followed Grice's rules, discourse would be insipid and dull. The elements that make ordinary conversation fun – exaggeration, jokes, deliberate mistaking of words, sarcasm and irony – are inappropriate in formal, structured discourse, just as the formally polite expression of the Committee Room would be out of place round a table in the pub, yet tiny elements of each are allowed to find their way into the other.
3 their failure to mention politeness, which Lakoff sees as almost the cardinal rule governing **discourse interaction** (the way we speak to one another).

Why are speakers allowed to violate Grice's rules without protest, for example? Because politeness allows communication to be maintained and confrontation would hinder it or bring it to an end (the whole idea of conversation is to keep the ball in play, passing it from player to player, rather than kick it into touch). The little formulae with which we introduce such violations prove that they are an accepted part of the game: Lakoff instances *By the way* and *As you know,* the first signalling the breaking of the rule of Manner, the second of Quantity. He sees politeness, therefore, as second only to the need to be clear.

Lakoff's rules for conversation

1 Be clear.
2 Be polite.
Politeness itself is then made to yield further rules:
a Don't impose. We have conventions that allow us to preserve a polite distance from our addressees:
i we ask permission to raise topics with them: *Do you mind my asking/saying . . .* (it's true that in asking if the addressee minds the question the speaker is already asking it, but it gives at least the impression of freedom of choice)
ii we use an impersonal mode of address, including sentences in the passive voice

- **iii** we use technical terms as far as possible, to avoid the emotional connotations that cluster round ordinary words. Lakoff, who is American, instances *copulation* rather than *making it.*

b Give options. Allow your addressee to make his or her own decisions; leave the options open. In other words, do not hint in your presentation of a subject how you feel your addressee should react.

c Make your addressee feel good – be friendly. Lakoff points out the difficulties that arise here. First names and verbal tags indicating intimacy – such as *Y'know, I mean, like* – are fine if the speaker using them is equal or superior to the addressee; if the speaker is of lower status, however, the addressee feels patronized or insulted.

There is in fact a pragmatic element to the politeness rule, as Lakoff points out. Use the formal address seen as polite under rule 2a in a situation where your addressee expects rule 2c to operate, for instance, and you will be thought rude.

Lakoff gives the further example of the 'conversational implicature': *It's cold in here* may or may not be a polite way of saying *Shut the window.* Under rule 2b, the request might be construed as polite, since it leaves the addressee's options open: he or she can choose to shut the window or not. A speaker superior in status to the addressee, however, will be taken as giving an order in an inappropriate way, and therefore guilty of a breach of politeness.

Conventions controlling discourse interaction

Introducing the topic

We cannot even begin to speak to people until we've checked that they are able and/or willing to give us their attention – usually by greeting them with their names, if known:

Peter, did you finish that essay?

or by introducing ourselves by our names, if not:

Hello! I'm [name], *your local Liberal Democrat candidate . . . Good morning!* [name] *speaking. I'm ringing about . . .*

We would be considered brusque and rude if we plunged straight in without such preliminaries.

In the same way, once introductions are over, the contributions each person makes to the conversation are governed by two over-arching principles: those of **politeness** and **co-operation**. We must be polite, or our addressees will not want to respond. We must co-operate with them, showing that we are listening by nods of the head or encouraging noises, helping them to repair breakdowns in their speech by seeking clarification of what we have failed to grasp, and uttering encouraging statements: *I see what you mean; Quite; Point taken*, and so on. If we do not, the mood may be judged hostile or cold at best, and communication may break down.

The main point for speakers to bear in mind is that conversation is not a competition – something that, in poet Wendy Cope's experience, some men appear to forget (some women do, too, of course).

> One man on his own can be quite good fun
> But don't go drinking with two –
> They'll probably have an argument
> And take no notice of you.
>
> What makes men so tedious
> Is the need to show off and compete.
> They'll bore you to death for hours and hours
> Before they'll admit defeat . . .
>
> ('Men and Their Boring Arguments' in *Serious Concerns*)

Opening a conversation

There are several conventional ways of opening a conversation:

a The request

Excuse me, but could you tell me something about the food here? Sarah, could you fill me in on what happened in the meeting this morning?

(Don't confuse requests like this with questions asking for some form of *yes* or *no* answer. The speakers aren't asking whether it's *possible* for their interlocutors to tell them these things – they know they can. They're requesting them to do it – a form of indirect command.)

b The question

Did you read my e-mail this morning, Alison? What do you think we should do?

c The offer

Shamin, I've just finished that book you recommended. It was good.

The speaker is 'offering' or volunteering a conversational topic here, showing that he or she wants to talk. Such offers are examples of the two-part conversational exchanges known technically as **adjacency pairs.** Greetings are normally met with greetings, questions with answers, offers with acceptances or refusals.

Failure to complete the second half of the exchange, breaking the adjacency pair, can be put down to the addressee's wish to annoy, tease, frustrate, or show hostility towards the speaker.

Once the conversation has been started, further conventions come into play.

Turn-taking

1. Listeners know when a speaker is coming to the end of an utterance because they hear the voice begin to fall.
2. Often the person who is speaking decides who shall be given the next turn. He or she shows this by such devices as

a mentioning the person's name;
b looking at the person enquiringly;
c talking about a subject that the person is known to be well briefed in.

(a) and (c) are often combined in a phrase, such as, *You've done a lot of work on this, Bob, haven't you?*

If the current speaker doesn't pick anyone out, the next turn goes to whoever gets in first, or manages to shout everybody else down. If nobody offers to say anything after the current speaker has finished, after a moment or two of silence he or she is free to speak again.

Skilled conversationalists know the rules of turn-taking so well that they can break them without damage. They can gauge exactly how much and at what point they can begin to speak over another person's utterance without ruining the conversation or antagonizing the person. This usually happens when the listener can see where the speaker's idea is leading and chimes in either to say the same thing or contradict. Alternatively, the listener may simply be anticipating the end of the sentence and wants to break in quickly without giving anyone else a chance. Interruptions of this kind have to be handled sensitively, or the interrupter will be seen to be self-centred, boorish and rude.

Running repairs

If two people find they are speaking simultaneously, one or both usually take steps to repair the breach of convention. Alternative strategies include the following:

- halting in the middle of a sentence
- apologizing
- inviting the other person to go ahead by a formula like *Please,* or *After you* or *Go ahead*
- the uttering of a phrase such as *I haven't finished yet*
- or, less politely, overriding the other speaker by carrying on talking in a loud voice.

Relevance

When new speakers take up their turns, convention demands that what they say shall be relevant to what has previously been said. New topics cannot be opened up until properly introduced.

Introducing a new topic

When they want to introduce a new topic, speakers use conventional signalling phrases like *incidentally; by the way; apropos of what we've just been talking about; that reminds me; well, I think we ought to move on to another point; is there anything else you'd like to bring up?* etc.

Repairing breakdowns in communication

When speakers find themselves at a loss for words, or when they have uttered something which is obscure or misleading or simply not what they meant to say, they have to repair the resulting breakdown. They try to do this as quickly as possible, before their addressees can point out the fault: *No, that's not quite what I mean,* or *I'm sorry, what I'm trying to say is . . .* and so on. It is also legitimate to try to help other people in this situation with formulae like *I think what you mean is . . .* or *Is what you're trying to say . . . ?* If the speaker has really ground to a halt and is lost for words, someone might offer to pick up the point: *I think what Blank is trying to say is that . . .*

Positive feedback

Positive feedback (technically, *back-channel feedback*) is the term for the signals that listeners send to speakers to assure them that attention is being paid and their message is getting through. These signals can range from non-verbal noises, through one-word responses (*Quite*, *Really?*) to short questions. (Requests for clarification of a point can be included under this heading.)

a Encouraging phrases

Really? You don't say! No! How interesting. I know.

b Non-verbal signs

Uh huh, Mmm, plus a wide range of expressive noises.

c Paralinguistic features

Changing facial expressions, head tilts, shakes and nods, etc.

In the same way, speakers have mechanisms for checking that people are listening to them:

- They try to make eye contact with their listeners, changing their position if necessary to do so.
- They look enquiringly at their listeners and check on their facial expressions.
- They try to keep their listeners involved by using phrases like *you know?, right?* and *do you see/know what I mean?*
- They use gestures and changing facial expressions to hold their listeners' attention; research shows that something of this kind occurs at five- to seven-second intervals in conversation between adults.

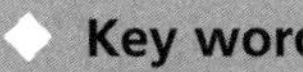

Key words
Paralinguistic features: the range of gestures, facial expressions, and tones of voice that accompany conversation. *Body language* is the popular name for unspoken paralinguistic features.

Closing a conversation

Unspoken rules also govern how we close a conversation. To get up abruptly and walk away without a word would signal anger and/or dislike. We soften the break by signalling our intention to leave several moments before we actually go. Mechanisms include:

Body language

Shifting from one foot to the other and half turning away if we're standing up; shifting about in our chair and/or moving forward on to the edge of the seat if we're sitting down; starting to collect books or bags or other belongings together, etc.

Conventional phrases

Well, it's been lovely talking to you; Oh well, can't stand here all day, I suppose; I've really enjoyed our chat, we must get together again soon/meet for lunch, etc.; *Well, if there's no other business I think we can call it a day*, etc.

Discourse interaction illustrated

Consider the following (fictional) dialogue between a radio presenter, P (young, trendy, cool) and a member of the public (M). The presenter asks his listeners why we extend greater tolerance to badly behaved media stars than to ordinary people, and kickstarts the discussion with an opinion of his own.

use of 'we' builds pseudo-personal relationship with listeners

subject formally introduced

P: So why do we let people off the hook when they're famous? Why is it 'Oh I see old Mick Jagger's been at it again' and 'Disgusting at his age isn't it?' when it's somebody down the street? I'll tell you why it is, it's because we identify with them, we feed off them and we put them on a pedestal, we want them to succeed and so maybe that's part of the reason why we seem more tolerant to them. Or are we? Mike in Doncaster's on the line. Morning to you Mike.

leaves options open for audience

adjacency pair: greeting

M: Good morning Alan, how are you?

adjacency pair: offer & acceptance

P: I'm very well. What's your point?

M: The point I want to make is I actually run a Youth Club and er er in my own little circle I'm a bit of a role model with the children I work with, and what happens I find when the children see me involving myself with leading all these activities they want to emulate me. I feel I have a big responsibility to give off the right and positive messages to these children, and likewise you know these stars that are in these high profile positions you know should take on responsibilities and send off the right messages to their fans instead of taking drugs and and getting drunk and abusing people, all these kinds of things you know, it's

point about responsibility well & economically made (quantity rule)

claiming common ground & seeking feedback

just despicable as far as I'm concerned, I can't understand why they do it . . .

P: So what do you want, Mike? You want your female celebs to be like Julie Andrews and your male celebs to be like Cliff Richard? Pure as the driven snow and blameless in every way?

M: No no no, you see you're not taking this seriously Alan, I've heard you do this before, you do this all the time on your programme, that's why you have all these jingles and terrible music –

P: Welcome to the 21st century, Mike.

M: No, the point I'm trying to make is that moral standards are declining and what I'm trying to do like a voice in the wilderness and I'm sure there's loads of other people out there who think like me is raise moral standards. These media stars are privileged people you know and they're just abusing their position . . .

P: I take your point, Mike, it's a good one and I don't mean to trivialize it but what I'm trying to suggest to you is that for good or ill we do seem to rather like the cheeky chappie who thumbs his nose at the kind of morality you're talking about, don't we? – the Oliver Reeds, the George Bests, the Jimmy Whites . . .

M: Yes yes yes yes, that's just it, that's just what we're doing, we're actually encouraging people like that to go on doing it and then the next generation of celebs will say well they got away with it, I'll do the same. You know we – we're – it's – by raising their profile we're lowering the morality that I'm so passionately concerned with and –

P: What about when we see pictures of celebs looking in rather a bad way – is that a good thing or a bad thing? Isn't that going to turn the fans off? Surely they'll look at that and say I'm never going to take drugs if you end up like that?

M: Okay, okay, and what will happen after? You're in the media Alan, you know. They'll be more famous than ever and end up on television or something . . .

P: That's the whole point, what Mike's just said, they may be on Charlie now but soon they'll be on Richard and Judy. I've got to cut you off in your prime now Mike because we're running out of time, but thanks for sharing those thoughts with us. And now the travel with Vanessa.

robs M. of options by pushing him onto defensive (breach of politeness rule)

M. repairs politeness principle by refusing to be nettled

'repairs' what he sees as faulty reception of his point

has made this point already so breaches Grice's manner rule: 'be succinct'

repairs conversational breach by reassuring him of good intentions

polite, reassuring him he understands – observes politeness & friendliness rules

leaves options open again

both now working co-operatively, obeying rules

breach of succinctness rule

shows skill in knowing how & when to break in

concedes M.'s point & expands on it – the in-group he's addressing now is made up of sensible, responsible people who dislike excesses

polite dismissal

Children's versus adult conversation

Children pick up the unspoken rules of conversation much as they learn to talk – by listening to adults and imitating them. Before they have had time to learn, however, they can be awkward conversational partners for adults used to observing the rules.

Children will do any or all of the following when they talk to other people:

- plunge straight into a conversation with a statement (instead of the conventional request or question or offer): *I've got new shoes*.
- fail to give the person to whom they are talking his or her turn to speak, for instance by asking two questions in a row, or by cutting across what somebody else is saying: *Are you washing your car?* [no pause for answer] *Is it a new one?*
- fail to give positive feedback; they will just stand there, staring;
- fail to involve their listeners by using questions like *you know?*, gesture, etc.
- fail to soften the ending of a conversation by the use of conventional mechanisms; they just walk away.

Activity

1. Find a child aged between three and five (visit the local playgroup if you don't have one in your family circle) and record or note down the conversation he or she has with an adult or teenager.
2. Make notes also on any paralinguistic features noticed. Does the child use gesture, facial expression, and so on?
3. Make a transcript of your recording or write out your notes in full.
4. Discuss any ways in which the child's conversation breaks the rules of adult conversation.

Note: the kind of role-models a child has is an important factor in developing conversational skills. The child of self-confident, articulate parents has an inbuilt advantage here.

Male and female conversation

> Men and women use much the same grammar and vocabulary in English, although each sex uses certain kinds of words and structures more frequently than the other. Most men, for instance, use more swear-words than most women, whilst far more women than men use such emotive adjectives as *super* and *lovely*, exclamations such as *Goodness me!* and *Oh dear!*, and intensifiers such as *so* and *such* (e.g. *It was so busy*).
>
> Crystal, *The Cambridge Encyclopedia of Language*

Greater differences emerge, however, when we look at the way in which men and women operate in male–female conversation.

Pamela Fishman claims that, just as women do all the chores around the house, so they do all the chores – the 'shitwork' – in mixed-sex conversation.

After listening to fifty-two hours of taped talk between men and women, she came to the conclusion that women made all the effort and that men joined in only when 'offered' a topic that interested them – after which they would take control and do all the talking. Her thesis is supported by Spender's transcript of a conversation at a social gathering:

> Female: Did he have the papers ready for you?
> Male: Mmm.
> Female: And were they all right . . . was anything missing?
> Male: Not that I could see.
> Female: Well, that must have been a relief, anyway . . .
> Female: I suppose everything went well after that?
> Male: Almost.
> Female: Oh. Was there something else?
> Male: Yes, actually.
> Female: It wasn't X . . . was it? . . . He didn't let you down again?
> Male: I'd say he did.
> Female: He really is irresponsible, you know, you should get . . .
> Male: I'm going to do something about it. It was just about the last straw today. How many times do you think that makes this week?
>
> Spender, *Man-Made Language*

Notice how the woman spends all her time talking about matters that relate to the man, and how he resists all her efforts to draw him out until he chooses to respond – after which he interrupts her in mid-sentence and then proceeds to dominate the conversation.

Women restrict their own opportunities for expression, Fishman argues, by concentrating on the development of male topics. They are required to be 'linguistically available' to men, to listen to them and to keep the conversation going. Women who go against this convention by holding their own in conversations with men are made to suffer for it:

> Women who consistently and successfully control interactions are criticized by men and are likely to be called 'bitchy', 'domineering' or 'aggressive'.
>
> Fishman, quoted in Spender, *Man-Made Language*

In case you should think this is merely female prejudice, Crystal reports that

> Women have been found to ask more questions, make more use of positive and encouraging 'noises' (such as *mhm*), use a wider intonational range and a more marked rhythmic stress, and make greater use of the pronouns *you* and *we*. By contrast, men are much more likely to interrupt (more than three times as much in some studies) to dispute what has been said, to ignore or respond poorly to what has been said, to introduce more new topics into the conversation, and to make more declarations of fact or opinion.

Most interpretations of these differences refer to the contrasting social roles of the sexes in modern society. Men are seen to reflect in their conversational dominance the power they have traditionally received from society; women, likewise, exercise the supporting role that they have been taught to adopt – in this case, helping the conversation along and providing men with opportunities to express this dominance.

However, Crystal is prepared to see shades of grey where Fishman and Spender see only black and white. He points out that each sex can be found to adopt the other's linguistic practices in different contexts.

> Men do not always hog the conversation; women are not always content to encourage them and draw them out.
>
> The danger . . . is that in the process of criticizing old sexual stereotypes researchers are in danger of creating new ones.

Activity

Try to observe (as unobtrusively as possible) a mixed-sex conversation, and assess whether:

1 it supports what Fishman claims about
 a women contributing more speech-acts than men;
 b men making longer contributions than women;
 c men interrupting women more;
2 women
 a use more paralinguistic features than men;
 b give more positive feedback than men.

The relative values of spoken and written English

In theory, written English scores over spoken English in two ways:

1 it is more carefully constructed, formally punctuated and so more clear;
2 it is 'frozen' on the page and so can be read:
 a at the reader's own pace;
 b as many times as is necessary to grasp the meaning.

Before the invention of recorded sound it was also the only way of passing information on to people who were not there to hear you speak, to later generations and to people in other parts of the world.

In practice, spoken English is usually easier to understand, partly because it is usually accompanied by the features described immediately below.

Suprasegmental features of spoken English

 **Key words**

Suprasegmental features: communicative activities in conversation which accompany language, but which are not themselves part of language, e.g. stress, pitch, and intonation. (*Segmental features* are the actual segments of language – vowels and consonants. *Supra* means *above, beyond*.)

Compared with a piece of written English, spoken English seems muddled and unclear. In practice, however, speech is almost always more immediately understandable. Speakers can use meaningful looks, winks, smiles and frowns, discreet coughs, and disparaging sniffs to show what they're really thinking, but more importantly, they can use the suprasegmental features called *stress*, *rhythm*, and *intonation*. We can separate these features from one another in order to examine them, but in reality they are inextricably linked and work together to get their effects.

Stress

Stress is the pronunciation of one particular syllable of a word with slightly more force than the other(s). In the following examples this syllable is marked by the symbol ●.

Word stress

1 English words have one syllable which is naturally stressed more than others, e.g.:

brother garden happy

2 When prefixes and suffixes are added, the stress remains on the same syllable in many cases, e.g.:

happy unhappy happily

pretty prettier

3 Notice that some word families have a shifting stress pattern:

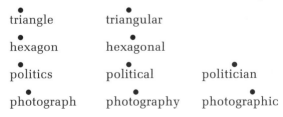

triangle triangular

hexagon hexagonal

politics political politician

photograph photography photographic

4 Generally speaking, English prefers the stress to fall close to the beginning of a word, either on the first syllable or, if that is a prefix, on the second.

Activity Write out the following words, and mark the accented syllable in each word by placing a large dot above it:

pencil big bigger biology biological

Changes in word stress

Words have a natural forward stress in English but there are two instances where the stress changes.

1 –*teen* words

When we count, or when there is a following noun, we stress the first syllable:

twelve thirteen fourteen fifteen sixteen

I've got nineteen hamsters.

However, when the number stands alone, we stress the *–teen*:

She's sixteen.

Turn to page seventeen.

2 Contrastive stress

When we want to correct what someone says or contrast our opinion with theirs, we can break the normal pattern by stressing the syllable that we think gives the correct information:

A: She was looking happy tonight.

B: She looked unhappy to me.

The fact that the accent in *unhappy* falls on the first rather than on the usual syllable shows the native English listener that the negative idea in *un* is the important one here.

Sentence stress

In a sentence, we normally stress *content words* such as nouns, verbs, adjectives, and adverbs more than the *structure* words that hold sentences together (words like articles, prepositions, and auxiliary verbs such as *was* and *had*.) Thus in the sentence

Sign here at the bottom of the document

the content words *sign*, *here*, *bottom*, and *document* are stressed, while the structure words *at the* and *of the* are not.

Contrastive stress may also be used, and a different sort of word stressed when we want to make a point:

I said in the cupboard, not on it!

Activity

To find out for yourself how different sentence stress can also indicate meaning, write out the following sentence three times, labelling the sentences (a), (b), and (c).

John could only see his wife from the door.

1. In sentence (a), mark the word that would be stressed if the speaker meant that John could not hear his wife from the door.
2. In sentence (b), mark the word that would be stressed if the speaker meant that John could not see the other person or persons in the room.
3. In sentence (c), mark the word that would be stressed if the only place John could see his wife from was the door.

Rhythm

Rhythm is created by our perception of prominent stresses in speech. English is said to be an *isochronous* or *stress-timed* language – that is, one in which stressed syllables are equally spaced in time, with the unstressed syllables reduced to fit between them. (Compare this with French, in which all syllables, stressed and unstressed, are equally spaced, thus giving a much more staccato rhythm.)

Because English speakers stress content or lexical words and leave structure or grammatical words unstressed, the same number of stresses can be found in sentences like the following:

•   •
He told his mother.

•   •
He sent it to his mother.

As Quirk points out, if these sentences were spoken by the same person under the same conditions, they would have the same number of stresses and take the same amount of time to say. *Sent it to his* would be said more quickly than *told his*, to make the intervals between the stresses roughly the same length.

Rhythm in speech is spontaneous and natural, whereas in some kinds of poetry there is a preconceived pattern. When a regular beat occurs in speech, the effect is oddly poetic. This example came from a conversation between friends:

Many a dish I've washed there, and many a bed I've made.

On the whole, however, rhythm plays only an incidental part in everyday communication. It has more to do in persuasive speech, in the language of advertising, and in poetry.

Intonation

> **◆ Key words**
> *Pitch*: the degree of highness or lowness in the voice, similar to the placing of different notes in music.
> *Intonation*: the rise and fall in the voice due to varying the pitch. When we describe an accent as 'sing-song', this is because we hear very clear rising and falling intonation patterns in it.
> *Tone units*: segments of spoken English, roughly corresponding to units of information.
> *The tonic syllable*: the syllable within a tone unit on which the strongest stress falls.
> *The onset*: the first prominent syllable in a tone unit; the voice begins to rise on the onset then rises further towards the tonic syllable.

Tone units

To clarify what *tone units* are, it may be useful to contrast the structure of spoken and written utterances.

Written English is made up of units with a clearly defined structure, called clauses and phrases:

> In reality [*phrase*] probably because he needed them so much [*dependent clause*] Lawrence hated women [*main clause*].

Punctuation is added, to make the connection or lack of connection between the units plain:

> In reality, probably because he needed them so much, Lawrence hated women.

Spoken English, on the other hand, is made up of groups of words with a less definite structure, called *tone units*. There are no punctuation marks to show where one tone unit ends and another begins; instead, they are separated by such things as brief pauses, obvious changes of pitch and/or loudness of voice, or the drawing out of the last sound in the unit.

Here, for example, is a short piece of spoken English. The boundaries of the tone units into which it can be divided are marked by vertical lines:

> Farmers | in Southern France | have lifted | their blockade of railway lines | which has stranded thousands | of passengers | on trains | and at stations. | Trains are now running again | twenty-four hours after groups | of farmers | erected | the barricades.

There may be several stresses in each tone unit, but one syllable always stands out more than the others – has *peak prominence* – because it is given a heavier stress. It is called the *tonic syllable*. The tonic syllables in the passage above are shown by ■.

The voice does not peak abruptly on this tonic syllable. The rise begins earlier in the tone unit, starting on a slightly less heavily stressed syllable, then rising with varying degrees of sharpness to a peak. (The stressed syllable on which the voice begins to rise is called the *onset*.)

Consider the following tone units, for example. The *onset* is shown by □ and the *tonic syllable* is shown by ■.

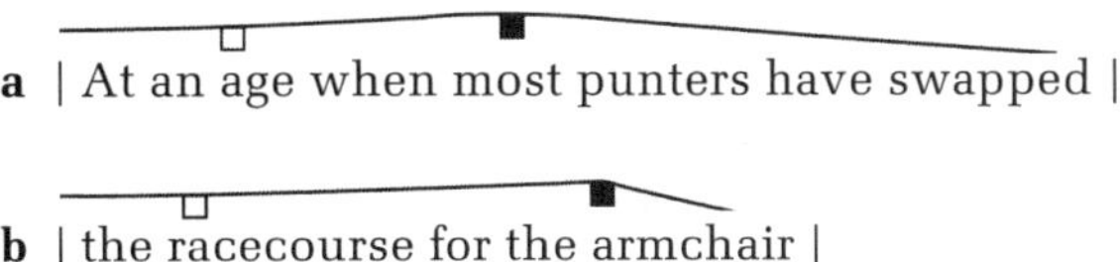

a | At an age when most punters have swapped |
b | the racecourse for the armchair |

Say (a) aloud and you should hear your voice begin to rise on *age*, then climb to a peak on *mo* before falling slightly to mid level on *have swapped*. Say (b) aloud and you should hear your voice rise on *race*, and go on climbing slightly until it reaches the tonic syllable, *arm*, before falling away to a much lower level.

The normal English intonation in a tone unit is therefore a rise followed by a fall.

Activity

for goodness' sake	for the time being	at the present moment
bread and butter	heaven and earth	collapse into a heap

1. Write out the above phrases, marking the tonic syllable. Then say them slowly and carefully to yourself and listen for the fall in pitch from the syllable you have marked as the tonic syllable – the one on which the stress is strongest, or most prominent. Mark it with a downward line.
2. If you think there is an *onset* – that is, a stressed syllable on which the voice begins to rise towards the *tonic syllable* – mark this syllable with □ and a line rising towards the tonic syllable.

Remember, the stressed syllable on which the rise begins is called the *onset*.

General patterns of intonation in English sentences

There are four intonation patterns in English speech:

1 falling, indicated by a downward arrow (↘);
2 rising, indicated by an upward arrow (↗);
3 rise–fall, indicated by a combination of the first two signs (⌒↘);
4 fall–rise, indicated by a combination of the first two signs (◡↗).

Falling intonation

Falling intonation is the most common in English, simply by default; it's the one speakers use when they have no reason for using any other. It might be described as the *neutral* tone.

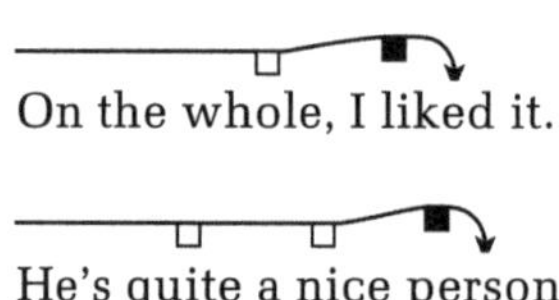

On the whole, I liked it.

He's quite a nice person.

The above examples show how English speakers drop their voices from high or medium pitch to low when they are coming to the end of what they have to say.

Since we spend a lot of time making simple factual statements like this, it is hardly surprising that the falling tone is so common in English speech.

By contrast, falling tones from a very high pitch can convey extreme exasperation coming to a head.

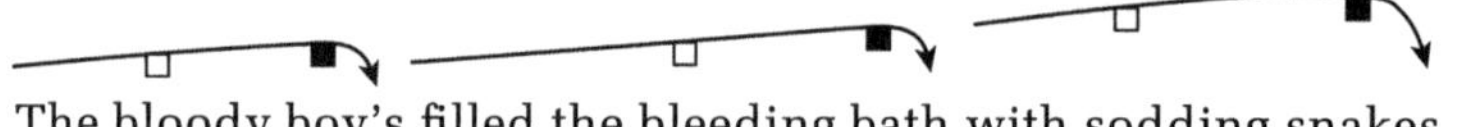

The bloody boy's filled the bleeding bath with sodding snakes.

On a more practical note, speakers drop their voice on the tonic syllable in most questions beginning with a *wh-* word:

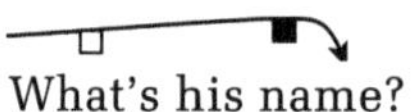

What's his name?

and in short responses to such questions:

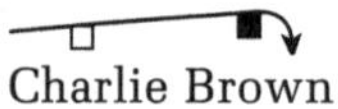

Charlie Brown.

Rising intonation

Rising intonation is the next most common intonation. Broadly speaking, it is used:

a to signal lack of finality; speakers are unsure of what they are saying and want to leave it open:

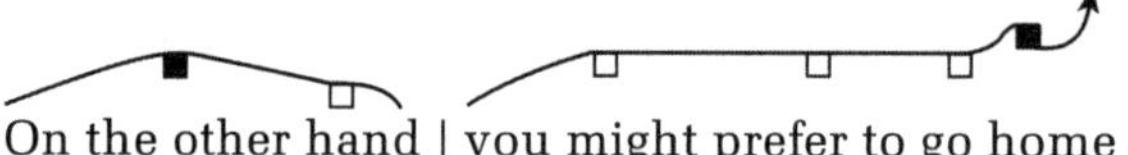

On the other hand | you might prefer to go home |

b to signal that speakers haven't finished all they've got to say:

We need to build more houses | we need to provide more jobs | . . .

c to ask declarative questions:

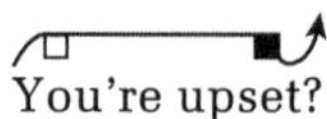

You're upset?

Rising and falling intonation

The next two intonations do not have such clear-cut uses as the ones just described, and individual speakers use them to express a variety of different meanings. Quirk discerns one or two patterns, however.

Rise–fall intonation

Quirk notes two main uses, both involving contrast:

1 To express an opinion contrary to the one uttered by a previous speaker:

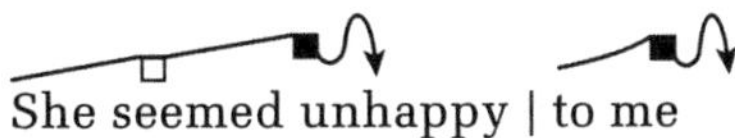

She seemed unhappy | to me

2 To express a contrast with something that has been said or implied in the previous sentence:

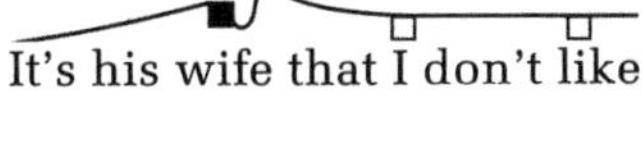

It's his wife that I don't like

It's his job that's worrying him

3 Knowles discerns a further use of the rise–fall: to hint at something instead of saying it outright, or to warn. Consider the following examples:

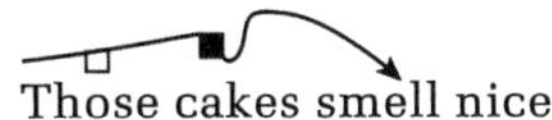

Those cakes smell nice

Uttered with a falling intonation only, this is a simple observation. Uttered with a rise–fall, it becomes a clear hint: 'I'd like one'.

Fall–rise intonation

1 The falling and rising intonation can be used to express doubt:

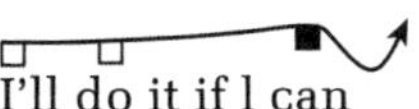

I'll do it if l can

2 It can also express a warning:

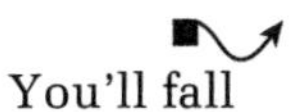

You'll fall

Uttered with a fall–rise intonation to a child doing something dangerous, this becomes an indirect command, 'Get off'; whereas uttered with a falling intonation it is a simple observation.

3 It is especially common on adverbs when they come at the beginning of sentences:

Hopefully, England will win.

Finally, we decided not to go.

Talking point

1 Which of the following is an invitation, which a command?

Come in   Come in

2 Which of the following versions of 'Goodbye' implies 'See you again', and which suggests the parting is final?

Goodbye   Goodbye

3 Which of the following shows genuine gratitude, which sarcasm?

Thank you   Thank you.

4 Which indicates that the play was quite good, which that it was mediocre?

It wasn't bad.   It wasn't bad.

Activity

1 Decide which of the tonic syllables in the following have a rising, and which a falling intonation.

If you like| I'll go with you

On the whole| I prefer to wait

You're not leaving already [disappointment, not surprise]

What's his name?

Please sit down [a persuasive request, not an order]

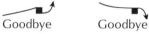

2 When you've decided, write down these sentences and indicate the rising intonations on the stressed syllable with this mark (↗), and the falling ones with this (↘).

Activity

1 Try to find or make a recording of someone
  a speaking emotionally about their country or their religion;
  b speaking angrily.
  Make a transcript of the recording.

2 Mark on your transcript every tonic syllable on which the intonation rises or falls. Do this by putting ■ above the tonic syllable, and an upward or downward facing arrow following it, like this: ■↗ ■↘

3 **a** Say the word *really* in such a way that you express the following attitudes:
  interest
  wondering surprise
  indifference
  anger
  cynical disbelief (a sort of 'who-do-you-think-you're-kidding' attitude)

b Draw lines to show the intonation for each pronunciation (the overall shape made by the rise and fall of the voice).

4 Listen to a newsreader reading one item of news. What level does his or her voice start on, what level does it go to in the middle, and on what level does it finish?

Tempo

Key words

Tempo: the speed or rate at which speech is delivered.

The rate at which speakers utter their words varies considerably. It depends on such factors as the amount of time available, the state of their emotions, the context in which they are speaking, and the audience they are speaking to.

Speakers tend to **speed up** their delivery when:

- time is running out;
- they are excited or enthusiastic about their subject;
- they fear someone will interrupt or disagree with them;
- they want to get an unpleasant item over with quickly;
- they realize they have made a gaffe or a mistake or have expressed themselves confusingly and hurry on to a new topic in the hope that their listener(s) will either fail to notice or simply forget;
- they think of another, more interesting topic and get rid of the old one as quickly as possible;
- they realize they've been droning on at a boring rate and overcompensate by then going too fast.

Speakers tend to **slow down** their delivery when:

- they have a captive audience and no time constraints;
- the occasion is a solemn one;
- they are trying very hard to find exactly the right way of expressing their meaning;
- they want to impress their listeners with their importance.

Suprasegmental features of speech in written English

Written English may be better organized than speech, but it is not so warm, so vivid, or so immediate. To compensate for this, writers try to indicate effects of stress, pitch, intonation, loudness, rhythm, and tempo in their work. The headlines of tabloids like *The Sun* and *The Mirror* are often referred to as 'screaming'. Their large, bold capitals are the written equivalent of someone speaking at the top of his or her voice. They resort to capitals too to indicate stress:

The Sun says 'Let them go NOW!'

It is novelists who try hardest to capture the living quality of speech. They usually resort to italics to show stress:

> 'A large girl like you must wear clothes that *fit*; and Elfine, *whatever* you do, always wear court shoes.'
>
> Stella Gibbons, *Cold Comfort Farm*

Pitch, loudness, and timbre of voice are indicated by appropriate verbs and adverbs. Low pitch is conveyed by verbs like *growled, muttered, mumbled, dropped his voice half an octave, his voice sank to a whisper, he spoke in a low murmur/muffled whisper*, etc.; mid pitch by phrases like *said evenly/ levelly, spoke in even tones*; high pitch by verbs like *cried, screamed, shrieked, shouted*, and by phrases like *spoke in rising tones*. Whether these devices add life and force or simply slow down the narrative depends upon the skill of the writer. At best, they seem contrived and clumsy when measured against the flow of living speech.

Summary

Spoken English is not an inferior version of written English but a different, parallel form. When we speak to one another we communicate as much through suprasegmental features as through the actual words we use. *Stress* is the most central of these suprasegmental features for the following reasons:

- it is perceived as a sequence of regular beats and therefore is the basis of *rhythm*;
- it requires some syllables to be pronounced with greater energy than others and consequently leads to changes in intonation.

Activity

1 To shape your thinking about the different qualities of speech and writing, discuss in pairs how you would prefer to learn a new subject – by correspondence course or by personal contact with a tutor. Explain your reasons.

2 Look again at the transcript of speech on pages 3–4. In the light of what you have read in this section, explain why it would be easier to understand when listened to than when read.

The acquisition of language

(The illustrations and quotations from other authors in this section are drawn from *Children's Language and Learning*, by J. Wells Lindfors.)

The two most striking facts about learning to speak are that

1 it takes place at a time when our cognitive faculties are barely developed;
2 it cannot be hurried or taught.

If children can't manage other complex systems like maths at this stage, how can they master the complexities of language, and in so short a time?

An outline of speech development

0–8 weeks

Babies start the process of learning to speak the moment they enter the world. They begin to cry and make little sounds referred to as *vegetative noises*, and this exercises the vocal organs and gives them practice in controlling the flow of air through mouth and nose – preliminary steps towards speech. Crying with lips stretched back and mouth wide open produces something that sounds like the vowel *a* (say *ant* and you'll see what I mean); smacking the lips together produces noises that sound rather like the consonants *p* and *b*. So, at a very early stage of their lives, babies have taken the first steps on the road to speech.

8–20 weeks

Fortunately, babies don't just cry. They make quieter, lower-pitched, and more musical sounds called *cooing*, too, from roughly eight weeks of age. Cooing gives rise to a wider range of vowel and consonant-like sounds – *u*s, *k*s and *g*s, for example, the *ch* sound as in *loch*, and even a sophisticated rolled *r* sound like the one used in French and German. Somewhere between two and five months babies start stringing these sounds together into sequences like *kuu* and *guu* – the characteristic 'cooing' sound.

So, during their first five months of life, babies use some of the sounds found in speech and vary the pitch and loudness of their voices. The noises that they make do not yet sound like speech, however. Two of the most important features of normal speech – intonation and rhythm – are still missing. Babies stop for breath at random intervals, and so their cooing lacks the normal rising and falling tones and stress-timed rhythm of adult speech.

20–30 weeks

Over the next two and a half months the babies' vocal organs develop and they begin to try out new positions for their tongues. Friction sounds like *fff* emerge, and the trilled *r* that sounds like a 'raspberry'. Sounds begin to be combined into longer sequences (the first signs of *babbling*) and long glides from high to low pitch are heard, but adult intonation and rhythm are still missing and speech is still a long way off.

25–50 weeks

At roughly six months, babies begin *babbling* – stringing together long sequences of repeated sounds such as *bababab, dadadada*. From about nine months more varied patterns of babbling (*variegated babbling*) are heard, in which consonants and vowels change from one syllable to the next: *ada*, *maba*, and so on. *S* and *sh* sounds begin to emerge for the first time. The babble is jerky and erratic. Some segments will be loud, some soft; some high in pitch, others low. Speed too may vary from very fast to quite slow.

36–72 weeks

At about nine months comes a very significant change. The suprasegmental features of melody and rhythm – the things that make speech sound fluent and natural – occasionally make themselves heard. A phrase with a definite melodic shape emerges from a welter of meaningless babble, and parents are sure that the baby has spoken its first word. In reality it is still just practising its sounds, and the first word is still some way away.

By the end of this period, the characteristic melodic shape (or *tones*) of questions, exclamations, greeting, and naming can all be heard in the child's speech, but it is still quite meaningless. In Crystal's words, 'it has got "its act together", but it has yet to learn what the act is for'.

Nevertheless, the emergence of rhythm and intonation in children's speech is the first sign that real language will soon be heard. Up to this point, all babies, whatever their nationality, have gone through the same stages of development and have sounded much the same. Now, thanks to rhythm and intonation (rhythm, you will remember, arises from the perception of stress), they begin to sound increasingly different from one another. The babbling of English babies can be described as *tum-ti-tum*, that of French infants as *rat-a-tat*, whilst the utterances of Chinese children have a more sing-song quality.

Somewhere around 52 weeks of age, short utterances of one or two syllables begin to be heard. These are called *proto-words*. Because they are uttered with the rhythm and intonation of normal speech they sound deceptively like real words, but they are not. As far as the babies are concerned, the sounds mean nothing, and real words – language – must have meaning.

Chomsky's Innatist theory

According to Noam Chomsky, children learn language easily because the brain is pre-programmed – wired up for language acquisition in the womb. In some mysterious and unspecified way, all human babies, simply by virtue of being human, 'know' what kind of a system language is, and 'understand' the universal principles on which it operates – all unconsciously, of course. All they have to do when exposed to their own particular language, therefore, is discover how these universal principles operate in it. They don't have to learn that strings of sound can be combined into words, for instance; only what particular sequences of sound are the ones used in their society.

Support for Chomsky came from Dan Isaac Slobin, who pointed out that both anatomically, through the specialized development of our oral and respiratory sytems, and neurologically, through the direct linking of these organs to Broca's and Wernicke's areas of the brain, human beings are 'specifically adapted to produce and process temporal sequences of distinct speech sounds' – i.e. talk. (Chimps and monkeys are not so adapted: chimps lack the necessary vocal equipment, and the equivalent areas of the monkey brain are detailed to control the workings of the hands, feet and tail.)

Skinner's Behavourist theory

Chomsky's theory was evolved in opposition to B.F. Skinner, who claimed that children learn to speak in the same way as they learn anything else: by reinforcement from the environment. (In the case of language learning, 'the environment' presumably includes the parents.) Children are born with a general learning potential which is shaped, in the case of language, by positive and negative feedback (rewards and punishment from their parents). Positive feedback for the child's simple early responses is given for a short time, then dropped in favour of increasingly sophisticated responses, until eventually the child's language comes to match that of its parents.

Difficulties were found in both these theories. If Skinner is right and response to the environment is the key, how do children born into impoverished surroundings acquire language as easily as more fortunate ones? How do mentally handicapped children learn language at all? Parental reinforcement didn't seem to be the key factor either, since observation shows that:

- **a** most parents correct for politeness and truthfulness of content, rather than for grammar;
- **b** parental corrections of grammar don't work in any case: children have to learn at their own pace. They can't be hurried into applying a rule until they've reached the stage where they're ready to do so. Witness the frustrations of the parent below (who might have been better occupied in assuring the child that she *was* liked.)

Child: Nobody don't like me.

Mother: No, say 'nobody likes me'.

Child: Nobody don't like me.

Mother: (*After eight more tries*) No, now listen carefully, say 'nobody likes me'.

Child: Oh! Nobody don't likes me.

(McNeil in *The Genesis of Language*, MIT Press, 1966)

Chomsky's theory was much more acceptable, but had one major stumbling block: if rules are built in, how are we to account for children applying a rule, then forgetting it, then applying it again at different stages of language development? No one questioned the existence of some kind of innate capacity for language, but no one was clear what the nature of it was.

From content to process

Since then, direct and intensive study of children learning language in natural settings has suggested that the innate capacity is nothing more mysterious than a specialized ability of the brain to work out the rules of the language it is exposed to. Slobin contrasts this 'process approach' with the 'content' approach of Chomsky.

> It seems to me that the child is born not with a set of linguistic categories but with some sort of process mechanism – a set of procedures and inference rules, if you will – that he uses to process linguistic data. These mechanisms are such that, applying them to the input data, the child ends up with something which is a member of the class of human languages. The linguistic universals, then, are the *result* of an innate cognitive competence rather than the content of such a competence.
>
> (in *The Genesis of Language*, 1966)

The Interactionist theory

The latest theories about language acquisition accept children's innate capacity for inference, but link it to their interaction with their physical and social environment. As Genishi and Dyson (1984) point out, 'every instance of language the child encounters is contextualized – that is, it occurs in some real situation for some real communicative purpose.' By listening to adult talk, children learn that language can help them to do a number of useful things. It can be:

- **a** **instrumental:** a means of getting them what they want or need;
- **b** **regulatory:** a means of controlling their own and other people's behaviour;
- **c** **interactional:** a means of socializing with other people;
- **d** **expressive:** a means of asserting their individuality and making their feelings understood;
- **e** **heuristic:** a means of learning things through *Why? What? Who?* and *Where?* questions;
- **f** **representational:** a means of conveying things about themselves to other people;
- **g** **creative:** a means of having fun by playing with words and making up stories.

Summary

Children:

1. listen to the sentences adults speak;
2. discern regular patterns in the language they hear;
3. deduce the rules governing language use from these patterns;
4. use these rules in the construction of new, totally original sentences of their own;
5. compare their structures with those of adults and revise any that reveal themselves to be wrong until
6. their speech matches that of the adults in their particular speech community.

Children, in other words, are now seen to be 'hypothesis makers, testers, and revisers', working always within an interactive environment.

The cognitive basis of speech

Children's ability to handle language depends upon their understanding of

a the physical environment;
b their relationship with that environment.

Once they have grasped the existence of separate, stable objects, they can proceed to the first step in language acquisition.

Nomination

The first words children speak are nouns, the names of things: *dolly, ball, Mummy, Daddy*. It takes them time to get all the names right, however, for reasons outlined in Eve Clark's 'semantic features' hypothesis. (E.V. Clark in *Cognitive Development and the Acquisition of Language*, ed. T. Moore, New York Academic Press, Inc., 1973).

Seeing, say, a dog for the first time, children pick out the feature that strikes them most about the creature – the fact that it has four legs – and, assuming that that is its definition, thereafter they call anything with four legs a dog. The same process is at work when anything round – e.g. clocks, gas meters and bathroom scales – becomes *moon*.)

Corrective feedback from adults allows them to add further, refining features to their original definition, until eventually their use of the word matches that of adults. (Jargon term: it *possesses the same bundles of semantic features* as the adult word.)

From physical to abstract

The progress of children's speech is always from the physical to the abstract: from simple content words like *cake, doggie* and *drink* to grammatical morphemes like the apostrophe *s*, which signifies the abstract concept of possession. Children get the *idea* of possession quite easily through seeing one thing in their environment constantly associated with another: *Mummy's shoes, Daddy's book*; but it is a long time before they can understand how it is signalled by that *s*.

Since the child is the centre of his or her own world, the language of personal deixis might seem easy for them to acquire. In fact, sorting out that they are *I* when other people constantly refer to them as *you* is difficult for them to handle, as is the fact that people who refer to themselves as *I* suddenly become *you* when it's the child's turn to speak. Some families avoid the problem altogether by referring to the child in the third person, by name:

Child: Donna want drink.
Father: Donna can have a drink in a minute.

The more remote and abstract deictic terms also give children problems: they quickly learn the temporal and locational terms that indicate things and events close to them – *here, near, this, that,* and *now* – but they have much more trouble with those more distant in space and time: *then, before* and *after, in front of* and *behind. Up* is learned later than *down,* and *bring* and *take* – signalling movement towards and away from them as speaker – may still be giving them trouble when they are six. Only the development of self-awareness, the concept of themselves as beings distinct from other people, allows children to solve the problem.

By the time their utterances extend beyond two words, however, most children are using *I* for the speaker role. (*Me* in the same place is grammatically incorrect, but an acceptable alternative at this early stage: e.g. *Me sitting down.*) A firm grasp of *I* also leads to the use of *me* and *my* to signal possession.

The acquisition of grammar: children's learning strategies

Children differ in the way they learn. Some use the **production strategy**, talking a lot and benefiting from the large amount of consequent feedback. Katherine Nelson gives the following example:

> Child: I sit down.
> Mother: Oh, you're sitting down?
> Child: I sit down with cup. I sitting. I sit here.
> Mother: Uh-huh. You're sitting down there.
> Child: Sit down there.

Notice how the mother extends her child's utterances into fully developed clauses, putting in the auxiliary in the clause *You're (You are) sitting down.* Notice too that the child's grasp of deictic language is still shaky: she uses *here* quite correctly, then changes it to *there* in imitation of her mother's usage. The child shows she understands the need for turn-taking, responding to her mother's promptings with pleasure and managing to take the change from *sit* to *sitting* on board at least once.

Others choose the **comprehension strategy**, preferring to observe more than talk, watching to see how words and meaning relate. These two methods, together with the **questioning strategy** – *What dis? What dat?* – produce a higher level of linguistic competence at the age of two than either the self-explanatory **imitation** or **repetition strategies.** But whichever method they choose to learn, they gradually acquire the structure words like *a, the, it, is, my* that fill the gap between content words like *Mummy, David,* and *car.* In doing so they escape from the limitations of the physical present – they can talk about what has happened in the past and what may happen in the future.

Speaking in sentences

If we are to assess the grammatical development of children's utterances, we need models with which to compare them. Since the majority of English sentences conform to the patterns given by Wells Lindfors, these would seem to provide us with the right criteria.

First, a little necessary grammar:

Grammarians divide the English sentence into two sections:

i the **subject** **ii** the **predicate** (what is predicated or said about the subject):

subject	*predicate*
grown-ups	drive

Since the subject is always a noun or pronoun, we call it a **noun phrase** (*NP*).

Since the predicate always contains a verb, we call it a **verb phrase** (*VP*).

NP	*VP*
Grown-ups	drive.

Four basic sentence patterns

We can distinguish four basic patterns of sentence:

1 a subject + the verb *to be* (*is, am, had been, was, will be,* etc.) + a complement:

NP	*VP*
Daddy	is gardening

(A complement complements, i.e. completes, a verb of incomplete predication – one that can't make a complete statement without the help of a complement.)

2 a subject + an intransitive verb + an optional adverb:

NP	*VP*	*adverb*
Daddy	has fallen	down

(Intransitive verbs are those that do not take an object.)

3 a subject + a transitive verb + an object + optional adverb:

NP	*VP*	*object*	*opt.adv.*
Daddy	has hurt	his knee	badly

4 a subject + a copulative verb + a complement:

NP	*VP*	*complement*	*opt.adv.*
The knee	seems	all right	now

(Copulative or linking verbs like *to be, look, seem, appear, become,* and *feel* are simply verbs that are incomplete without a complement.)

The adverb in sentence 3 presents young children with difficulty as they learn to use that particular part of speech at a fairly late stage of their development. Whereas nouns and adjectives relate quite obviously to things that can be touched and seen, adverbs denote abstract things such as relationships and degrees of intensity, which are difficult for the childish mind to grasp.

The last sentence form is obviously the most complex, and therefore the most difficult to handle. By the time children can use this pattern they will have largely mastered the main principles of grammar.

Activity

Measure the following utterances against the sentence forms above and explain what the child is as yet unable to do.

daddy garden	fall-down daddy	daddy hurt knee
garden daddy	all-gone train	daddy knee hurt

Sentence transformation

No sooner have children learned to handle the word order outlined in the sentence patterns above than they have to learn to reverse it for the following purposes:

a To give commands

The noun phrase moves to the end of the sentence and the verb phrase to the front.

Thus, the constructions

NP	*VP*
Daddy	strokes the dog
Daddy	does not stroke the dog

become

VP	*NP*
Stroke the dog,	Daddy.
Do not stroke the dog,	Daddy.

This is sometimes known as the 'flip-flop' reversal.

b To ask questions

The normal positions of noun/pronoun and verb are reversed:

I can't play	Why can't I play?
Daddy is in the garden	Where is Daddy?
Hester has two sweets.	Why has Hester got two sweets?

Children naturally confuse the two patterns and come up with hybrid utterances like

Why I can't play? Why Hester has two sweets? Where Daddy is?

Matters get even more complicated for the child when the verb itself seems to change from the normal singular form *am* to the plural form *are*:

I am playing   Why aren't I playing?

Faced with the double whammy of reversing word order and transforming the verb form, no wonder children are defeated early on and use the simple formula:

Why I no playing?

Checklist of features at different stages of language development

One-word utterances

The first stage is marked by one-word utterances, e.g. *Me, Here*. These stand for the longer sentences children are not yet capable of forming, such as: *Give it to me*; *I want it*; *Let me do it*; and *Put it down over here*.

At this stage, language is rooted in physical experience, and children's facial expression, body language and actions are the only clue to what their monosyllabic utterances mean.

Word-combining

In the next stage children move on to word-combining, uttering phrases like: *Bricks fall down*.

Their speech is as much for themselves as for anyone else, as they report and comment on what they are doing. Nouns and verbs are the main currency of speech at this stage, with the structure words that make their relationships plain largely absent.

As in stage 1, therefore, utterances are ambiguous and can be read in a variety of different ways:

see dog (I want to see the dog; I can see the dog; I did see a dog.)
one house (I'm building a house; I live in a house; I saw a house.)

Utterances involving the verb *want*, however, are very clear:

want drink   want dinner   want down.

The locational expressions *on, where,* and *down* may come into play at this stage, but language is still basically rooted in physical action.

The introduction of structure words

This stage is marked by the introduction of structure words. These include:

- determiners: *the, a, these, those, some, my*
- modals and auxiliaries: *may, might, should, would, to have, had, will have*
- negative: *not*
- intensifiers: *quite, really, fairly*
- conjunctions: *and, but, so*
- subordinatives: *after, because, if, until*
- prepositions: *by, on, for, over*
- personal pronouns: *I, me, mine, theirs*

Unlike nouns, adjectives and adverbs, structure words carry no semantic information. They do, however, help to clarify the meaning of an utterance, and contribute greatly to smoothness and fluency of expression. *I want some dinner* is a level up from the basic *want dinner.*

The following elements begin to appear at this stage:

- articles (*a, the, some*)
- forms of the verb *to be* (*It's my game*)
- the plural marker *s* on the end of nouns (*games*)
- the possessive morpheme *'s* (*dog's*)
- prepositions like *on, with* and *through*
- auxiliary verbs like *can* (*I can do it*)
- negatives in a variety of forms (*I can't, I didn't, No, uh uh, I not like*)
- interrogatives with no reversal of the subject–verb order (*Why I can't have?*)
- simple imperatives (*Go away! Stop it!*)

The growth of reasoning

At this stage progress is revealed by the following:

- the use of interrogatives in the reversed as well as the unreversed order
- *why?* questions of a more speculative kind: *Why is the sky blue? Why does Daddy do that?* – showing that attention is switching from purely physical to more abstract matters, such as people's reasons and motives for behaving as they do
- the appearance of modal verbs like *might* and *will* to discuss the future
- the third-person singular inflection *-es:* e.g. *Can I go swimming? Tim **does**.* (Not having mastered the rule for the negative form, however, they are likely to apply the *s* inflection to it, too, coming up with versions like *Mummy don't likes; Her don'ts.*)
- the use of conjunctions like *and* and *because* to link two statements in one sentence: *Tim wants to **and** I does. Let's go to sleep **because** we tired.*

Regular and irregular verb forms

In the course of the above progress towards mature expression, children will begin by using irregular verbs correctly in imitation of their parents:

I held the hamster; Mummy saw it.

They then assimilate the *-ed* rule for the regular past tense ending, and assume that it applies to every verb they use:

The wasp stinged me so I hitted it till it was dead.

Further experience of adult talk shows them their mistake and they return eventually to the correct forms.

Summary

Children's speech progresses from telegrammatic utterances / through incomplete clauses with few inflections / to fully inflected words / in complete clauses / that are smoothly linked with the help of conjunctions / and devices such as pronoun back-reference.

Describing children's speech patterns

It is useful to remember formulations such as the following for describing children's speech.

The child expresses [possession, plurals, negation, questions, etc.] through the pattern [. . .].

At this stage the child is using elements like [. . .], [. . .] and [. . .], that were not present at earlier stages.

'Elements' is an all-purpose term that can be used for any word in an utterance.

Checklist of features to look for

- The child expresses himself or herself through telegrammatic or block language, with one- or two-word utterances: *teddy, me, dolly; want down, want dinner.*
- The child omits to use noun phrases, e.g. [I] *want down.*
- The child omits the personal pronoun *I* of person deixis: [I] *want down*; [Me] *sit here*; [I] *want* [my] *dinner.*
- The child reverses the normal subject–verb order: *cake eat* for *eat cake.*
- The child shows that he or she is not yet able to handle auxiliary verbs in the following ways:
  - expressing the continuous present tense through the use of the participle only
  - leaving out the auxiliary verb *to be* that helps to form it: *I* [am] *sitting here; I* [am] *eating cake.*
- The child expresses negation with a simple *no* or *not*: *no sit there/not sit there*; he or she could be attempting any one of the following constructions, but the utterance lacks auxiliaries to make the exact intention clear:
  - a direct command: [Do] *not sit there*

  - an indirect command: [You are] *not* [to] *sit there*
  - an assertion: [I am] *not* [going to] *sit there.*
- The child expresses possession with the appropriate apostrophe *s* marker: *Daddy's chair.*
- The child expresses plurals by using the *s* inflection: *two cars.*
- The child expresses interrogatives by reversing the normal subject–verb order: *Why can't Tim play?*
- The child expresses interrogatives using the normal subject–verb order for a statement: *Why Tim can't play?*
- The child uses the appropriate endings for irregular verbs: *I caught the ball,* not *I catched it.*
- The child applies the *-ed* ending of regular verbs to irregular forms: *I seed the car; We goed swimming.*
- The child uses modal auxiliaries to express
  - obligation (*you must, you should, you ought*)
  - permission (*you can, you may*)
  - prohibition (*you can't, you mustn't*)
  - necessity (*you must*)
  - possibility (*you can, you may, you could*); and ability (*you can, you could*)
- The child uses the special set of indeterminate pronouns that adults use in sentences expressing negation (*anything, anyone, any*): *I haven't got any money.*

Activity

1 Describe the grammatical characteristics of the data samples given below, and comment on how the children's utterances differ at each stage. No correlation is intended between the stages here and those outlined above.

Stage 1	**Stage 2**	**Stage 3**
want biccy	me want biccy	may I have a biccy please?
where teddy?	where teddy is?	where's teddy?
no dirty (of sock)	no the sun shining	I don't want it

2 Comment on the development of the child's language in the two sets of utterances below:

There no squirrels	I can't see some squirrels
He no bite you	You can't dance
I no want envelope	I don't know his name

3 Comment on the child's handling of negation in the utterances below:

I'm not scared of nothing
Little puppies can't bite no one, right?
Don't never leave your chair
He can't have nothing
I never have none

4 Describe the grammatical characteristics of the data samples given below, and comment on how the children's utterances differ at each stage.

Stage 1	Stage 2	Stage 3
I rides train?	See my doggie?	Did I saw that in my book?
Sit chair?	You can't fix it?	Will you help me?
Ball go?	Mummy pinch finger?	Can't it be a bigger truck?
What that?	What the dolly have?	Where I should put it?
What cowboy doing?	Why you waking me up?	What I did yesterday?
Where kitty?	What me think?	Why kitty can't stand up?
Where horse go?	Why not . . . me *can't* dance?	What he can ride in?

Activity

Below are extracts in chronological order from the conversation of speakers of various ages, taken from Crystal, *Listen to Your Child*.
Point out the features that make their speech characteristic of their different age groups.

3 months

Michael: (*loud crying*)
Mother: Oh my word! What a noise! What a noise! (*Picks up Michael.*)
Michael: (*sobs*)
Mother: Oh dear, dear, dear! Didn't anybody come to see you? Let's have a look at you. (*Looks inside nappy.*) No, you're all right there, aren't you?
Michael: (*spluttering noises*)
Mother: Well, what is it, then? Are you hungry, is that it? Is it a long time since dinner-time?
Michael: (*gurgles and smiles*)

18 months

Child (*at breakfast table*): Bun. Butter. Jelly. Cakie. Jam.

21 months

Child (*coming in from garden*): Daddy-knee.
Mother: What's that, darling? What about daddy's knee?
Child: Fall-down daddy.
Mother: Did he? Where did he fall down?
Child: In-garden fall-down.
Mother: Daddy's fallen down in the garden! Poor daddy. Is he all right?
Child: Daddy-knee sore.
Mother: Daddy's fallen over and his knee's sore? I'd better come and see, hadn't I?

28 months

Child: Me want – Look! Balls. You like those balls?
Mother: Yes.
Child: Ball. Kick. Kick. Daddy kick.
Mother: That's right, you have to kick it, don't you?

Child: Mmm. Um. Um. Kick hard. Only kick hard . . . Our play that. On floor. Our play that on floor. Now. Our play that. On floor. Our play that on floor. Now. Our play that. On floor. No that. Now.
Mother: All right.
Child: Mummy, come on floor me.

3 years
Child: Hester be fast asleep, mummy.
Mother: She was tired.
Child: And why did her have two sweets, mummy?
Mother: Because you each had two, that's why. She had the same as you. Ooh dear, now what?
Child: Daddy didn't give me two in the end.
Mother: Yes, he did.
Child: He didn't.
Mother: He did.
Child: Look, he given one to – two to Hester, and two to us.
Mother: Yes, that's right.
Child: Why did he give?
Mother: Because there were six sweets. That's two each.

4 years 7 months
Susie: Oh, look, a crab. We seen – we were been to the seaside.
Baby-sitter: Have you?
Susie: We saw cr-fishes and crabs. And we saw a jelly-fish, and we had to bury it. And we – we did holding crabs, and we – we holded him in by the spade.
Baby-sitter: Did you?
Susie: Yes, to kill them, so they won't bite our feet.
Baby-sitter: Oh.
Susie: If you stand on them, they hurt you, won't they?
Baby-sitter: They would do. They'd pinch you.
Susie: You'd have to – and we put them under the sand, where the sea was. And they were going to the sea.
Susie: And we saw some shells. And we picked them up, and we heard the sea in them. And we saw a crab on a lid. And we saw lots of crabs on the sea-side. And I picked the – fishes up – no, the shells, and the feathers from the birds. And I saw a pig.

5 years 6 months
Dad: What do you want to play, then?
Lucy: I'll be the waitress and you have to eat in my shop. You come in, and sit down, and I can come and see you.
(*Dad acts his part obediently. Lucy walks over, clutching an imaginary notebook and pencil.*)
Lucy: Good afternoon.
Dad: Good afternoon.
Lucy: What do you want to eat?

Dad: Ooh, I'd like some cornflakes, and some sausages, please.
Lucy: We haven't got any sausages.
Dad: Oh dear. Well, let me see . . . Have you got any steak?
Lucy: Yes. We got steak.
Dad: I'll have some steak, then.
Lucy: O.K. 'Bye.

Writing skills

Children's brains are programmed to speak, but not to write, and fluent speakers take far longer to become properly fluent writers. When writing about things that have happened to them personally, even eleven-year-olds write in much the same style as children of seven speak: in short, declarative sentences strung together with *and*, *so*, and *and then*. Witness the following examples:

a Today it's my birthday and I had a spiaragrath and a airfix Bumper Books and I played with my spiaragrath and when daddy brought me to school hes going back and his going to play with my spiaragrath and today Gary is coming to tea and we will play subuiteo and football and with my spiaragrath and we might have a game at table soccer and Gary will have to go at about 8 o'clock and I will go and help him cary his things then I will go home and go to bed.
David, aged 7

b Dear Mrs Smith,
My monster is late because I did not finish it in English and I only had a cuple of lines to do and I finished it off in geography so my house tutor mister mordred taw it up and I had to take it home and do it. I hope you like it from Stephen Tolley yours faithily.
Stephen, aged 11

Quoted in Jones and Mulford, *Children Using Language*

Notice that the writers of these pieces describe the events:

- in the order in which they occurred;
- in short, blunt, declarative statements.

In (a) there is no logical connection between the events, and only the continuous use of *and* binds them together into some sort of whole. Older, more sophisticated writers might single out one event as more important or interesting than the others and deal with it first, going back to describe earlier ones later on. They might also put in the kind of asides and linking phrases that would express their feelings about the events – *I had to go in to get my tea then, unfortunately*. This writer is writing simply as he speaks, and all the things that might make the accounts more interesting if they were heard rather than read – changes of intonation, stress, and rhythm – are of course missing.

When asked to write about things outside themselves, nine- and eleven-year-olds use fewer conjunctions. This makes the writing sound more controlled, but at the same time rather monotonous and clipped:

a On Thursday we went to have a look round the Tithe Barn. We went through the woods and we saw a grey squirrel which jumped from a branch to a very thick branch. The trees were not all out, but the flowers were. The Tithe Barn is on Cupfield Hall Farm. The outside of the barn is made of flint and stone, and the tiles are very uneven. A lot of the barn is the arridginal material. At the tops of the roof there were nests, the tiles had moss and grass growing on them. There were holes in the roof. It was very dark in there.
Mary, aged 9

b What kind of world is a fish world? Imagine living in water all the time. There are many kinds of insect that crawl about the weeds and mud. Many are unearthly like creatures. Illustrated opposite is a caddis larvae made up of bits and bobs such as sticks and stones. Also there is the water scorpion which kills its enemys. First it kills them and then sucks out all the juices. Fish are streamlined for swimming. They breath by swallowing water and extracting the oxygen from the water and pushing it out through his gills.
Neil, aged 11

from Jones and Mulford, *Children Using Language*

This last piece does have a coherent logical structure – that of question and answer. Again, however, the techniques that more sophisticated writers use to weave clauses into longer, smoother sentences – subordinate clauses and linking words – are largely missing. For something much closer to adult writing, see the account written by a fourteen-year-old, below.

School trip to the South of France
After an exhausting eighteen hour journey by coach and ferry we arrived at Marseilles to meet the families we were going to stay with for the rest of the week. We were all called off the coach in pairs to be greeted by our very enthusiastic French families. We were kissed on the cheek twice by each person, a strange, but friendly experience! Despite the frenzied last minute practice of our French on the coach we found that, at first, all we could say was oui or non. However, over the next few days our French improved, especially when we realized we needed it to survive. The next day we set off early to the Camargue and St Marie de la Mer. At the Camargue, the landscape was very flat, marshy, and rather boring, until we spotted a group of pink flamingoes! Later on during the journey we saw herds of wild black bulls and the occasional white horse. In St Marie de la Mer we visited Arles and looked around two old Roman bull fighting rings, where bull fighting still sometimes continues.

Activity Rewrite (a) above in a more sophisticated prose style. Make any alterations you see fit.

Accent and dialect

 **Key words**

Regional dialect: a variety of English distinguished by its own characteristic features of vocabulary and grammar, spoken in a particular geographical region.

Standard English (*SE*): the dialect (i.e. the vocabulary and grammar) used by well-educated people throughout the British Isles.

Ideolect: the linguistic system of an individual speaker (i.e. the speech habits peculiar to an individual speaker) within a particular dialect.

Regional accent: a variety of pronunciation peculiar to people who live in a particular geographical region.

Received Pronunciation (*RP*): a variety of pronunciation used by a small number of people throughout the British Isles who constitute a social elite.

Differences between accent and dialect

The first thing to note is that *dialect* and *accent* refer to distinctly different things. *Dialect* is the term used to describe the different kinds of vocabulary and grammar used by different groups of speakers. *Accent* refers to the way in which they pronounce words.

Thus, if you compared non-standard forms of the past tense, like *I seen* and *I done,* with the standard forms *I saw* and *I did*, you would be discussing *dialect*. If you compared the Lincolnshire word *frit* with its southern English counterpart *frightened* you would also be discussing dialect. But if you compared the way in which people in east London pronounce *things* (*fings*) and *well* (wɛʊ) with RP versions of the same words, you'd be talking about *accent*.

Regional dialects and Standard English

The second thing to note is the difference between *regional dialects* and the dialect known as *Standard English*. This is the dialect used by educated people throughout the country, whether they speak with a regional accent or not. It is the dialect in which all official documents, textbooks, instruction manuals, 'quality' newspapers and magazines are written, and the dialect that children are taught to use in school. It is also the form of English taught to foreigners, and therefore a model for English users world-wide.

Since Standard English is the written norm, we tend to think of regional dialects as deviations from it. In fact, each dialect has a stable grammar of its own, derived from the dialect of the tribe that originally settled the region in which that dialect is used.

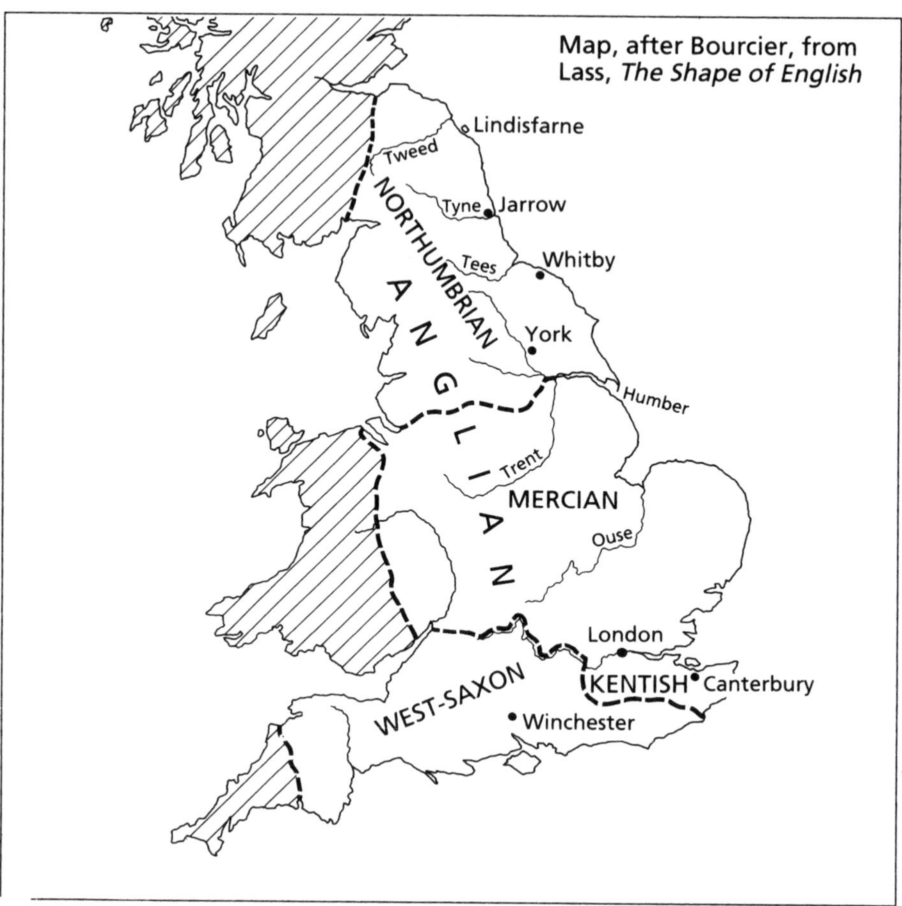

What seem to be 'errors' when measured against Standard English may actually be usages unaltered since Anglo-Saxon times. Double negatives, for instance, such as 'I haven't got no time', are actually relics of Old English. It used to put a negating particle *ne* in front of the verb, and an intensifying word *noht* after it, in effect, saying the same thing twice:

And ne bið ðær nǣnig ealo gebrowen mid Estum, ac ρær bið medo genoh.

Literally, 'There is not there no ale brewed amongst the Esthonians, but there is plenty of mead.'

What many people do not know is that Standard English itself started out as 'only' a regional dialect – that of Anglo-Saxon Mercia, the south-eastern part of England. Together with the accent in which it was pronounced – *Received Pronunciation* – it spread outwards from the south-east into all areas of the British Isles.

Activity

Below are some non-standard dialect forms (from Hughes and Trudgill, *English Accents and Dialects*). Divide a page into two columns labelled *Non-Standard English* and *Standard English*. Write out the non-standard forms in the appropriate column, then fill in their Standard English equivalents:

Being on me own had never entered me head.
We was forever having arguments.
I hadn't got nothing to fall back on.
Go to the pub is it?
Where's it by? Over by here.

Standard English itself is not completely uniform throughout the country. Hughes and Trudgill (*English Accents and Dialects*) have shown that variations exist between north and south, for example, in the use of contracted negative forms:

North	**South**
I've not got it	I haven't got it
She'll not go	She won't go
Does he not like it?	Doesn't he like it?

But if there are variations within Standard English itself, there are many more between Standard English and regional dialect forms. A checklist of these variations is given below for those who might wish to do project work in this area.

Checklist of regional dialect variations

You may find dialect speakers using one or more of the following non-standard features:

1. Double or triple negatives where SE uses only one: *I didn't have no money* (I didn't have any money/I had no money/I hadn't any money), *I couldn't get none nowhere* (I couldn't get any anywhere)
2. *Ain't* where SE has *aren't*: *I ain't going* (I'm not going), *I ain't seen him* (I haven't seen him), *she ain't got it* (she hasn't got it)
3. *I aren't* where SE has *I'm not*: *I aren't going* (I'm not going)
4. *No* or *nae* in Scottish dialects, where SE would use *not* or *no*: *he's no nice* (he isn't nice), *I've nae got time* (I haven't got time), *I cannae come* (I cannot come)
5. The past participle where SE would use the past tense: *I seen it last night* (I saw it last night), *I done it yesterday* (I did it yesterday)
6. *Never* used to make the past tense negative, where SE would have *not*: *she said she'd come, but she never* (she said she'd come, but she didn't), *You did it. No, I never* (You did it. No, I didn't)
7. Omission of SE *-s* from third-person singular of present tense of verbs: *she go to see her mother every day* (she goes to see her mother every day),

he work in Norwich (he works in Norwich)
(This is mostly found in East Anglian, Afro-Caribbean, and southern American dialects, but one example – *don't* for *doesn't* – is said to be common among English speakers, including the upper classes.)

8 Addition of non-standard *-s* to all persons of the verb: *I likes it. We sings it. You plays it* (I like it. We sing it. You play it)

9 Different relative pronoun patterns from SE: *that's the house what/as I told you about* (that's the house that/which I told you about), *that's the woman which I told you about* (that's the woman who/that I told you about), *that's the man which/what his wife left him* (that's the man whose wife left him)

10 Possessive case (*hisself* and *theirselves*) in reflexive pronouns where SE uses the object case (*himself* and *themselves*): *he shot hisself* (he shot himself), *they blamed theirselves* (they blamed themselves)
(It is SE that seems to be illogical here. It uses *myself, yourself*, and *ourselves*, but doesn't carry it through consistently. Dialect users are simply making things consistent.)

11 Double comparatives and superlatives where SE uses single: *he's more nicer than her* (he's nicer than her), *she's the most kindest person I know* (she's the kindest person I know)

12 Subject or object case of personal pronoun *they* (*they, them*) where SE would use the demonstrative pronouns *those* and *these*: *I don't like them cigarettes* (I don't like those cigarettes), *look at they pictures* (look at these pictures)

13 Unmarked plurals where SE uses *-s* in plural nouns of weight and measure: *she earned a thousand pound* (she earned a thousand pounds), *the river is two mile wide* (the river is two miles wide), *the pond was three foot long* (the pond was three feet long)
(This is a usage coming down from Middle English. Old English said 'a thousand *of* pounds/two *of* miles' instead of the simpler modern versions above. The plural of the possessive case was *-a*: *punda*, *mila*, and when this ending was eroded in the Middle Ages, it left us with the dialect forms *mile* and *pound* instead of SE's plural marker, *-s*.)

14 Different preposition patterns from SE: *she lives at London* (she lives in London), *I'm going up the market* (I'm going to the market), *he got off of the bus outside Smiths* (he got off the bus outside Smiths), *I bought it off of him* (I bought it from him), *she was attacked with a man* (she was attacked by a man)

15 Different adverb patterns from SE: *wait here while the light goes green* (wait here till the light goes green), *he read the paper while she was ready* (he read the paper till she was ready)

16 Adjectives where SE uses adverbs: *he says it too quick for me* (he says it too quickly for me), *she did the tea nice* (she did the tea nicely), *it was built good* (it was built well)
(Although Standard English users would never do this in writing, they frequently use constructions like 'The car's running smoother now it's been serviced' in casual conversation.)

This is by no means a complete list. In parts of the north-west they use *hoo* and *shoo* instead of SE *she* (a hangover from Old English *heo*) whereas speakers in a broad band from Shropshire down through Wiltshire into Dorset, Somerset, and Devon prefer *her*, accompanied by uninflected *be*, as in *Her be a real good sort, her be*. *Thou* is still used in large areas of the north, with *thee* as a variant; areas of Yorkshire and Lincolnshire contract SE contractions even further (*isn't – int*, *doesn't – dunt*); Liverpool goes in the opposite direction and extends *you* into *yous*; Bradford uses *were* for all persons of the past tense of *to be* (*I/you/he/she/it were*); and Geordie has its own version of the SE forms *didn't*, *doesn't*, *don't*, *divn't*. The north also has many dialect words not understood south of the Wash: there, children *laik* instead of *bunk off* from school; they *go on messages* rather than *run errands*, get their *tabs rattled* (ears boxed) for *chelping* (cheeking) their parents. There, tea is *mashed*, sulky people are called *mardy* and asked to *get out of the road* (out of the way); *bairns greet* (babies cry), and *yes* and *no* are *aye* and *nay*, *anything* is *owt* and *nothing*, *nowt*.

In spite of the homogenizing effect of television, regional dialects are still going strong. I hope they never die out.

Activity

Conduct a research project. Your aim is to collect data which will help you to assess the truth of the claim that people at the lower end of the social scale are more likely to use non-standard grammatical forms than those above them. Your method will be a questionnaire.

1 Select a cross-section of your local community to respond to your questionnaire. Include young as well as old, male as well as female, from the following categories:

Social class	Typical occupations
1	people from the higher professions (solicitors, doctors, university lecturers, architects, accountants, lawyers)
2	people from the lower professional and technical class (managers of banks and other business organizations, middle managers, engineers, aircraft pilots, fire brigade officers, teachers, nurses)
3a	people from other non-manual occupations (bank clerks, sales reps, supervisors, and other white-collar workers)
3b	skilled manual workers who have gained qualifications through apprenticeships, City and Guilds examinations, etc.
4	semi-skilled workers (farm workers, postal delivery staff, telephone operators, and so on)
5	unskilled manual workers (kitchen hands, driver's mates, hospital porters, window cleaners, labourers, and so on).

Adapted from Selfe, *Sociology*

1, 2, and 3a are generally considered to be the 'middle classes', and 3b, 4, and 5 the working classes.

2 Try to identify some of the non-standard dialect forms in your own locality.

3 Construct
a sentences that contain these non-standard forms,
b equivalent sentences containing Standard English forms.

4 Write out these pairs of sentences at the head of a questionnaire. Underneath, set out the following questions. Your respondents can tick the appropriate box to indicate their answers to these questions:
- ◆ Would you yourself use this sentence? Yes No
- ◆ Would any members of your family use this sentence? Yes No
- ◆ Would any of your close friends use this sentence? Yes No
- ◆ Do you know anybody who might use this sentence? Yes No

In case none of these applies, you should also include the question:
- ◆ Who do you think might use this sentence?

5 Conduct your research.

6 Assess whether your results confirm or disprove the claim that the lower down the social scale you go, the more likely you are to find people using non-standard forms.

7 Assess whether your respondents claim different practices for themselves and for their friends. If they do, speculate on their motives.

Regional accents and Received Pronunciation

Prescriptivists believe that regional accents are sloppy deviations from the 'correct' standard of pronunciation – *Received Pronunciation*. It is truer to say that they are based on the pronunciation of Middle English in their particular area, or even, in some cases, of Anglo-Saxon. In my own area of south Lincolnshire, *mister* is pronounced *mester* – a clear link with the earlier long vowel, combining the *a* of *apple* and the *e* of *egg*, in Old English *mæster*.

Linguists usually distinguish four main dialects of Middle English: Northern, East Midland, West Midland, and Southern. The Northern extended as far south as the Humber; West Midland and East Midland (including London) between them occupied the area from the Humber to the Thames, while Southern covered the area south of the Thames, together with Gloucestershire and Hereford. Although Kent was included in this area, it always retained individual features of its own, making it a distinct variety of southern English.

The most obvious division in Britain today is between north and south, and differences in pronunciation between these two areas can be traced back to the different dialects of Middle English. Old English *a*, for example, remained unchanged in the north and persists today in the Scottish forms *stane* and *hame*. South of the Humber, however, it was modified into *o*, giving southern *stone* and *home*. (The Lowland Scots dialect actually springs from the early Northern Middle English of the twelfth century, Gaelic having retreated to the Highlands and Islands.) Similarly, *f* and *s* at the beginning of words in the Northern dialect were often turned into *v* and *z* in the Southern, giving *vor*, *vrom*, *vox*, instead of *for*, *from*, and *fox*. This difference can be seen in Modern English *fox* and *vixen*, the former coming down from the Northern and Midland dialects, the latter from the Southern. These differences can be seen in the dialect poetry of the Dorsetshire poet, William Barnes, the first verse of one of whose poems is given below, and in the speeches of Edgar, disguised as a peasant, in *King Lear*. These also reveal the grammar of the Dorsetshire dialect, in which 'I will' is contracted to 'chill', and 'I shall' to 'ice':

Chill not let go, zi, without vurther cagion.
Ice try wither your costard or my ballow be the harder.

The wife a-lost

Since I noo mwore do zee your feäce,
Up steärs or down below,
I'll zit me in the lwonesome pleäce,
Where flat-bough'd beech do grow;
Below the beeches bough, my love,
Where you did never come,
An' I don't look to meet ye now,
As I do look at hwome.

William Barnes

Sometimes, variant forms of the same word occur in different dialects, one deriving from Old English, one from Scandinavian. *Ch*, for example, in the Southern dialect often corresponds to a *k* in the Northern, giving *bench/benk*; *church/kirk*.

On the other hand, Received Pronunciation (or RP) is the accent used by a small elite (somewhere between five and three per cent of the population). A random sample of the population of the city of Norwich, for example, produced one RP speaker out of sixty people interviewed. In contrast, a massive eighty per cent of the population speak with regional accents of varying degrees of strength, whilst the remainder speak some form of modified RP.

Activity Go out into the major shopping centre/precinct of your locality and take a random sample of sixty passers-by. Assess the percentage that falls into the following categories:

- pure RP speakers;
- modified RP speakers;
- speakers with regional accents.

RP is the voice of the upper classes, of authority and of power. It is used by brigadiers and generals, by judges and barristers, and by those who read the national news on radio and television. All accents, like all dialects, are the products of particular regions, and RP was originally the regional accent of the south-east of England – the Mercia of Anglo-Saxon times. When wealth, power, and culture became concentrated in the south-east (it had the port of London, the Court, and the universities of Oxford and Cambridge), the accent and dialect of the region came to be associated with these things. They suggested power, culture, and wealth. From the 1300s onwards, therefore, people with social ambition learned to speak in the style of the south-east, just as in the 1100s they had had to learn French. Two further factors then helped to spread RP and SE more widely:

1 the setting up of public schools in the south-eastern region in Victorian times – these took in boys from all over the country and sent them home speaking with a standardized accent that became the mark of the middle class
2 the establishment of the British Broadcasting Company in 1927. Director-general John Reith set his organization the task of achieving 'the very best thing we could do' in both speech and writing, which in effect meant the use of immaculate SE and RP in all 'serious' programmes and the banishing of regional accents to the more trivial area of comedy shows. The experiment of having the news read in a Yorkshire accent by Wilfred Pickles during the Second World War outraged many listeners, and even as recently as 1987 an announcer with a Highland Scots accent was moved from the news-desk because some listeners complained that they couldn't understand a word she said.

Thanks to these two factors, Robert McCrum remarks, Standard English and RP became '. . . the voice of the officer, administrative, and consular class throughout the Empire – the voice of authority.'

It became detached from the region which bred it and became instead the badge of a particular social class. No one can tell which part of the country an RP speaker comes from simply by listening to his or her voice, whereas most of us can recognize speakers from such regions as Birmingham, Newcastle, and Liverpool.

Talking point

1 The Lairds of many famous Scottish clans still live on estates that their ancestors have held for centuries. They claim to be Scottish to the core, yet they have no trace of a Scottish accent. Why?
2 Read the following poem, then explain why
   a listeners with RP accents and
   b listeners with regional accents

react against having the news read in a regional accent such as that of Glasgow.

3 Discuss how Leonard manages to get across

a what he sees as the arrogance of the RP speaker, and

b his own feelings of resentment in reaction to it.

This is thi
six a clock
news thi
man said n
thi reason
a talk wia
BBC accent
is coz yi
widny wahnt
mi ti talk
aboot thi
trooth wia
voice lik
wanna yoo
scruff. if
a toktaboot
thi trooth
lik wanna yoo
scruff yi
widny thingk
it wuz troo.
jist wanna yoo
scruff tokn.
thirza right
way ti spell
ana right way
ti tok it. this
is me tokn yir
right way a
spellin. this
is ma trooth.
yooz doant no
thi trooth
yirsellz cawz
yi canny talk
right. this is
the six a clock
nyooz. belt up.

Tom Leonard

Standard English and Received Pronunciation

The terms *Standard English* and *Received Pronunciation* are often confused with each other, perhaps because the use of Received Pronunciation almost always implies the use of Standard English. It would be strange indeed to hear someone speaking in a regional dialect using the sounds of Received Pronunciation – try saying 'Just walk up the streets and you'm out of Dudley' (the dialect of the Birmingham area) in the RP accent of a radio or television news-reader and it will sound ridiculous. Standard English, on the other hand, is spoken by many educated people whose voices reveal traces of the accent of the region in which they were brought up. Their accent is said to be a modified form of RP. One well-known Professor of Linguistics speaks with a largely RP accent but still uses the flat 'a' vowels of his northern county, saying *bath, laff, path* instead of *barth, larf,* and *parth.* He sees no reason to change his accent any further in the direction of RP, but he does, like almost all well-educated people, use Standard English on all formal occasions.

Prescriptivists, who spend most of their time worrying about 'correctness', teach that regional dialects are inferior to Standard English. (Do they know that Standard English was itself originally 'only' a dialect?) This is largely because standards of correctness in our society are set by the written language, and most important writing uses Standard English vocabulary and grammar. (I know that many novels and plays contain characters who speak regional dialect with regional accents, and that Robert Burns and William Barnes wrote their best poetry in dialect – Barnes even put in marks to show how it should be pronounced in the Dorset accent – but for the most part novels are written in Standard English, and so is most poetry. There is very little important dialect writing in English.)

Even prescriptivists, however, if pushed, would have to admit that regional dialects add pungency and force to the language, and that the world would be blander and less interesting without them.

Talking point

1 Are speakers who use only Received Pronunciation likely to use regional dialect forms?
2 Do regional dialect users ever use full Received Pronunciation?
3 Do regular Standard English users ever have regional accents?
4 In the film musical *My Fair Lady,* Eliza, exquisitely dressed and using the purest RP, is made to say, 'It's my belief she done him in'. Explain why this is funny.

Dialect, accent, and social prestige

George Bernard Shaw observed in *Pygmalion* in 1912, that the moment an Englishman opens his mouth, some other Englishman begins to despise him. From the early 1900s until well into the 1950s, Received Pronunciation was the badge of entry into middle- and upper-class society. Listen to news bulletins from those days and you will hear a very formal, precise, and clipped English pronunciation, with the vowel *a*, for example, as in *that*, flattened to something closer to *e*: *thet*. Formality of speech was matched by formality of dress: announcers had to wear evening dress to read the news – even on the radio!

Things have changed a lot since then, thanks to the influence of American media stars with transatlantic accents, English working-class anti-heroes in books, plays, and films, and television personalities, chat-show hosts, and comedians speaking with accents as diverse as southern and northern Irish, Scots, Geordie, Scouse, and London. In media circles, RP stopped being king in the late 1950s. Regional accent and dialect were 'in', RP speakers 'out' – seen as either pompous, camp, or phony. Some people have taken the reaction against RP to such extremes that they show a kind of inverted snobbery. One well-known violinist, for example, has swapped his natural RP for the accent and dialect of a London street-market trader (Cheers, Nige). Even the younger Royals – Andrew and Edward – have 'ordinary' accents, very different from the *affected RP* of the Queen. (This is probably due partly to the media stars they mix with, partly to their need to play down their social status in a modern democratic state.) Outside media circles, however, Britain is still a remarkably snobbish country, and people are still frequently judged on the way in which they speak.

Some people argue that the link between accent, dialect, and social status is weakening, pointing out that Dukes have been heard to speak of 'flogging their Canalettos', like any barrow-boy. Others argue that they persist in all social circles, and that the key to prestige and social success is still smart clothes and a 'good' (i.e. as close to RP as possible) accent. A television documentary in the 1980s revealed how a candidate for the Foreign Office was selected on the basis that 'with that voice, anyone would believe anything she said'. Her rival for the post clearly knew far more, but spoke RP flavoured with flat northern vowel sounds. This idea is supported by Canadian research into the way in which people evaluate various dialects:

> . . . we know that there may be three 'rewards' for the speaker who upgrades his accent one or two notches towards his partner. These are: (i) an increase in perceived status; (ii) an increase in perceived favourability of personality (i.e. they like him more), and (iii) an increase in the perceived quality and persuasiveness of the content of the message (he seems more convincing).
>
> Howard Giles, *New Society*

The process of upgrading your accent to match that of the person you are talking to is *upward divergence of accent*. The opposite process, by which RP speakers might deliberately coarsen their accents to show friendship or the desire to make their interlocutor feel more comfortable, is known as *downward divergence*.

Accent, dialect, gender, and social class

Research seems to suggest that:

a Men and women have slightly different attitudes towards the use of dialect forms and regional accents; women (perhaps because they have been trained by social pressure to conform to standard norms?) tend to seek what is called *overt prestige*, that is, prestige that fits in with socially approved norms of behaviour. On the other hand men, or at least men from the three bottom social classes, prefer *covert prestige*: the respect and admiration of their peer group for standing out against those very ideals of respectability and good behaviour so important to their girlfriends and wives.

b This difference shows itself more clearly at the border-line between upper working class and lower middle class – the point where those at the bottom of the lower middle class have the least to lose, and those at the top of the upper working class have the most to gain, in terms of social success. Both gender and social class, therefore, help to determine how people speak.

Activity

Devise some research of your own into attitudes towards language.

1 How could you discover whether people in your neighbourhood were self-conscious about using such words as *toilet* and *serviette*? A questionnaire? If so, would you ask only about specific words, or ask an open question such as, *Are there any words that you as parents would not like your children to use?/ Are there any words that your parents do not like you to use (excluding swear words)?* (Before you start you might find it useful to read the short chapter on language – eighteen very small pages – in *Debrett's U and Non-U Revisited,* ed. Buckle, The Viking Press, New York.)

2 It is a well-known fact that some people assume a 'posh' accent when they answer the telephone. Ask a cross-section of people
a if they do this,
b why?
Analyse and discuss your results.

3 How could you discover whether non-RP speakers upgrade their accent to match that of someone who speaks 'better'? Could the telephone help you here? Could you set up some kind of experimental situation in which you involve an RP speaker in conversation with someone with a 'less good' accent? Would observation of real-life situations serve your purpose better? Where might you find two such people interacting? A student talking to a head teacher or principal? A customer asking for information in a very smart shop? Someone asking for a loan from a bank manager? (Students can get all kinds of help, including overdrafts, now. Take one of your friends, without telling him or her what you're up to, and see what happens.)

4 Check people's reactions to accent by getting two speakers to give the same short talk to a group who have no idea what you are trying to discover. Try to

make your two speakers look and dress very much alike, but get one to speak in an accent as close to RP as possible, and the other in some kind of regional or urban dialect. Afterwards, ask the group which speaker struck them as being:

- more intelligent;
- more self-confident;
- more ambitious;
- more hard-working;
- more determined;

(assumptions usually made about RP speakers on the basis of their accent alone)

- more honest;
- more sincere;
- more friendly and warm;
- more likely to have a good sense of humour;
- more likely to make a good friend.

(assumptions usually made about regional dialect speakers on the basis of their accent alone)

5 Check whether people adapt their accent to fit formal and informal contexts by performing either or both of the following experiments:

Experiment A

1. Set up a small discussion group (four or five people) and either record it if possible, or make notes on the kinds of vocabulary and grammar used.
2. Introduce a tutor, counsellor, or other older person into the discussion to lift it on to a more formal plane. Again, record or make notes.
3. Assess whether any of the speakers changed their accent, grammar, and idiom in the second session.

Experiment B

1. Identify some of the non-standard (i.e. non-RP) features of your local accent. (Hughes and Trudgill give thorough checklists of all the major English accents and dialects.)
2. Set up a group of as many people as you think you can handle from the following social classes:
   - Upper middle class
   - Lower middle class
   - Upper working class
   - Middle working class
   - Lower working class.

   Ask them one by one to perform the following tasks, and record or make notes on each.

   a Read out a list of words (a page from a dictionary will do) (WLS).
   b Read out a passage from a book (RPS).
   c Respond to some questions put to them in formal interview style (FS).
   d Talk casually with the others involved in the experiment on the question of accents (CS).

   Key: WLS = Word-List Style; RPS = Reading-Passage Style; FS = Formal Style; CS = Casual Style.

3 Analyse your results. You should find that accent and grammar diverge more noticeably from SE and RP standards the more relaxed and less formal the situation and task become.
4 Assess whether there was any noticeable difference between the accent and grammar of males and females in your group in any of the different styles.

6 a Read the advertisement for Trophy beer on page 61, then draw character sketches showing the impression you gain of
- the dialect speaker,
- the user of SE and RP.

b Assess how far their portrayed accent and dialect have influenced your opinions of each kind of speaker.

Talking point

In the light of what you have just read, which of the following attitudes seems to you to be the most sensible:

a Since Received Pronunciation is the most prestigious accent and Standard English has the most correct vocabulary and grammar, all children should be taught to use them all the time, regardless of their family background and the region where they live.
b Since Received Pronunciation and Standard English are really only dialects themselves, we should teach children who don't already use them to ignore them and carry on speaking in their own way.
c Since Received Pronunciation and Standard English are the forms of language that everyone is likely to meet in formal situations, children should be taught to use them so that they can be self-confident in such contexts. We should teach them to use different styles of speech for different audiences in the same way that we teach them to use different written registers for different readers.
d We should teach all children to write 'correctly' in Standard English, because this will help them to pass exams and to please employers, but we should leave their accents alone. The way you speak is a part of your personality, and as long as you're using Standard English, nobody will worry about your accent.

The sounds of English

Look again at the Trophy advertisement and the Tom Leonard poem and you'll see that combinations of ordinary letters can give you quite a good impression of the way regional speakers pronounce words. A more exact method, however, is to use the symbols of the *International Phonetic Alphabet* (the IPA). These are based on the vowel and consonant sounds of Received Pronunciation, and give us a fixed standard against which the varying pronunciations of regional speakers can be assessed. The columns below show

1 the individual symbols of the IPA
2 a sample word in which RP speakers use the sound represented by that symbol
3 the phonetic transcription of that word (i.e. the writing out of the word using phonetic symbols instead of ordinary letters).

Bristol barmaid sings praises of locally-brewed Whitbread Trophy bitter:

"Nuthin' can touch moy lovely Bristol Bigheads fer flavour, natsa fact."

Translation:

("I firmly believe that the Trophy bitter brewed for the Bristol area has a taste superior to that brewed elsewhere.")

"Strewy nuff to say that every drarp a-Big'ead oi'm a-servin' 'ere's a-brewed special fer th'West Vingland."

(All Trophy 'Bighead' bitter sold in Bristol has, in fact, been brewed in and especially for the West of England.)

"An' we're much 'bliged ta Whitbread, thassall oi can say, a-coz wee 'preciate people 'oo 'preciates our e-fined tastes."

(Whitbread's policy of brewing Trophy to suit local tastes pleases us greatly. Peoples' tastes do vary from area to area, you know.)

"Aft trawl, snice to know yer understud."

(Whitbread's sensitivity in this delicate matter is touching, don't you think?)

"S'warm in 'ere, innit, wine chew get stuck inter one o'moy lovely Bristols?"

(But enough of this careless chatter. Allow me to pull for you a pint of our own local Trophy brew.)

Whitbread 'Bighead' Trophy Bitter. Brewed to understand the local tongue.

Trophy is brewed by local Whitbread breweries in Blackburn, Cardiff, Castle Eden, Cheltenham, Faversham, Kirkstall, Liverpool, Luton, Marlow, Portsmouth, Rhymney, Romsey, Salford, Samlesbury, Sheffield and Tiverton.

Phonetic transcriptions, whether of single symbols or whole words, are always contained within two oblique lines. This indicates that the sounds represented by the phonetic symbols refer to the sounds of an actual language. Phonetic symbols enclosed within square brackets represent sounds in the abstract, not attached to a particular language.

Although they look very strange and intimidating at first, phonetic symbols have two advantages over ordinary spelling:

1 they don't change from word to word, as many ordinary letters do. In RP, *u*, for instance, is pronounced one way in *but*, another in *put*; however, the phonetic symbol for the sound in *but* is always the same: /ʌ/.

2 the phonetic spelling of a word is shorter and simpler than the ordinary spelling: *beach*, for example, uses five letters, but only three phonetic symbols: /bitʃ/.

Don't try to learn by heart all the phonetic symbols given below. Just go through them slowly and carefully, listening to the different sounds each makes. If you then do a little practice on each category in turn, starting with vowels, phonetic symbols will soon become familiar to you.

Single vowels

i as in RP	b**ea**d	/bid/	ɔ	b**oar**d	/bɔd/
ɪ	b**i**d	/bɪd/	ʊ	p**u**t	/pʊt/
e	b**e**d	/bed/	u	sh**oe**	/ʃu/
æ	b**a**d	/bæd/	ʌ	c**u**p	/kʌp/
ɑ	b**ar**d	/bɑd/	ɜ	b**ir**d	/bɜd/
ɒ	c**o**d	/kɒd/	ə	**a**bout, port**er**	/əbaʊt/, /pɔtə/

Note: the one very common vowel sound that is not represented on its own in the table is the one that looks like an upside-down *e*: /ə/. This is a sort of all-purpose sound found in words like *another* (/ənəðə/), and the many different words that end in *ent* or *ant*: /prezənt/, /kleimənt/. It is called *schwa*.

Activity

Copy out the following paragraph, replacing all the ordinary vowel letters – a, e, i, o, u – with phonetic symbols that represent the way the words would be spoken by an RP speaker. You will find that some symbols – ɑ and ɔ for example – cut down the number of letters in the word by sounding like a vowel and consonant combined: *r* isn't needed in words like *yard* and *sort*.

Whenever Willy was in trouble his thoughts turned towards planting seeds in his back yard. He resented his boss, was fed up with his work, and sad that Biff, his son, was just bumming along instead of planning ahead. For Willy, true success meant earning hundreds of dollars and winning respect from other men.

Not all the vowel sounds of RP can be represented by single vowels, however. When writing the paragraph for the Activity above, for instance, I couldn't use words like *out*, *around*, *thousands*, and *go*, because the sounds in these words are made up of *combinations* of vowels, called *diphthongs*. Say 'go' aloud and you will hear your voice glide from the neutral *schwa* sound to the more rounded vowel represented by /ʊ/.

◆ **Key words**

Diphthong: two vowel sounds combining to produce one syllable of a word; during the pronunciation of the syllable the tongue moves from one position to another, causing a continual change in vowel quality: as for instance in the pronunciation of the syllable *a* in *late* during which the tongue moves from the position of *e* towards that of *i*.

A *triphthong* combines three vowels sounds to form one syllable; e.g. fire (/faɪə/).

The full list of diphthongs is given below. Look carefully at each one, pronounce them, then do the practice suggested.

Diphthongs

eɪ	p**ay**	/peɪ/	aʊ	h**ou**nd	/haʊnd/
aɪ	p**ie**	/paɪ/	ɪə	b**eer**	/bɪə/
ɔɪ	b**oy**	/bɔɪ/	ɛə	b**ear**	/bɛə/
əʊ	g**o**	/gəʊ/	ʊə	c**ure**	/kjʊə/

Activity

Write out the following paragraph, representing *all* vowels and diphthongs with phonetic symbols.

Lynda did not know what to say to her husband. She sighed and took up her darning. If only Biff would stop his bumming around and settle down. Willy would be happy then, it would give him something to cheer about. He cared so much for Biff, and she could not bear to watch his slow drift towards death. It was pure torment to her.

Finally, look at the list of consonants. Apart from the fact that there are two different symbols for the two different sounds of th, these are quite straightforward and should give you little difficulty.

Consonants

p	**p**it	/pɪt/	ʃ	**sh**oe	/ʃu/
b	**b**it	/bɪt/	ʒ	mea**s**ure	/meʃə/
t	**t**ip	/tɪp/	h	**h**ot	/hɒt/
d	**d**i**d**	/dɪd/	tʃ	**ch**arge	/tʃɑdʒ/
k	**k**ic**k**	/kɪk/	dʒ	**g**in	/dʒɪn/
g	**g**ive	/gɪv/	m	**m**ouse	/maʊs/
f	**f**ive	/faɪv/	n	**n**ice	/naɪs/
v	**v**ine	/vaɪn/	ŋ	si**ng**	/sɪŋ
θ	**th**umb	/θʌm/	l	**l**eaf	/lif/
ð	**th**is	/ðɪs/	r	**r**un	/rʌn/
s	**s**ome	/sʌm/	j	**y**acht	/jɒt/
z	**z**oo	/zu/	w	**w**et	/wet/

Activity

Complete your practice of phonetic transcription by adding the symbols for consonants to the paragraphs in the Activities above about Willy and Lynda Loman. You will end up with something that looks like a foreign language.

There is just one other symbol to notice: the *glottal stop*: ʔ. This represents not a consonant, but a sound used instead of a consonant. Where RP speakers pronounce /t/ in the middle of a word like *butter*, for example, some non-RP speakers produce a sound at the back of the throat by closing the space between the vocal cords. Try producing it yourself:

1 say the word *letter*, taking care to pronounce the /t/; notice how it is produced at the front of the mouth, with your tongue high on the ridge above your teeth on /l/, and on the top of the teeth themselves on /t/;
2 now say the word again, being careful to keep your tongue away from your teeth; you will feel the movement in your throat that produces the *glottal stop*, and will find your tongue ending up below your bottom teeth.

The sounds of RP

There are variations of pronunciation within RP. At the top of the continuum is the most exaggerated form, *affected RP*. This is practised not only by the Queen and old-fashioned members of the aristocracy, but also by members of the upper middle class who are very conscious of their dignity and importance. The connoisseur and art critic Brian Sewell, often to be seen on TV and heard on Radio 4's *Loose Ends*, speaks a form of RP that can only be described as exquisite.

The Queen herself has moderated her accent only slightly to suit the informality of the times. Her pronunciation differs enormously from that of most of her subjects, /æ/, for example, being closer to /e/ in words like *that*.

Lower down the social scale, changes are taking place between the pronunciation of older, more conservative users of Received Pronunciation and younger, trendier ones.

One tendency is for younger speakers to turn diphthongs and triphthongs into monophthongs. Where older speakers have /ʃiə/ for *fire*, younger ones have /ʃɑ:/. As a result, the distinction between the pronunciation of words such as *paw*, *pore*, and *poor* is being lost.

According to Hughes and Trudgill, this is particularly true of the single word *our*, which many young RP and non-RP speakers now pronounce /ɑ:/. (This is having the secondary effect of causing students to misspell *our* as *are*.) For some unknown reason, /a/ remains untouched in other words such as *hour* and *flower*.

Despite these variations, however, most RP speakers sound fairly similar in style and give little or no indication of what part of the country they come from. It is when we listen to regional speakers that the real differences are heard.

Differences between RP and regional accents

The most obvious difference between the accents of north and south, for instance, involves the following two letters. Both are pronounced short in the north but long in London and the Home Counties.

1 -*a* as in *chaff*

North	**South**
/æ/	/ɑ/

Words containing -*a* that are pronounced differently include:

path, laugh, grass, dance, grant, demand, plant, branch, example

Words containing -*a* that are pronounced the same include:

gaff, raffle, gas, lass, maths, ass, mass, chassis, pant, romance, band, camp, shambles

Words containing -*a* that can be pronounced either way include:

plastic, transport

Note: speakers with strong south-western accents either do not distinguish between long and short -*a*, or do it inconsistently. The Welsh use long -*a* in some words, e.g. *grarse*, but not in others, e.g. *dance*; the Scots and the Irish do not use long -*a* at all, unless imitating RP in the search for higher social status.

2 -*u* as in *bun, put*

In the south, this has two distinct forms, represented by the phonetic symbols /ʌ/ and /ʊ/. In the north, /ʊ/ only is used most of the time. This means that while southern speakers can distinguish between pairs of words like *put* and *putt*, northern speakers cannot.

North	South
/pʊt/	/pʊt/
/pʊtt/	/pʌtt/
/cʊd/	/cʌd/
/cʊd/	/cʊd/

Some older northern speakers, however, use a further *-u* sound never found in RP: /u:/. This allows them to distinguish between /u:/ and /ʊ/ in such pairs as book (/bu:k/) and buck (/bʊk/), pronounced in the south as /bʊk/ and /bʌk/.

Activity

1 Look for characters with a London accent in TV programmes such as *Birds of a Feather*, *Minder*, or *Only Fools and Horses*, and listen to the way they pronounce the words *no* and *poor*. What vowel sounds can you find in them?
2 Now try to describe the sounds, using symbols from the tables on pages 62–63.
3 Sometimes an RP diphthong is changed into a single other vowel in London and other south-east accents. Listen to the way they say *poor* and write it down in phonetic symbols.

Talking point

Other letters to look at in regional accents are *-a* and *-i*. How does a cockney or an Australian pronounce -a in words like *lady*? (Where did the first main settlers in Australia come from?) How does a dialect user from East Anglia or the Bristol area pronounce the personal pronoun *I* and other syllables containing *-i*?

Consonants in RP and in regional dialects

Except when they are speaking quickly, RP speakers pronounce most consonants. The exception is the letter /r/, which is dropped:

1 after vowels, as in *bar*, *carpet* (pronounced /bɑ:/, /kɑ:pet/);
2 before consonants, as in *car-port* (pronounced /kɑ:pɔ:t/).
(It is still pronounced between vowels, however, as in car engine – /kɑ:r'enjɪn/.)
Note: when /r/ occurs in the middle of a word it is known as *inter-vocalic* /r/. When it occurs at the end it is called *post-vocalic* /r/.

The Scots, the Irish, people who live in Bristol and the south-west and in parts of Lancashire still pronounce post-vocalic /r/ – you will hear *thurr* for *there* and *their*.

Activity

Explain the confusion that arises in this conversation between a Hebridean Scotsman and an English incomer:

> 'Maybe we'd all have time to play at the peats if we had a cart [like him],' I pointed out.
> 'How would that help him?' demanded Erchy, looking puzzled.
> 'Well, having a cart means he can get his peats home in his own time. He doesn't have to carry them himself or wait for a lorry like the rest of us.'
> 'I'm not gettin' your meaning,' said Erchy, still puzzled.

'His peats – in his cart. He has a cart, hasn't he?' I repeated testily.
'He has two or three but I don't see how they'd help him get home his peats,' said Erchy.
'Miss Peckwitt's meanin' to say a carrrt,' interpreted Morag.
Erchy's face cleared. 'Ach, is that it? I thought she was goin' mad herself talkin' about a cat helpin' him to get home the peats. Honest, you English folk do speak a funny language sometimes.'

Lillian Beckwith, *A Rope in Case*

Many speakers with regional accents, on the other hand, do not pronounce the consonants found in RP. Some consonants are simply dropped:

1 /h/ Many speakers with regional accents drop their aitches. *Hat* and *at*, *heart* and *art*, *hit* and *it* are therefore pronounced the same. Exceptions to this rule are those who live in Newcastle and parts of the north-east, the Scots, and the Irish.

2 /ŋ/ Most regional accents do not pronounce /ŋ/ in the suffix *-ing*: instead we find *singin'*, pronounced /siŋin/; *walkin'*, pronounced /wɔ:kin/. (This is said to be true also of members of the aristocracy, who talk of *huntin'*, *shootin'*, and *fishin'*.)

3 /j/ In the past, /j/ used to be used after /r/ and /l/ in words like *rude* and *Luke:* /rju:d/, /lju:k/.

At the moment, /j/ is being lost after /s/, even in RP, so that we find *super* /su:pə/, for instance, side by side with suit /sju:t/.

People with regional accents drop /j/ more often than RP users: parts of the north have lost /j/ after *th*: e.g. *enthuse*. London has lost /j/

- after /n/: /nju:z/ becomes /nu:z/;
- after /t/: /tju:n/ becomes /tu:n/;
- and after /d/: /dju:/ becomes /du:k/

(The same thing also occurs in many American accents.)

Speakers in a large area of eastern England have dropped /j/ before /u:/ after all consonants, so that pronunciations like those below are now the norm: *pew* /pu:/; *few* /fu:/; *beauty* /bu:ti/.

Some consonants are replaced by glottal stops: Hughes and Trudgill find that non-RP speakers use glottal stops in the following places:

1 at the end of words before a following vowel or consonant:
that man – /ðæˀ mæn/;
that apple – /ðæˀ æpəl/;
2 before an /n/: *button* – /bʌˀən/;
3 before an /l/: *bottle* – /bɒˀəl/;
4 before a vowel: *better* – /beˀər/.

Some consonants are replaced by other, different consonants:

1 Cockney speakers substitute /f/ for the *-th* sound we find in *thought* at the beginning, in the middle, and at the end of words:
   thin becomes /fin/; *Cathy* becomes /kæfiː/; *both* becomes /bouf/
2 They often use /v/ to replace the *-th* sound we hear in *then* in the middle and at the end of words:
   together becomes /təgɛvə/; *bathe* becomes /baɪv/
3 They use /d/ instead of the *-th* sound we hear in *then* at the beginning of words like *the*, *these*, and *then*.

Some consonants, strangely enough, are turned into vowels or diphthongs:

1 Speakers from London and the surrounding area change /l/ into a vowel when it occurs in the following places:
   - at the end of a word and after a vowel: *Paul* becomes /poʊ/;
   - before a consonant when it is part of the same syllable; *milk* becomes /miʊk/;
   - when /l/ is a syllable in itself in words like *table*: /tæɪbʊ/.
2 When /l/ follows the vowel /ɔː/ it may be dropped altogether; thus *Paul's* may become /pɔːz/ and sound exactly like *pause*.

Hughes and Trudgill note that:

> The vowels which represent /l/ can alter the quality of the vowels preceding them in such a way as to make homophones of pairs like:
>
> *pool/pull; doll/dole; peal/pill.*

This tendency, like turning diphthongs and triphthongs into monophthongs, seems to be spreading – evidence of the rising tide of 'estuary English' that is sweeping the southern half of the country.

Activity Find the three phonetic symbols that, put together, will give the sound of 'well' in the accent of the London area.

Exceptions to the general trend

There are two exceptions to this practice of dropping consonants:

1 Non-RP users in Birmingham, Manchester, and Liverpool not only pronounce /ŋ/ at the end of words; they add an extra /g/ for good measure: *singer* becomes /sɪŋgə/, *thing* becomes /θɪŋg/.
2 Speakers of both RP and regional dialects are in the habit of adding *intrusive* /r/ in places where no /r/ was ever used. The source of *intrusive* /r/ seems to have been the dropping of /r/ before a consonant in words like *carport* and the retention of /r/ before a vowel, in compounds like *car engine*, where it is known as a *linking* /r/. If /r/ is pronounced before a vowel in places like this, the unconscious reasoning seems to run, it should be inserted before all vowels. We therefore find examples like *draw up* /drɔːr ʌp/, which used never to have an /r/, side by side with *soar up* /sɔːr ʌp/, where /r/ is customary.

Activity

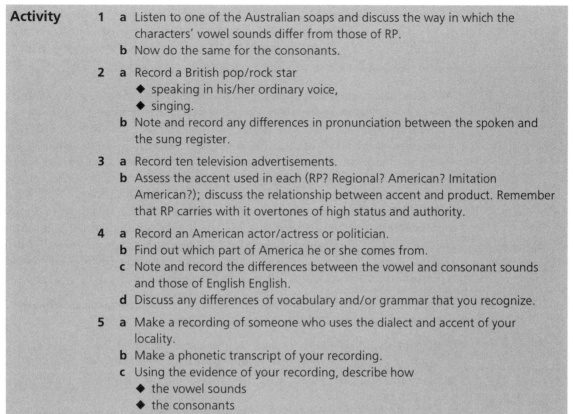

1. a Listen to one of the Australian soaps and discuss the way in which the characters' vowel sounds differ from those of RP.
   b Now do the same for the consonants.
2. a Record a British pop/rock star
   - speaking in his/her ordinary voice,
   - singing.

   b Note and record any differences in pronunciation between the spoken and the sung register.
3. a Record ten television advertisements.
   b Assess the accent used in each (RP? Regional? American? Imitation American?); discuss the relationship between accent and product. Remember that RP carries with it overtones of high status and authority.
4. a Record an American actor/actress or politician.
   b Find out which part of America he or she comes from.
   c Note and record the differences between the vowel and consonant sounds and those of English English.
   d Discuss any differences of vocabulary and/or grammar that you recognize.
5. a Make a recording of someone who uses the dialect and accent of your locality.
   b Make a phonetic transcript of your recording.
   c Using the evidence of your recording, describe how
   - the vowel sounds
   - the consonants

   used by your speakers differ from those of Received Pronunciation.

Black English

Over one per cent of the British population today is of British West Indian or, as many now prefer to call it, Afro-Caribbean descent. Most of them speak some form of the dialect known as British Black English.

Key words

Creole: creoles begin as *pidgins* – artificial languages specially invented to allow peoples who do not know each other's language to talk to each other. At first only good for passing simple information, they blossom eventually into *creoles* – fully developed languages capable of expressing anything their users want to say; in some cases, they replace the original language spoken by one of the peoples concerned and become mother-tongues.

Creoles from different parts of the world share many common features – a fact that has led to two different theories about their origins:

1. they all spring ultimately from one fifteenth-century Portuguese pidgin used in Africa, Asia, and the Americas;
2. they all arose out of the same innate human tendency to pare language down to its essentials when communication has to be quick

and simple. (See the account of how children handle prepositions, page 110, and the remarks on telegrams on page 137.)

Patois: synonym for *creole*.

As earlier chapters of this book have shown, very few people in this country speak completely pure Received Pronunciation and Standard English, or use exclusively dialect forms of grammar and regional accents. The majority use some form of modified RP and SE, diverging upwards or downwards as the situation demands. Exactly the same is true of people of Afro-Caribbean descent. *Black English*, like any other dialect, is a continuum, with full creole at one end, RP at the other, and modified forms of each in the middle. Most British Blacks born in this country since the 1970s, for instance, use only certain elements of creole or patois, and then only in informal contexts. And the same is true of pronunciation. Afro-Caribbeans might pronounce SE *town* (/taun/) for example as *tong* and *brown* as *brong* among friends, but would use a pronunciation closer to RP in most formal situations.

Like the rest of the British nation, therefore, Afro-Caribbeans have several varieties of accent and dialect from which to choose:

1 RP and Standard English, used by the more educated, like barrister and MP Paul Boateng or newscaster Moira Stewart;
2 Standard English spoken with the accent of the regions in which they happen to live;
3 Modified Jamaican creole, spoken by young Blacks when they feel in high spirits, or angry, or aggressive, or for any of the following reasons:
- to establish a group identity/racial solidarity (Rasta or 'Dread-talk' is an extreme form of this)
- to reject white (or black) outsiders
- to show contempt for people who think black culture inferior.

4 Full Jamaican creole, spoken largely by older members of the Afro-Caribbean community.

Far from being able to speak only creole, then, many young Blacks can use all these dialects, changing their register to suit context and audience. It therefore makes much more sense to talk of Jamaican creole (JC) and Black English (BE) rather than lump both together under the common label West Indian English.

The extreme end of the continuum: Jamaican creole

Jamaican creole (often called *patois*) is a language in its own right, with a full range of grammatical features and its own *lexis* (vocabulary) and *phonology* (system of pronunciation). (Afro-Caribbean immigrants did come from other islands of the West Indies, but the majority were from Jamaica, and so Jamaican creole has come to dominate the very similar dialects of Barbados, Guyana, St Vincent, and so on.)

Spoken largely by the older generation, full JC is difficult for English people to understand. Try your hand at the following example. (You will find you can recognize many of the words if you say them aloud, quickly. Black English is largely an oral language, and when it is written down, it is spelt as it is pronounced.)

> We go luk aan di difran wie hou di langwij we wi taak mos impaatan fi di blak pikni-dem iina skuul.

Literal translation

We (are) go(ing to) look at the different ways how the language that we talk (is) most important for the black children in school.

Standard English translation

We shall consider various aspects of language as they pertain to the education of West Indian children.

Creole, age, and gender

You might expect that West Indian immigrants to this country would bring up their children to speak creole like them, at least in the home. In fact, many Afro-Caribbean parents speak creole to their children but refuse to allow their children to use it to them in return, because:

a they think it unseemly for children to speak in such a familiar way to their parents;

b older West Indians are conscious of the undesirable associations that cling to creole: slavery, poverty, lack of education, and so on.

Edwards quotes typical reactions to this parental attitude:

> 'Dem a stop me and say, "We bring you over here fi h'educate you, a learn fi speak better", and all this kind of thing. Well, me used to listen to dem, but after dem gone, me used to speak the same.'
>
> 'Every couple of months Mum will go, "Look at Mrs Grant or somebody's children down the road, they speak lovely Henglish. A what wrong with unu?" . . . Then we go, "How now brown cow, the rain in Spain falls mainly on the plain." So she goes, "A what you a do? Lef' me alone!" '
>
> Viv Edwards, *The West Indian Language Issue in British Schools*

Hewitt mentions another factor that operates against the learning of creole:

> Really dense creole is used strictly for men-talk. The girls, as in other British dialects, tend to use Standard English with either a regional or modified RP accent.
>
> Roger Hewitt, *White Talk Black Talk*

The middle of the continuum: modified creole

Most young Afro-Caribbeans use a modified form of creole, generally referred to as patois, among their friends in informal situations. However, they can diverge upwards towards more ordinary English speech when necessary, as the following examples from Edwards, *Language in a Black Community*, show:

1 Don, a young Afro-Caribbean, is talking informally to friends and a black fieldworker doing research into young black people's use of patois:

> Dem [the questions] alright in a way, right. Dem reasonable. Dem could be lickle better, but dem reasonable. Me na bex [angry] wid dem, dem alright . . . When white people ready fi write some rubbish bout black people, dem can do it, dem can do it, right. So dat's why me say dem reasonable. Notn wrong wid dem.

2 Here, the same speaker is talking to black friends about some tickets for a dance that he has lost:

> Me still naa get in, mi still naa get in because a na fi-dem fault. Dat no have notn fi do wid dem.
>
> (I still won't get in, I still won't get in because it's not their fault. That hasn't got anything to do with them.)

3 Here, Don is again talking to black friends:

> Me say, 'Do it! Flash it!' Dat mean seh im a go beat im.
>
> (I say, 'Do it! Flash it!' That means he's going to beat him.)

These short extracts contain many patois features:

- the patois pronouns *mi* and *dem*;
- adjectives used as verbs: *bex, reasonable, alright;*
- *fi* before an infinitive;
- *no* in the form of *naa* instead of *is not*;
- the focusing particle *a*;
- the patois possessive *fi-dem* (their);
- the continuative particle *a* to form the present continuous tense: *im a go beat him*;
- *seh* after stative verbs.

4 Talking to white researchers, however, in a formal interview situation, Don's language was much closer to SE:

> I say it come from Africa really. It started from dere true slavery. Dat's di way I see it. It started from there, yeah. But those kids what born over here right, they don't want to admit it. Like Paddy, they don't want to admit it right that our culture started from Africa.

His pronunciation is still very Afro-Caribbean – *tru*, *dere*, *di* rather than *true*, *there*, and *the* – but he inflects his verb endings to show the past tense, uses the SE negative form *don't* instead of *naa*, and puts in linking verbs (copulas like *come*).

Code switching

Many young Blacks, especially girls, do not stick as closely to patois as Don does. They switch easily, often in mid-sentence, between patois words and patois pronunciation, often to show affection or to tease or to jazz things up a bit.

Creole and 'correctness'

The prescriptivist attitude towards both JC and BE speakers is that they use English sloppily, dropping inflexions, and refusing to do as SE users do out of sheer laziness. (They say the same about regional dialect users, too, of course.)

The wrongness of this idea has been pointed out by Loreto Todd in *Modern Englishes, Pidgins and Creoles.* Afro-Caribbeans cannot fairly be accused of dropping inflexions, she points out, because no such inflexions existed in the West African languages that formed the base of their creole. Other grammatical 'errors', such as using the wrong case of the pronoun, may well be due to the same reason.

Creole and slang

Creole has a vivid and immediate quality that makes it very appealing to white children and adolescents. Patois slang like *bad, wicked*, and *safe* has found its way into every London school and college. Researching the use of Black English in Camden schools, Maria Manning found children of many different ethnic backgrounds all using it as slang.

> Barney (aged nine), lip curled in contempt: 'You a *lame* chief, well lame, *serious* lame!'
>
> 'You say that to annoy someone, for instance if they don't score a goal. It's a cuss.'

'EEzee!' and 'rare!' are both terms of praise. The first means relaxed, laid-back, or 'cool', but is pronounced in the same way as the football chant, with both vowels given equal weight. 'Rare!' is an expression of wonder, gasped rather than spoken, and probably coming from DJs' patter at rap parties.

Why should Black English have such a strong influence on the informal speech of these multi-ethnic groups? Manning suggests two reasons:

1 'the spare, emphatic style of Black English' gives it a dynamic, forceful, immediate effect suited to the hard, fast life of city kids;

Creole and slang

2 Black English gives them the chance to thumb their noses at Standard English and all the things that go with it: respectability, conformity, passing examinations, and so on.

Black English, then, is being used by both white and black children to rebel against a culture that seems to have little to offer them.

Maria Manning writes:

> All the children I spoke to are white, but Black English speaks to them because they also feel excluded from the mythical 'British culture' enshrined in Standard English.

Activity

1 Ask Afro-Caribbean students in your school or college if they are willing to help you with some research into their own or their family's use of patois. This is a sensitive area, so be tactful and be ready for a refusal.

2 Devise a questionnaire in which you ask them:
a if they ever use any or all of the following;
b if so, how often;
c where they use them (i.e. home or elsewhere);
d in whose company.

Speakers of light patois will use *d* for *th* and *fi* instead of *to* with the infinitive. Speakers of moderate patois may, in addition to these, also use *fi* to show possession, *mi* for *me*, *im* for *him*, and *dem* after nouns as a plural marker. They may also use *seh* before certain verbs. The greater the number of non-standard features used after these, the fuller the creole. Non-standard features are listed below.

Differences between Jamaican Creole and Standard English

- no *-s* ending on plural nouns: *3 gal* (3 girls)
- *dem* used to mark plural nouns: *di gal dem* (the girls)
- word order and *fi* used to show possession: *Alvin woman* (Alvin's woman), *fi-mi records* (my records)
- no inflection on pronouns to show cases:
  mi (I, me, and my) *yu* (you, your) *im* (he, him, his, she, her)
  i (it, its) *we* (we, us, our) *unu* (you, your)
  dem (they, them, their)
- no *-s* ending on third-person singular of verb: *go* (goes), *taak* (talks)
- no inflection to show tense of verbs: *tel* (tell) is used for the past as well as the present
- *-a* used
  1 to mark the present participle: *a fight* (fighting)
  2 to mark the progressive tense in which actions are continuous: *mi a taak* (I am talking)
- *did*, *don*, and *ben* used to indicate the simple past tense (I have finished work) and the past perfect tense (I had finished work): *I did see her just now* (I saw her just a moment ago), *mi don sliip* (I have finished sleeping), *mi ben waak huom aredi* (I had already walked home)
- *wi* or *go* plus the verb stem used to indicate future tense: *they wi let you know/they go let you know* (they will tell you)
- *fi* used instead of *to* with infinitives: *you ask im how fi cook rice im no know* (if you ask him how to cook rice he doesn't know)
- lack of linking verbs, e.g. *is, seem, become: di gal happy* (the girl is happy), *who im?* (who's he?)
- the use of *seh* after verbs like *know*, *say*, *talk*, *hear*, and *be*, in place of *that* in English sentences: *A glad seh im gaan* (I'm glad that he's gone)
- unconventional negatives: use of *noh* before the verb to make it negative: *she decide seh she noh want it any more* (she decided she did not want it any more)

- multiple negation: *she decide seh she no want none no more* (she decided she didn't want any more)
- passives that look like actives: *this can't share* (you can't share this), *that record play a lot* (that record is played a lot)
- actives that look like passives: *he ain't easy to beat up* (he doesn't beat people up easily), *he's easy to annoy* (he annoys other people easily)
- *de* and *deh* used instead of *there*: *it deh* (it's there)

3 Ask your respondents where they learned any patois they may speak.

4 **a** Make a recording of a speaker with a creole accent.
b Make a phonetic transcript of part of your recording.
c Discuss the major differences in pronunciation between creole and RP.

5 Working from your notes, write a report on the use of patois within your locality.

2 Language and Grammar

The vocabulary of English

The family background of English

English belongs to the Germanic branch of the great Indo-European family of languages.

One theory suggests that all these languages evolved from one earlier one, spoken by a people who farmed Anatolia in eastern Turkey at some time before 6500 BC. The influence of this early ancestor can be seen in the table below, showing obvious similarities in the conjugation of verbs within the Indo-European family:

English	Sanskrit	Greek (Doric)	Latin	Old High German	Old Slavonic
I bear	bharami	phero	fero	biru	bera
(thou bearest)	bharasi	phereis	fers	binis	beresi
he bears	bharati	pherei	fert	birit	beretu
we bear	bharamas	pheromes	ferimus	berames	beremu
you bear	bharata	pherete	feris	beret	berete
they bear	bharanti	pheronti	ferunt	berant	beratu

F. Bodmer, *The Loom of Language*

The evolution of one language into many

The theory also suggests that the Indo-European language was spread, not by war and conquest, but by a peaceful process of expansion known as 'the wave of advance'. The process worked like this:

1 The farmers moved outwards from Anatolia, field by field, carrying their language first into Greece and Crete, then west across Europe to the British Isles and south-east into India.
2 As new areas of land were colonized, dialect forms of the original Indo-European language began to evolve.
3 These dialect forms began to harden into distinct sub-families of language, such as Old High German and Latin.
4 These sub-families evolved in turn into the separate languages spoken in various parts of Europe, India, and the Middle East. The 'Romance' languages, for example – French, Italian, Spanish, Portuguese, Catalan, and Romanian – all began life as 'dog-Latin', the form of the language spoken in the streets and bars, as opposed to the elite written form studied in schools and colleges: *horse*, for instance, is *equus* in classical Latin, *caballus* in the common form (Fr. *cheval*, Sp. *caballo*, It. *cavalto*). Dog-Latin would have been spoken with a different accent in the different regions of

the Roman Empire, but it was recognizably the same language. In the same way, German, English, Dutch, Danish, Swedish, and Icelandic all began as the same form of Old German before evolving their own identities and going their separate ways. The unmistakable signs of this common ancestry are shown below:

Da nobis hodie panem nostrum quotidianum	(Latin)
Donne-nous aujourd'hui notre pain quotidien	(French)
Danos hoy nuestro pan cotidiano	(Spanish)
Dacci oggi il nostro pane cotidiano	(Italian)
O pão nosso de cada dia dai-nos hoje	(Portuguese)
Gib uns heute unser täglich Brot	(German)
Geef ons heden ons dagelijksch brood	(Dutch)
Giv os i dag vort daglige brød	(Danish)
Giv oss i dag vårt dagliga bröd	(Swedish)
Gef oss i dag vort daglegt brauð	(Icelandic)

F. Bodmer, *The Loom of Language*

The arrival of English in Britain

Because of its situation on the western fringes of Europe, Britain has always been a last resort for peoples escaping from wars and famines on the Continent itself. Wave after wave of Celtic tribes colonized the country in prehistoric times, known only by vague labels such as the *Beaker People* (from archaeological finds). When the Germanic Angles, Saxons, and Jutes arrived in about 450 AD, they soon came to dominate the Celts, many of whom were driven into the mountains, islands, and coastal fringes. (The Romans, who had ruled them for five hundred years – a period equal to that between the early days of Elizabeth I and 1937 – had just gone, leaving them unprotected.)

The Celtic stock survived – not only among the Irish, the Welsh, and the Scots, but also among the people we now think of as 'English' – but the old Celtic language was overwhelmed by Anglo-Saxon and has left few traces: the element *coombe* (a deep valley) in place names like *Ilfracombe*; a few river names such as *Dart* and *Nene*; and a small number of nouns such as *ass*, *bannock*, *brock*, and *binn*.

An indication of the language that evolved out of the dialects of the Angles, Saxons, and Jutes – Anglo-Saxon or Old English – will be given in the section 'The grammar English has lost', on page 95.

The nature of English

Modern English is made up of three layers of vocabulary:

1 Anglo-Saxon (with additions from the Viking language, Old Norse)
2 French
3 Latin (with additions from Greek, often through Latin).

The Anglo-Saxon basis of English

Look at the passage below and you will see how much of the oldest part of our language has survived into the present day (words of Anglo-Saxon origin are in italic):

> *English was not* merely *the* product *of the* dialects *brought to England by the Jutes, Angles, and Saxons. These* formed *its* basis, *the* sole basis *of its* grammar, *and the* source *of by far the* largest part *of its* vocabulary. *But there were other* elements *which* entered *into it.*

Look at what is left when these are removed –

> merely . . . product . . . dialects . . . formed . . . basis . . . sole basis . . . grammar . . . source . . . largest part . . . vocabulary . . . elements . . . entered

– and you will see that it would be impossible for us to speak or write intelligibly without the help of Old English, simply because all the little *structure words* that hold sentences together – like *a*, *the*, *in*, and *that* – are Anglo-Saxon.

Other indispensable English structure words are:

- the personal pronouns *I*, *you*, *he*, *she*, *we*, *us*;
- the demonstrative pronouns *this*, *that*, *these*, *those*;
- the auxiliary verbs *can*, *shall*;
- the conjunctions *as*, *and*, *but*, *so*, *then*;
- the prepositions *on*, *in*, *under*, *over*, *down*, *up*, *to*, *by*;
- the adverbs *when*, *while*, *where*.

Many of our most familiar **content words** (the words that carry ideas) are also Anglo-Saxon in origin. For example:

Nouns

house (hūs)	love (lufu)	heart (heorte)	wife (wīf)
husband (hūsbonda)	father (fæder)	son (sunu)	friend (frēond)
ship (scip)	food (fōda)	grass (græs)	leaf (lēaf)
fowl *or* bird (fugol)	saddle (sadol)	water (wæter)	moon (mōna)
sun (sunne)	winter (winter)	spring (spryng)	fall (feall)
day (dæg)	night (niht)	king (cyning)	

Adjectives

right (riht)	evil (yfel)	cold (cald)	busy (bisig)
bloody (blōdig)	bitter (biter)	broad (brād)	black (blæc)

Verbs

eat (etan)	drink (drincan)	sleep (slǣpan)	live (libban)
fight (feohtan)			

Most names for parts of the body, most numbers, and most strong verbs also come from Anglo-Saxon. (Strong verbs are those that form their past tense by changing the vowel, e.g. *speak/spoke*. Examples include *ride, sing, think, fight, find, sit, stand, drink, have, hold, do, be.*)

Finally, most rude names for parts of the body and its functions – *arse* and *fart*, for example – are Anglo Saxon in origin (these two are found across the whole range of Indo-European languages). So are most of the 'four-letter words' that used to be written with initial and final letters and a row of asterisks in between: *sh**t*, *c***t*, and *f***k*, for example, although there are no written records of the last two before the twelfth century. Once perhaps terms acceptable in ordinary conversation, they have acquired obscene connotations over the centuries and cannot now be used in ordinary social contexts, nor on the television at peak viewing times.

Old Norse additions to Anglo-Saxon vocabulary

No sooner had Angles, Saxons, and Jutes begun to unite into one nation under Alfred the Great than they began to be invaded by Scandinavian Vikings. After harassing the English continuously from 787 to 1014, the Danes finally conquered them, and ruled the country for twenty-eight years.

The effect on the English language was relatively slight. The Germanic language spoken by the invaders – Old Norse – was so like Old English that Danes and Anglo-Saxons could understand one another as readily as Danes and Swedes do today, and the two languages eventually blended into one.

The following words, remarkably similar in sound and style to Old English vocabulary, all derive from Old Norse:

bank birth brink bull leg loan dirt dregs race root
steak thrift trust window fellow freckle gap guess seat
skill skin skirt sky awkward flat ill loose low meek
rotten tight weak muggy crawl die droop gasp get give
glitter raise rake scare scowl snub sprint take thrive thrust

The stylistic qualities of Old Norse words

As the above lists show, Old English and Old Norse words generally have a direct, forceful, no-nonsense quality. Many are monosyllabic; many, such as *sky*, *skin*, *skill*, *scrape*, *scrub*, *screech*, *bask*, *whisk*, contain consonants that sound harsh to the ear. (The Romans remarked, rather rudely, that listening to the speech of Germanic tribes was like listening to the cawing of crows.) Many of the harsher sounds of English derive from Old Norse. While Old English modified sharp Germanic 'sk' to a softer 'sh' sound, Scandinavian kept 'sk': hence, for example, OE *shirt*, ON *skirt*. The same is true of 'k' and 'g': when these are pronounced hard, as in *kid*, *dyke* (cf *ditch*), *get*, *give*, *egg*, etc., the words in which they occur are generally Old Norse in origin.

The sounds of Old Norse have made their contribution to English poetry. The English county of Yorkshire was once part of the Danelaw – the kingdom ceded to the Danes by King Alfred – and many Scandinavian words linger on in its dialects – *gill* for stream, for instance. The most famous poet born in that region, Ted Hughes, ignores actual dialect words but exploits the harsh sounds of Anglo-Saxon and Old Norse in poems like the following:

Thistles

Against the rubber tongues of cows and the hoeing hands of men
Thistles spike the summer air
Or crackle open under a blue-black pressure.

Every one a revengeful burst
Of resurrection, a grasped fistful
Of splintered weapons and Icelandic frost thrust up

From the underground stain of a decayed Viking.
They are like pale hair and the gutturals of dialects.
Every one manages a plume of blood.

Then they grow grey, like men.
Mown down, it is a feud. Their sons appear,
Stiff with weapons, fighting back over the same ground.

Ted Hughes

Only ten words of this poem – *hoeing*, *blue*, *revengeful*, *resurrection*, *pressure*, *pale*, *gutturals*, *dialects*, *plume*, and *appear* – are from Latin or French; with the exception of *rubber* (origin unknown), the remaining eighty-one are either Old English, Old Norse, Old Swedish, or Old German in origin.

Activity Explain the similarities Hughes sees between thistles, Viking warriors, and the old Germanic dialects.

French additions to English vocabulary

Although the Norman French who ruled England from 1066 onwards were from the same stock as the Danes who had invaded England three centuries earlier, they were by now a very different people: thoroughly civilized and thoroughly French. (*Norman* means Northman or Viking.)

For three hundred years the Normans lorded it over the English in every way, controlling the government, the legal system, the army, and the church, and laying the foundations of the class divisions that have plagued English society ever since.

Activity

1. **a** Look up the entry under *punishment* in Roget's or any other thesaurus.
   b Check the derivation of the word and its given synonyms (words that have similar meanings).
   c Write a paragraph on what this indicates about the Conquest.
2. Read the first two pages of *Ivanhoe* by Sir Walter Scott.
3. Look up the word *marshal* in an encyclopaedia such as Longman's *English Larousse* and write a paragraph on what it reveals about French control of English society.

The English language suffered, too. For two hundred years after the Conquest, the kings of England spoke French, governed part of France, and took French women for their wives. Since French was the language of the Court, the upper and middle classes spoke French also, leaving only the unambitious and the peasants to speak English.

Nevertheless, although it took them a lot longer than it did their earlier Scandinavian kin, the Norman French did eventually settle down to become English and speak the Anglo-Saxon tongue. In the process, hundreds of French words passed into English, covering a wide range of contexts from cookery to religion to heraldry and the law. The resulting language, known as Middle English, is far closer to the language we speak today than was its Old English predecessor.

The stylistic qualities of French loan words

Although many humble words such as *bucket* come originally from French, most French borrowings are elegant words, with connotations of chivalry, courtliness, refinement, and romance. The French brought new and softer sounds into English, and, because they stressed their words differently, more varied rhythms also.

The rhythms of Middle English poetry and prose could be rather monotonous, thanks to the Anglo-Saxon habit of forward stress – the habit of placing the strongest stress on the first syllable of most words (or on the second if the first was a prefix; e.g. *bóard*, but *abóard*). Early borrowings from French were Anglicized by being stressed in this way: *góvernment*, *míracle*, *próperty*. Later ones, however, retained both a little of their original French pronunciation and the French system of giving equal stress to all the syllables of a word, as in *chócólát* (English *CHOClate*): *prémíére*, *clíché*, *néglígée*, *élíte*, *débútánte*, and so on.

Activity

Here is a list of English words and phrases which mean the same as words we have borrowed from the French. The first letter of each French word is given in brackets as a guide:

an illicit sexual affair (l)
a secret meeting (r)
remission given to a convict (p)
face fungus (m)
girl with dark hair (b)
public eating place (r)
an engaged person (f)
what success brings (p . . . . . . e)

1 Write down the appropriate word against its definition.
2 Check that you
a pronounce it with something of a French accent,
b distribute the stress over its several syllables.

The process reversed

> **Sound Bites**
>
> Un scoop, un one-man-show, une duty-free shop, un escalator, le fast-food, un jumbo-jet, un ferry, hot money, le Walkman, le bulldozer. **'Barbarous Anglo-Saxon terms' proscribed by the fifth edition of the Official Dictionary of Neologism, published by French Government this week**
>
> The Guardian, 31 December 1988

Latin and Greek additions to English vocabulary

Greek has been included with Latin here rather than treated separately in its own right. This is because Latin words are

a more numerous than Greek,
b more relevant to most people's experience.

It is true that twentieth-century scientists have drawn on Greek rather than Latin for words to name their inventions and discoveries. Medicine, for instance, has adapted the Greek suffixes *-itis* and *-osis* to signify disease, creating words like *arthritis*, *appendicitis*, *bronchitis*, *halitosis*, *neurosis*, *tuberculosis*, and *psychosis*. But the fact remains that Latin has made a far deeper and wider impact on the English language. Greek borrowings have to do with more specialized and esoteric concerns, as the following sample will show:

grammar logic rhetoric arithmetic geometry astronomy
music academy atom acrobat Bible diphthong harmony
ecstasy nymph tyrant drama theatre comedy tragedy climax
catastrophe episode scene dialogue chorus prologue
epilogue irony alphabet elegy dilemma caustic basis pathos
epic theory orchestra pandemonium museum hyphen dogma
clinic bathos philander phase pylon therm agnostic

Activity Look up the derivation of *homo* in words like *homosexual* and *homogeneous*, and of *hetero* in words such as *heterosexual*, *heterogeneous*. You will need to know the latter for the next section.

Although English was once a largely homogeneous Germanic or Teutonic language, well over half its vocabulary today is derived from Latin. We began to borrow wholesale from Latin during the Middle Ages, when scholars throughout Europe wrote and spoke to one another in that language. As a result, we lost our habit of coining new words out of existing English elements (*hand-book* for L. *manual*, for instance, and *Threeness* for *Trinity*) and started taking words directly from Latin texts instead. Interestingly, modern German, although sprung from the same Teutonic roots as Anglo-Saxon, has kept this ability. Where we borrowed from Latin, they formed new words out of existing German elements:

English	**German**
contradict (from L. *contra* = against, *dicere*, *dictum* = to speak)	widersprechen (from G. *wider* = against *sprechen* = to speak)
solidarity (from L. *solidus* = of dense consistency, firm, substantial)	Zusammengehörigkeitsgefühl (from G. *zusammen* = together *Gehörigkeit* = belonging *Gefühl* = feeling)

Just how widely we've borrowed from Latin is shown in the following list. (Those of you who are studying German or French or Spanish might like to check the equivalent words in those languages.)

pauper proviso equivalent legitimate index scribe simile
memento requiem collect (noun) diocese mediator tolerance
abject adjacent allegory conspiracy contempt custody
distract frustrate genius gesture history homicide immune
incarnate include incredible incubus incumbent index
individual infancy interior infinite innate innumerable intellect
interrupt juniper lapidary legal limbo

Note: not all of these words came directly from Latin. Some, like *equivalent*, *collect*, *diocese*, *mediator*, *tolerance*, *conspiracy*, and *homicide*, are Latin words which found their way into Old French before they were borrowed by English. In the same way, *allegory* and *history* originally came into Latin from Greek. Words borrowed from the Romance languages have a mixed parentage: the Romans borrowed from the Greeks, the French borrowed from the Romans, and we in turn have borrowed their borrowings. Loan words may therefore have been taken straight from the original language or have entered indirectly via another language, in a slightly modified form.

Activity

1 Look up any words in the above list that you do not know.
2 Write clear definitions of the first six words on the list.
3 What is the most striking difference between the Latin words and your definitions of them?
4 Argue the case for and against getting rid of Latin loan words by 'translating' them into native English elements – *ungettatable* for *inaccessible*, say; *unseethroughable* for *opaque*. (Don't forget to take spelling as well as comprehensibility into account.)

Today we would find it hard to manage without such Latin prefixes as *anti*, *re*, *pro*, *trans*, *post*, *pre*, *sub*, and *de*; and suffixes such as *-ate*, *-ic*, and *-al* (as in *educate*, *elastic*, *normal*, *abysmal*). And to appreciate the importance of Greek and Latin roots, we have only to look at Greek *logos* (a speaking or discourse on, i.e. the science or study of), and *-nomia* (arrangement, management, regulation, i.e. classification of, science of), found in the form of *-ology* and *-onomy* in words like *biology*, *astronomy*, and countless other scientific terms. The academic world would collapse without them.

The stylistic qualities of Latin loan words

Generally speaking, the words we have borrowed from Latin are lengthy, impressive, and polysyllabic. They carry prestige and authority.

The advantage of a heterogeneous language: precision

Thanks to the mingling of Latin, French, and native Anglo-Saxon elements, English is rich in synonyms. The French have a word for everything, we are told. We have at least three, with different qualities that fit them for different purposes in different contexts. We have:

- ◆ Anglo-Saxon words that are familiar, immediate, and therefore warm in tone;
- ◆ French borrowings that are more formal and polite;
- ◆ more esoteric and learned Latin loan words, that seem weightier, solemn, and more remote.

In theory, therefore, English speakers can always find the exact word they need for a particular context: the Saxon word for ordinary situations; the sophisticated French word for more fashionable contexts; the more recondite Latin word for more abstract, metaphysical concerns. The distinctive qualities of these different kinds of word can be seen in the following sets, where the first word is always native English, the second French, and the third Latin in origin:

ask–question–interrogate	thin–spare–emaciated	folk–people–nation
help–aid–assistance	goodness–virtue–probity	fast–firm–secure
fire–flame–conflagration	holy–sacred–consecrated	time–age–epoch

Baugh, *A History of the English Language*

Activity

1. Put the following groups of three into the same English–French–Latin sequence as above, judging which word belongs to which language purely on sound and 'feel'.
   a impecunious, needy, financially distressed
   b inept, incompetent, gauche
   c residence, domicile, house
   d reserved, close-mouthed, uncommunicative
   e harden, solidify, coagulate
2. Check that you are correct by consulting *The Concise Oxford Dictionary*.
3. Write sentences using all the words of each set.
4. Discuss the different tone and atmosphere of the sentences you have created out of each set of synonyms. What impression do they make on you? How do they sound?

The use of Latinate words in English literary writing

Writers who use a predominantly Latinate style do so for one or more of the following reasons:

1 They find a sensuous appeal in the quality of Latin words. They love the fullness and richness of their vowels, the strength (without harshness) of their consonants. (Examples: Sir Thomas Browne, John Milton, Thomas Babington Macaulay, Henry James, Joseph Conrad.)
2 They feel that nothing less than elevated Latinate diction can match the dignity and importance of their subject-matter. (Johnson criticized Shakespeare for using the humble word 'blanket' in the context of a tragedy.) (Examples: Jonathan Swift, Samuel Johnson.)
3 They have no choice but to use Latinate diction since the metaphysical nature of their themes – the nature of love, the conflict in the heart between good and evil, the concept of individual responsibility, the problem of guilt, for instance – can be fully discussed only in such terms. (Examples: Milton, Swift, Johnson, James, Conrad.)
4 The education of their time being based upon the study of Greek and Latin, they believe a Latinate style to be the mark of an educated man. (Examples: Alexander Pope, John Dryden, Joseph Addison, Richard Steele.)

To describe the styles that result, however different, critics use adjectives of an appropriately Latinate kind: when critics are in favour, *sonorous, resonant, magnificent, dignified,* and *eloquent* are used; when they are not, *over-elaborate, unnatural, inflated, pretentious, pompous* and *excessively formal.*

Below are brief extracts from the work of three of the main exponents of the Latinate style in English: Milton, Conrad, and Henry James. (Latinate words in all three extracts are printed in italics.)

A

Him the Almighty Power
Hur'ld headlong flaming from th'*Ethereal* Sky
With *hideous* ruin and combustion down
To bottomless *perdition*, there to dwell
In *Adamantine* Chains and *penal* Fire,
Who durst defy th'*Omnipotent* to Arms . . .

Milton, *Paradise Lost*

B

She was *savage* and *superb*, wild-eyed and *magnificent*; there was something *ominous* and *stately* in her *deliberate progress*. And in the hush that had fallen *suddenly* upon the whole sorrowful land, the *immense* wilderness, the *colossal* body of the *fecund* earth and *mysterious* life seemed to look at her, *pensive*, as though it had been looking at the image of its own *tenebrous* and *passionate* soul.

Conrad, *Heart of Darkness*

C

> Felix had *observed* on the day before his *characteristic pallor*, and now he *perceived* that there was something almost *cadaverous* in his uncle's high-featured white face. But so clever were this young man's quick *sympathies* and *perceptions* that he had already learned that in these *semi-mortuary manifestations* there was no cause for alarm. His light *imagination* had gained a glimpse of Mr Wentworth's *spiritual mechanism*, and taught him that, the old man being *infinitely conscientious*, the *special operation* of *conscience* within him *announced* itself by several of the *indications* of *physical faintness*.
>
> Henry James, *The Europeans*

Each is a great writer in his own particular way; none of the three should be judged on little snippets taken out of context.

The rise and fall of Latinate vocabulary

Latin words began to flood into English at the beginning of the Renaissance, from the 1430s onwards. During the seventeenth and eighteenth centuries English writers and scholars modelled their work on classical literature and borrowed still more. Philosophers such as Francis Bacon and scientists like Sir Isaac Newton wrote their treatises in Latin, and attempts were even made to teach grammar school students in that language. (Shakespeare learned his 'little Latin and less Greek' at Stratford Grammar and got his revenge later by mocking pedants who talked in Latin, in plays like *Love's Labours Lost*.)

Nevertheless, up to 1650, English writers could take or leave Latin borrowings. If a Latin word was useful in making a point it would find a place in a sentence, but the surrounding vocabulary would be predominantly English.

The situation changed dramatically in the second half of the seventeenth century, when the roles of the two languages were almost reversed. A glance at the table below will show the percentage of native English and Latin loan words in the work of the 'best' English writers:

		English %	Latin %
The Authorized Version of the Bible	1611	94	6
Shakespeare	1564–1616	90	10
Spenser	1552–1599	86	14
Milton	1608–1674	81	19
Addison	1672–1719	82	18
Swift	1667–1745	75	25
Pope	1688–1744	80	20

Johnson	1709–1784	72	28
Hume	1711–1776	73	27
Gibbon	1737–1794	70	30
Macaulay	1800–1859	75	25
Tennyson	1809–1892	88	12

Baugh, *A History of the English Language*

The larger the number of Latinate words in a piece of writing, therefore, the greater the likelihood that it was written between 1650 and 1800. The main exceptions to this rule of thumb are Sir Thomas Browne, 1605–1682, who took to Latinisms rather earlier than most other writers, and Thomas Babington Macaulay, who took to them in a much later period. (The five-year-old Macaulay, asked how he was feeling after being scalded by a cup of hot tea, replied, 'Thank you, ma'am, the agony is much abated'.) Not until Wordsworth's stand for 'language such as men do use' did things begin slowly to change, and he was soundly criticized for his efforts. Here is an example of Wordsworth's 'common' language, 'such as men do use':

> In the sweet shire of Cardigan,
> Not far from pleasant Ivor-hall,
> An old man dwells, a little man,
> I've heard he once was tall.
> Of years he has upon his back,
> No doubt, a burthen weighty;
> He says he is three score and ten,
> But others say he's eighty.
>
> William Wordsworth, *Simon Lee, The Old Huntsman*, 1798

And here is a contemporary critic's opinion of it, full of the kind of Latinate vocabulary he would have preferred Wordsworth to use for the dignity of English poetry:

> Long habits of seclusion, and an excessive ambition of originality can alone account for the disproportion which seems to exist between this author's taste and his genius . . . Solitary musings [among his lakes and mountains] might no doubt be expected to nurse up the mind to the majesty of poetical conception, – (though it is remarkable, that all the greater poets lived, or had lived, in the full current of society): – But the collision of equal minds – the admonition of prevailing impressions – seems necessary to reduce its redundancies, and repress that tendency to extravagance or puerility, into which the self-indulgence and self-admiration of genius is so apt to be betrayed, when it is allowed to wanton, without awe or restraint, in the triumph and delight of its own intoxication.

English as a world language

Whether they are learning English in their own countries or as emigrants to an English-speaking country, speakers of Germanic and Romance languages find English readily accessible and easy to pick up because they find echoes of their own languages in its mixed vocabulary.

As a result, English, rather than German, French, Spanish, or Italian, is fast becoming the *lingua franca* of a common European civilization, and the major language of the world.

Latin and Greek elements

Since so many of our most important words are drawn from Latin and Greek, knowledge of the elements that make them up improves writing and reading skills enormously. Teachers in New York ghetto schools recently tried teaching low-achieving black children the most important Latin and Greek elements and roots; their vocabulary, reading ability, and behaviour all improved dramatically. They had been given a key to understanding language, and it helped.

Browse through the following list of Latin and Greek elements and then carry out the activities suggested below.

Prefixes

a, an (Gk) *a-*, *an-* not, un-, -less, without: *agnostic*, *amoral*, *amorphous*
ab, abs, a (L) *a*, *ab*, *abs* away, from, away from: *abduct*, *aberration*, *abstinence*
ad, a (L) *ad* towards, against, at: *adhere*, *adjacent*, *admire*, *advent*
amb(i) (L) *ambo*, *amb(i)* both, around, about: *ambidextrous*, *ambiguous*, *ambivalent*
ant(e) (L) *ante* before: *antecedent*, *antediluvian*, *antenatal*, *anteroom*
ant(i) (Gk) *anti* against, opposite: *Antarctic*, *antibiotic*, *antidote*
aut(o) (Gk) *autos* self, by oneself: *autistic*, *autobiography*. *autograph*
bene (L) *bene* well: *benediction*, *benefactor*, *benefit*, *benevolent*
bi, bin, bis (L) *bi* two, twice: *biceps*, *biennial*, *bilateral*, *bilingual*
circa, circum (L) *circum* around: *circuit*, *circumcision*, *circumlocution*
com, con, co (L) *co* with, together: *coeducation*, *cohabit*, *compatriot*
de (L) *de* down from, away from, off: *decelerate*, *declivity*, *decrease*
dis, di (L) *dis-*, *di-* apart; different, *digress*, *discordant*, *dislocate*, *disrupt*
dys (Gk) *dys* badly, ill-: *dysentery*, *dysfunction*, *dyslexic*, *dyspepsia*
en, em (Gk) *en* in: *emblem*, *empathy*, *energy*, *enthusiast*
equ(i), iniqui (L) *aequus* equal: *equanimity*, *equidistant*, *equilibrium*
eu (Gk) *eu-* well-: *eulogy*, *euphonious*, *euphuistic*
ex, e (L) *e*, *ex* from, out of, away from: *effluent*, *effulgent*, *effusion*
hyper (Gk) *hyper* over: *hyperactive*, *hyperbole*, *hypercritical*
in, im, i (L) *in-* in, into, upon, un-: *illicit*, *immure*, *impose*, *incarnate*
orth(o) (Gk) *orthos* straight, right: *orthodox*, *orthography*, *orthopaedics*
par(a) (Gk) *para* beside, beyond: *paramedic*, *paramilitary*, *paranormal*
poly (Gk) *poly-* much, many: *polygamy*, *polyglot*, *polygon*, *polymath*

post, poster (L) *post* after: *postdate, posterity, posthumous, postprandial*
pre (L) *prae* before, in front: *precede, preclude, precursor, predict*
re (L) *re-* back, again: *recline, recurrent, regress, reject, rejuvenate*
retro (L) *retro* backwards: *retroactive, retrograde, retrogress, retrospective*
sub (L) *sub* under: *subaqua, subhuman, subplot, suburb, suffix, suppress*

Roots

acer(b), acid, acri(d), acu (L) *acer, acr-* sharp, bitter: *acerbic, acrimony, exacerbate*
amic, am(or), imic (L) *amor* love, *amicus* friend: *amateur, amicable, inimical*
anim (L) *animus* mind, *anima* mind, spirit, soul: *animated, animosity, magnanimous*
ann, enn (L) *annus* year: *annuity, biennial, centennial, millennium*
arch (Gk) *-arches/os* ruler, ruling: *anarchy, hierarchy, oligarchy, patriarch*
arch(i) (Gk) *archi-* first, chief: *archbishop, archduke, archetypal, architect*
ast(e)r(o) (Gk) *aster* star: *asterisk, astrology, astronaut, disastrous*
aud(io) (L) *audire, audit-* to hear: *audible, audience, audition, auditorium*
bio (Gk) *bios* life: *amphibious, antibiotic, biochemistry, biography*
capit (L) *caput, capit-* head: *capital, capitation, capitulate, decapitate*
chron(o) (Gk) *chronos* time: *anachronistic, chronic, chronological, synchronize*
cosm(o) (Gk) *kosmos* world, universe: *cosmic, macrocosm, microcosm*
cred (L) *credere, credit-* to trust, believe: *credible, creditable, credulous*
cur(r), curs (L) *currere, curs-* to run: *concur, concurrent, precursor*
dem(o) (Gk) *demos* the people: *demagogue, endemic, epidemic, pandemic*
dic(t) (L) *dicere, dict-* to say, speak: *contradict, dictator, diction*
duc(t) (L) *ducere, duct-* to lead: *aqueduct, deduce, educate, seduce*
exter(n), extr(a), extrem (L) *exterus* outside, outward: *exterior, extracurricular*
fac(t), fect, fic, fiat (L) *facere, fact-* to make, do: *affect, benefactor, fact*
fin (L) *finis* boundary, end: *affinity, confine, define, finite*
hetero (Gk) *heteros* other: *heterodox, heterogeneous, heterosexual*
(h)om(o) (Gk) *homos* same, *homalos* even, level: *anomaly, homogeneous*
hydr(o) (Gk) *hydor* water: *dehydrate, hydrant, hydraulic, hydrophobia*
labor (L) *labor* work: *collaborate, elaborate, laboratory, laborious*
loc (L) *locus* place: *allocate, dislocate, local, location, locum*
magn(i) (L) *magnus* big: *magnanimous, magnate, magnificent, magnum opus*
mal(e) (L) *male* badly, ill, *malus* bad, evil: *malaria, malediction, malfunction*
mar(in) (L) *mare* the sea: *marinade, marine, maritime, submarine*
medi (L) *medius* middle: *intermediary, medi(a)eval, mediate, mediocre*
mon(o) (Gk) *mono-* alone, single: *monarch, monastery, monograph, monolith*
nom(ic) (Gk) *-nomia* arrangement, management: *astronomy, economy*
nom(in) (L) *nomen, nomin-* name: *denomination, ignominy, misnomer, nomenclature*

omni (L) *omnis* all: *omnibus, omnipotent, omniscient, omnivorous*
oper, opus (L) *opus, oper-* a work: *cooperate, magnum opus, modus operandi*
pass, pat (L) *pati, pass-* to suffer: *compassion, impassive, patience*
phot(o), phos (Gk) *phos, phot-* light: *phosphorus, photograph, photosynthesis*
sci (L) *scire* to know: *conscience, conscious, nescient, prescience*
scrib, script (L) *scribere, script-* to write: *describe, inscription, scribe*
spir (L) *spirare, spirat-* to breathe: *aspire, conspire, expire, inspire, spirit*
super, suprem (L) *super* above: *insuperable, superfluous, supernatural*
syn (syl, sym, sys, sy) (Gk) *syn* with: *synchronize, synonym, synthesis*
tel(e) (Gk) *tele* far: *telegram, telepathy, telephone, telescope*
ter(r)(estr) (L) *terra* the earth: *terrestrial, extraterrestrial, Mediterranean*
the(o), thus (Gk) *theos* God: *apotheosis, atheist, enthusiasm, pantheist*
tract (L) *trahere, tract-* to draw, drag: *abstract, attract, contract*
tra(ns) (L) *trans* across: *trajectory, transact, transatlantic, transcend*
urb (L) *urbs* city: *conurbation, suburb, urban, urbane*

Mary Byrne, *Eureka*

Activity

1. Using *The Concise Oxford Dictionary*, look up the meaning of any unknown words in the above list.
2. The element *jur* from L *jurare*, to swear, occurs in several important English words. Find words containing this element with the following meanings:
   - to swear away or renounce
   - to perform magical tricks
   - a body of people sworn to deliver a verdict
   - the swearing of a falsehood.
3. Use the element *liber* (L for *free*) to form words with the following meanings:
   - generous
   - to set free
   - free thinker or person of loose morals.
4. Using the elements *man(i)* and *manu* (from L *manus*, hand) create words with the following meanings:
   - to control things (by hand)
   - hand care
   - to influence someone's behaviour for one's own ends
   - an instruction booklet
   - to produce something commercially
   - (thing) written by hand.
5. *Inter* derives from the Latin word for *among, between*. Find words containing this element with the following meanings:
   - among other things (two Latin words are used for this)
   - a go-between
   - between nations
   - mutually communicating
   - (cause a) break between

- between continents
- scatter between
- mutual dependence
- period between two events
- to throw in, interpose (remark, etc.)
- to come between.

6 Use the elements *jug*, *junct*, and *jung* from Latin *jungere*, to join, to form words that mean the following:
- relating to a married pair
- a word that joins other words or clauses
- a joining
- a crucial moment or point in time
- to bring under control, conquer.

7 Bigamy means the state of being married to two people at the same time. What is meant by *monogamy*, *polygamy*, and *hypergamy*?

8 *Dogma* and *dox* come from Greek *dokeein*, to think, and *doxa*, opinion. What do the following words mean: *dogma*, *dogmatic*, *heterodox*, *orthodox*, *paradox*?

9 Look up the meaning of *panacea*, *pandemonium*, *panorama*, *pantheism*, and *pantheon*. What is the derivation of the element they all have in common?

10 *Path(o)* from Gk *pathos* signifies *suffering*, *experience*, *feeling*. What kinds of feeling are indicated by the following words with this element: *antipathy*, *sympathy*, *empathy*, *apathy*, *telepathy*?

11 **a** Look up the derivations of *citizen*, *civil*, *civilization*; *savage*, and *primitive*.
b Define as clearly as you can the difference between a primitive and a civilized society.
c What other meaning can you find for *civilized*? Can the natives of certain primitive societies be called civilized in this sense of the word? Can the industrialized societies of the West?

12 The following elements are particularly useful to students of English language and literature. Look them up and make notes on them for your own use:

bath(y) (Gk) *bathos* depth
cris, crit (Gk) *krisis* judgment
gram (Gk) *gramma*, *grammat-* thing written, writing, letter, line
graph (Gk) *graphein* to write
loc, loq (L) *loqui*, *locut-* to speak
log (Gk) *logos* a speaking, speech, saying, word, discourse, thought, reasoning, reckoning, ratio
morph (Gk) *morphe* form, shape, figure
onym, onomast, onomato (Gk) *onoma*, *onomat-* name
or(at) (L) *orare*, *orat-* to speak, make a speech, plead, pray
phras (Gk) *phrasis* a speaking, speech
romanc, romant (L) *Roma* (Rome) romance
thes(is), thet (Gk) *thesis* a placing, setting
verb (L) *verbum* word

The prescriptivist attitude towards vocabulary

Like pronunciation and grammar, vocabulary undergoes a constant process of change. We make up new words to express new ideas or to dress up old ones (*interface*; *state of the art*); we extend the meaning of existing words by using them metaphorically (*the bottom line*); we alter the meaning of existing words by using them in mistake for others. *Prevaricate*, for example, is presently being confused with *procrastinate* by speakers as diverse as Margaret Thatcher (she accused General Galtieri of prevaricating when he was playing for time – enough to start a war in itself had his English been good enough) and a Radio 2 sports commentator – a fair indication that a shift of meaning is under way.

This last practice rouses the anger of prescriptivists – people who would like words to be used only with their 'original' meanings.

Activity

Read the passage that follows, written in the 1960s, and carry out the suggested tasks.

It is certainly a rather sterile pursuit to attack what we know (or what dictionaries could tell us) are thoroughly established words. Despite strong opinion to the contrary, it is futile to try to stop words from being used in a sense different from that in which they were used at some earlier period. Such an 'etymological fallacy' betrays, in any case, a lamentable ignorance of the nature of language. We are still occasionally told that it is incorrect to use *tremendous* in the sense of huge because the word 'really' means 'that which causes trembling', the 'really' deriving its force from the fact that *tremendous* comes from the gerundive of the Latin verb *tremere*, to tremble. If such pedantic considerations are taken as the basis of 'correctness', then the 'correct' meaning of style is a pointed instrument and the 'correct' meaning of like, a body. One could not speak of arriving at King's Cross, because King's Cross has no shore, and the word's derivation shows that at one time it meant to come to the shore . . . Change of meaning is commonplace, and indeed it would appear to be fundamental in living language. One reason for the futility of objecting to a modern meaning lies in the fact that almost every word we use today has a slightly different meaning from the one it had a century ago: and a century ago it had a slightly different meaning from the one it had a century before that. Or rather meanings. For it is natural for a word to have more than one, and we can even say that, the commoner the word, the more meanings it has: and this is a further reason for seeing the search for a 'correct' or 'basic' meaning as futile. In his fascinating, recent book, *Studies in Words*, Professor C.S. Lewis explains the steps by which even an apparently simple word like 'sad' has radically changed its meaning over the years. It once meant 'full to the brim', 'well-fed'; one could be thoroughly 'sad' with food and drink (sated, satiated, satisfied, and saturated are etymologically related to it). From this it came to mean 'solid' as well; a good spear could be sad, and one could sleep sadly. This idea of solidness was then metaphorically applied to human character, and a person who was reliable and firm could be called sad. It is now easy to see how the chief modern sense could come into existence; a well-fed person may feel solid, heavy, and dull, and thus be sober-faced on that account: we must not forget the slang use of the expression 'fed-up' which offers something of a semantic parallel. Alternatively, a person who is reliable and firm is a serious person, and serious is the opposite of light-hearted and gay.

In the face of so universal a natural process, one may as well sit on the shore and order back the advancing tide as attempt to turn back the tide of semantic change. The conclusion is obvious (and has been accepted by dictionary makers for generations): the only practical and reasonable standard of a word's acceptability at all or in a particular sense is usage. If lay-by is in use among lorry-drivers, Ministry of Transport and local Government officials, that is enough: the word can be recorded in our dictionaries with the meaning that is current among those who use the word. If guts is used for courage, but with some contextual restriction, the lexicographer will still record this sense, but will add a note on the particular restriction he has noticed ('informal' or 'colloquial' perhaps). In either case, he will be accurately and objectively representing the usage as he observes it: he will not be sitting as a magistrate, frowning upon the 'ugly', 'atrocious', or vile.

Randolph Quirk, *The Use of English*

1 In paragraph I the writer castigates prescriptivists for ignorance and pedantry.
- **a** What etymological fallacy are prescriptivists working on if they suppose that words can always be used in their original meaning?
- **b** Why could their 'pedantic considerations' never be taken as the basis of 'correctness'?

2 With particular reference to the second half of the last sentence, 'he will not be sitting . . .' discuss what the writer thinks of prescriptivist attitudes towards the use of words.

3 What do you understand by a 'contextual restriction' (line 45)?

4 Look up the following words in the micro-print edition of *The Oxford English Dictionary*, tracing their change of meaning through the centuries:
horrible awful enormous extravagant disgusting nice
modern admiration sophisticated gay

5 Use the following words in sentences of your own devising:
aggravate, chronic, disinterested.
Look up the dictionary definition of these words and make notes for your own use.
If your use of the above three words agrees with one of the formal definitions given, does that make it correct? If so, in what way is it correct?
If your use of the words corresponds to the entries followed by the note '(coll.)', does that mean it is wrong? If not, in what sense can it be said to be right?
If these three words eventually survive only in their colloquial meaning, will anything be lost?
Do you agree with the writer when he says that the sole criterion of a word's acceptability is usage?
If not, what methods could you suggest for preserving important meanings?

Grammar and syntax

The grammar English has lost

Note: you are not asked to learn the grammar discussed in this section, but simply to be aware that it once existed.

Some people complain that English 'has very little grammar'. What do they mean?

They mean that the structure of individual words in modern English is less interesting than in certain other languages such as modern German and French because we have lost our habit of inflecting words: that is, showing their meaning by altering their form.

Inflections

Words can be inflected:

1 by changing the vowels inside a word, as we do with irregular plurals such as *feet* (singular 'foot');

2 by adding letters at the end, as we do when we add *-s* to regular nouns to make them plural, and *-s* and *-ed* endings to verbs to show number and tense:

(I) walk, (he/she) walk*s*, (you/we/they) walk*ed*.

Languages that inflect their words are called *synthetic* languages, as opposed to *analytical* ones that don't, like English.

Take for example the Latin sentence, *Nero interfecit Agrippinam.* (Nero murdered Agrippina.) The fact that the word *Nero* has no inflection shows that he is the **subject** of the sentence – the agent or doer of the action. The *-m* inflection on *Agrippina* on the other hand shows her to be the **object** of the sentence, the receiver of the action. It would make no difference therefore if we altered the word order and wrote *Agrippinam interfecit Nero*, for the *-m* inflection on *Agrippina* gives it only one possible meaning: she was the victim of Nero's action – the murderee, as an American might say.

In modern English, on the other hand, we use word order to show meaning: subjects are always placed first and objects second. Change *Nero killed Agrippina* to *Agrippina killed Nero* and you change completely the meaning of the sentence.

Like Latin, Old English was a highly inflected language. Its words changed their forms to show

a their function,

b their agreement with other words in a sentence.

For example, Old English nouns had four inflections (or case-endings) to show their function in a sentence.

Inflections of noun and pronoun in Old English

- the **nominative** or **subject** case (showing that it was the subject)
- the **accusative** or **object** case (showing that it was the object. This case is sometimes also called the *direct object.*)
- the **genitive** or **possessive** case (showing that something belonged to it)
- the **dative** (showing that something was being done by, or to, or for it; it would also cover the meanings *in* and *on*, for which there was no separate *ablative* case, as there was in Latin. The dative case is sometimes also called the *indirect object.*)

For example:

N stān (*stone*)	cyning (*king*)
A stān	cyninge
G stānes	cyninges
D stāne	cyninge

Baugh, *A History of the English Language*

To see how the system worked, imagine having to inflect a common noun like *cat*. Instead of using the same form of the word whenever we mentioned the animal, we should have to vary it to suit its function in the sentence, like this:

The cat [*nominative case*] is hungry.
We have a nice cate [*accusative case*].
The cates [*genitive or possessive case*] food is in the cupboard.
Give some to the cate [*dative case*].

Any other nouns used in the sentence would also have to be inflected, of course: in the examples above involving the cat, *food* would take the accusative case-ending, *cupboard* the dative, for instance. And even then the complexities were not over: there was the **declension** to take into account.

Declension

Nouns that ended in a vowel took the case-endings of the weak declension; those that ended in a consonant took those of the strong. Thus, *stan* (see below) belongs to the strong declension, *gièfu* and *hunta* to the weak.

Singular	N	stān	gièf-u	hunt-a
	G	stān-es	gièf-e	hunt-an
	D	stān-e	gièf-e	hunt-an
	A	stān	gièf-e	hunt-an
Plural	N	stān-as	gièf-a	hunt-an
	G	stān-a	gièf-a	hunt-ena
	D	stān-um	gièf-um	hunt-um
	A	stān-as	gièf-a	hunt-an

Baugh, *A History of the English Language*

So, you had to remember

a to give each noun in a sentence the ending appropriate to its function:
b to make sure that that case-ending was in the correct declension.

And even then your work was not finished; there was still gender to cope with.

Gender

Regardless of its natural sex (or lack of sex if inanimate), every noun was given a masculine, feminine, or neuter gender. Thus, *stone* and *hunter* (above) were masculine while *gift*, for no particular reason, was feminine. More absurdly still, *sunne* (sun) was feminine, *mōna* (moon) masculine, *wīf* (wife) neuter, and *wīf-mann* (woman) masculine (following the gender of the last element of the word).

The business of gender was made even more complicated by the fact that you didn't alter the nouns themselves, but the words that qualified those nouns. Demonstratives such as *this* and *that*, the definite and indefinite articles, *the* and *a* – all had to be given a masculine, feminine or neuter ending to suit the gender of their nouns:

the man	the woman	this man	this woman	(modern English)
se mann	ρaet wif	ρes mann	ρis wif	(Old English)

Modern German and the languages derived from Latin still inflect to show gender in this way, which may be one reason why we find them so hard to learn.

l'homme	la femme	cet homme	cette femme	(French)
der Mann	die Frau	dieser Mann	diese Frau	(German)
l'hombre	la mujer	este hombre	esta mujer	(Spanish)
l'uomo	la donna	questo uomo	questa donna	(Italian)

All adjectives were inflected also, so if we wanted to expand our original sentence into 'We have a nice black cat', both *nice* and *black* would have to be made masculine, feminine or neuter to match the gender of *cat*, and inflected either strong or weak according to the word that preceded them – in this particular instance, the indefinite article *a*.

Finally, having got your nouns, articles, and adjectives into agreement you would have to cope with verbs, which were rather more heavily inflected than ours today.

Inflections of the verb

Tense

Like the nouns, Old English verbs were divided into two categories: strong and weak. Strong verbs formed their past tense and past participle by modifying (i.e. changing) their stem vowel, as some still do: for example *dr**i**nk*, *dr**a**nk*, *dr**u**nk*. Weak verbs on the other hand formed their past tense and past participle by tacking a suffix on to the end of their stem: for example, *burn*, *burn**ed***, *burn**t***.

Number

Old English also had seven endings to show number (i.e. how many people were involved in the action of the verb): four endings in the present tense, and three in the past:

		present tense	**past tense**
1st person sing.	(I)	ic luf-i(g)e	ic luf-ode
2nd person sing.	(you)	ϸu* luf-ast	ϸu luf-odest
3rd person sing.	(he/it/she)	he/hit/heo luf-aϸ*	he/hit/heo luf-ode
1st person plur.	(we)	we luf-iaϸ	we luf-odon
2nd person plur.	(you)	ge luf-iaϸ	ge luf-odon
3rd person plur.	(they)	hie luf-iaϸ	hie luf-odon

Sweet, *A First Middle English Primer*

Can you see now what people mean when they say that Modern English has very little grammar?

Activity

1 Look at the text of any Shakespeare play and see how the old second and third person singular endings survived into the seventeenth century:
dost, hast, didst, beginst, etc. (contracted from *doest, havest, didest, beginnest*);
doth (contracted from *doeth*), *loveth, pleadeth*, etc.

2 Write out all the *persons* of the verb *to talk* in order to discover how many inflections to show number we use today (e.g. *I, you, she/he/it, we, you, they*).

3 Read the following passage and summarize its ideas in no more than seventy of your own words.

I can't help feeling that the current TV series, *The Story of English*, is making rather heavy weather of the question of why English is so universally popular. The class of students I used to take in English as a foreign language had no doubts at all. English was incredibly easy; it had no grammar at all.
These foreign students – from Spain, Portugal, France and Germany – were used to a language that operated as a system. Each sentence in most European languages is a machine, like a gearbox, in which one moving part affects every other part. All the words are altered, or inflected, to agree with all the other words. English, on the other hand, is an almost entirely un-inflected language. Where German has three genders for nouns, English has one. Where German nouns have four cases to show their function in the sentence, English nouns rely entirely on pronouns to tell you what they are doing. If you take a regular English verb like *to jump* it only has three inflections, which are: *jumps, jumping, jumped*. Stick these together with a group of simple auxiliaries like *may, will* and *should*, and you can form every tense and person that you need with about thirty words. To do the same in French would take around three hundred. This makes English very easy to learn. It is more like learning a list than a system, which is why various forms of pidgin English, and the bastard

* Anglo-Saxon had two letters to represent modern *th*: ð and ϸ. Either could be used to represent the two sounds of *th*, as in *thin* and *then*.

English of computer languages and airline-speak are so popular. It also makes English very very corruptible, which is why we have more jargon, neologisms, and foreign importations than anybody else. A hideous neologism in a French sentence will make the gearbox grind, whereas an English sentence can swallow almost anything from a megadeath to a cul de sac. On the positive side, because English has no grammar it is highly compressible, which makes it the ideal language for advertising men, headline writers, and poets. 'Sex-tangle vicar slams street-crime link' is utterly untranslatable, as is a fine line from Yeats like 'A lonely impulse of delight, drove to this tumult in the clouds.'

The period of levelled inflections, 1150–1500

At the beginning of this period, English was so fully inflected that it looks like a foreign language. By the end of it, it had clear similarities with the language that we use today.

The different stages of this transition are illustrated in the three extracts that follow, taken from Roger Lass's book, *The Shape of English*. All are versions of the same biblical passage (St Luke 2:8–9), but (a) is in Anglo-Saxon or Old English, (b) in Middle English, and (c) in early modern English.

a And hyrdas wæron on þam ylcan rice waciende, and nihtwæccan healdende ofer heora heorda. Þa stod Drihtnes engel wiþ hig, and Godes beorhtnes him ymbe scean; and hi him mycelum ege adredon.

b And scheeperdis weren in the same cuntre, wakynge and kepynge the watchis of the nyȝt on her flok. And lo! the aungel of the Lord stood bisidis hem, and the cleernesse of God schinede aboute hem, and thei dredden with greet drede.

c And there were in the same countrey shepheards abiding in ye field, keeping watch ouer their flocke by nyght. And loe, the Angel of the Lord came vpon them, and the glory of the Lord shone round about them, and they were sore afraid.

The only connection between (c) and (a), written four hundred years earlier, is the verb *were* (from Old English *wæron*). Both the vocabulary of (a) (*ylcan* for *same*, *Drihtnes* for *God's*, *ymbe* for *about*) and the order in which its words are arranged (notice the position of the verbs) make it look to us like a foreign language.

Far more resemblance can be seen between (c) and (b), written three hundred years earlier, mainly because the words are familiar (though oddly spelled). Even here, however, you will notice major differences: (b) uses the possessive pronoun *her* where we use *their*, and the object pronoun *hem* in place of modern *them*; it also inflects its verbs to distinguish between singular and plural, which we gave up doing long ago: *stood* and *schinede* are singular; *weren* and *dredden* have the *-en* ending that makes them plural.

The inflections we have lost

The noun

All the original case endings have been lost. (Neither of the two inflections we have now is original.)

The pronoun

The *thou*, *thee*, *ye*, *thy* and *thine* forms of the second person singular and plural have all been lost. These are now written indiscriminately as *you* and *yours*.

Singular: nominative or subject case: *thou*
Thou seydest this, that I was lyk a cat.
Singular: accusative or object case: *thee*
I love *thee* wel.
Plural: nominative or subject case: *ye*
Now herkneth . . . *ye* wise wyves, that kan understand.
Plural: accusative or object case: *you*
Ye know what was commanded *you*.
Singular: genitive or possessive case (before consonants): *thy*
I trowe thou woldest loke me in *thy* cheste.
Singular: genitive or possessive case (before vowels): *thine*
Keep *thyn* honour, and keep eek myn estaat.
Plural: genitive or possessive case: *your*
Dishonour not *your* mothers.

Grammatical gender

The masculine, feminine, and neuter endings of adjectives, demonstratives, and definite and indefinite articles have all been lost. Once nouns had lost their gender, there was nothing for these words to agree with.

The verb

Most of the three hundred or so old strong verbs have been lost, and all new ones entering the language since the seventeenth century have been given the regular *-ed* ending of the weak verb. For example, we say *I telephoned* rather than *I telephane*; *I have telephoned* rather than *I telephene*.

The endings for the second and third person singular of the verb that lent such flavour to the writings of earlier centuries have also disappeared:

Dost thou think, because thou *art* virtuous,
There shall be no more cakes and ale?

Time *hath*, my lord, a wallet at his back,
Wherein he puts alms for oblivion . . .

Allas! Whiche folie and whiche ignorance mysle*deth* wandrynge wrecchis fro the path of verray good!

The replacement of this old *-eth* ending with *-s* has left us with a grammatical illogicality:

- plural nouns end in *-s*, yet take plural verbs that do not: e.g. *Comedies make us laugh*;
- singular nouns do not end in *-s* yet take verbs that do: *Tragedy makes us cry*.

Activity

After the Conquest, influenced by the French practice of using *tu* to indicate familiar relationships and *vous* to show respect, the distinction between *thou*, *thee*, and *you* took on another use. *Thou* and *thee* were used to address friends and inferiors; *ye*, *your* and *you* were reserved for acquaintances and people of higher rank.

1 Write a letter to someone in the familiar *thee* and *thou* forms of the past, inviting him or her to dine with you. Then reply to this letter, rejecting the invitation, using the more distant *you* and *ye* forms. Remember that *thou* takes an *-st* ending (*thou knowest/dost/thinkst/findst*, etc.), *he*, *she* and *it* take an *-eth* ending (*hath/knoweth/doth/thinketh/findeth*, etc.), while the endings going with *I*, *you*, *we*, and *they* are written as today.

2 Discuss whether English is the poorer for the loss of these older pronouns.

Inflections remaining in modern English

Nouns

Only two inflections have survived to the present day, both in an altered form:

1 the *s* that marks the genitive or possessive case: the man*'s* house;
2 the *s* that marks the plural: house, house*s*.

Even these may not last for ever, since, strictly speaking, neither is really necessary for clear understanding of what is being said. If someone writes,

> He goes to his mother house for dinner every day

we understand him; if people talk of 'three pound ten' instead of 'three pounds ten', their meaning is not obscure.

Adjectives

We still retain the comparative and superlative forms (technically called *degrees*) of the adjective. Adjectives with one or two syllables are given the inflections *-er* and *-est*. Adjectives with three or more syllables are preceded by *more* and *most*. For example:

	Comparative	**Superlative**
fast	faster	fastest
near	nearer	nearest
interesting	more interesting	most interesting
Exceptions		
good	better	best
bad	worse	worst

Pronouns

The personal and relative pronouns are still inflected.

Personal pronouns

Nominative (subject) case:	I, you, he, she, it, we, they
Accusative (object) case:	me, you, him, her, it, us, them
Genitive (possessive) case:	mine, yours, his, hers, its, ours, theirs

Relative pronouns

Nominative (subject) case:	who
Accusative (object) case:	whom
Genitive (possessive) case:	whose

Verbs

In Old English, as we remarked above, verbs were inflected to show

a person,
b tense.

Only the *s* of the third person singular now remains, having supplanted the old *-eth* ending current throughout Middle English. Found everywhere in Chaucer – *telleth*, *saith*, *doth*, etc. – and still fairly common in Shakespeare, it had disappeared for ever by the end of the seventeenth century

Will this remaining *-s* also disappear, leaving us one day with the kind of perfectly regular verb system George Orwell thought could happen only in a totalitarian state? Will it make any difference to our understanding of a sentence if it does?

Disadvantages of the loss of inflections

As Bodmer points out in his *Loom of Language*, the loss of inflections has forced 'the introduction of roundabout expressions involving the use of particles such as *of*, *to*, *more than*, *most*, or of a special class of verbs some of which (e.g. *will*, *shall*, *can*, *may*) have more or less completely lost any meaning unless associated with another verb.' This has increased the number of monosyllables in a language that was already monosyllabic in character.

Some linguists accept the streamlined efficiency of modern English yet still mourn the flexible movement and rhythm given to prose and verse by the old inflections. One of them writes:

> . . . on the grounds of lilt and flow . . . I claim that the straightforward sentence 'The good lads went to the black mill' is inferior to the Chaucerian version, 'The goode lads wenten to the blake melle',* where the three sounded final *-e* inflexions stand respectively for a plural adjective, a weak adjective after a definite article, and a dative noun (melle = *to* the mill).

* The *-e* on *goode*, *blake*, and *melle* should be sounded as an extra syllable.

Advantages of the loss of inflections

The loss of inflections makes learning the language much easier, both for English schoolchildren and for foreigners. Only the following inflections are absolutely necessary in English today:

1 *-s* for the third person singular of the present tense of the verb (e.g. *sees*), or for the plural form of nouns (e.g. *glasses*);
2 *-ed* for the past tense verbs (e.g. *ordered*);
3 *-t*, *-en*, or *-ed* for the past participle (e.g. *burnt*, *eaten*, *disturbed*);
4 *-ing*, which can be added to the end of verbs to make present participles;
5 the different forms of the verb *to be*: *am*, *are*, *is*, *was*, *were*, (*have*/*has*/*had*) *been*, (*will*) *be*;
6 irregular noun plurals like *sheep*, *men*, *women*, and *children*;
7 the dozen or so common strong verbs mentioned below (page 108).

(We can get round the possessive apostrophe *s* by writing 'of the [something or other]', and round the *-er* and *-est* of comparatives and superlatives by writing 'more' and 'most'.)

Consider by contrast the plight of the French, who still have number and gender to cope with. They speak their language very fluently but find it difficult to write down correctly, since fifty per cent of its inflections exist only on paper and are never pronounced. Take the simple verb *aimer*, to love: the forms *j'aime* (I love), *tu aimes* (you love), *il/elle aime* (he/she loves), and *ils aiment* (they love) are all spelled differently but are pronounced exactly the same, while the infinitive *aimer* sounds exactly like the second person plural, *vous aimez*.

Activity

Read the following extract from Orwell's *Nineteen Eighty-four* and discuss whether the loss of all remaining inflections would be good or bad.

> The grammar of Newspeak had two outstanding peculiarities. The first of these was an almost complete interchangeability between different parts of speech. Any word in the language could be used either as verb, noun, adjective, or adverb . . . The word 'thought', for example, did not exist in Newspeak. Its place was taken by 'think', which did duty for both noun and verb. No etymological principle was followed here: in some cases it was the original noun that was chosen for retention, in other cases the verb. Even where a noun and verb of kindred meaning were not etymologically connected, one or other of them was frequently suppressed. There was, for example, no such word as 'cut', its meaning being sufficiently covered by the noun-verb 'knife'. Adjectives were formed by adding the suffix '-ful' to the noun-verb, and adverbs by adding '-wise'. Thus, for example, 'speedful' meant 'rapid' and 'speedwise' meant 'quickly' . . .
> The second distinguishing mark of Newspeak grammar was its regularity. With a few exceptions . . . all inflexions followed the same rules. Thus, in all verbs the preterite and the past participle were the same and ended in '-ed'. The preterite of 'steal' was 'stealed', the preterite of 'think' was 'thinked', and so on throughout the language, all such forms as swam, gave, brought, spoke, taken, etc., being abolished. All plurals were made by

> adding '-s' or '-es' as the case might be. The plurals of 'man', 'ox', 'life', were 'mans', 'oxes', 'lifes'. Comparison of adjectives was invariably made by adding '-er', '-est' ('good', 'gooder', 'goodest'), irregular forms and the 'more', 'most' formation being suppressed. The only classes of words that were still allowed to inflect irregularly were the pronouns, the relatives, the demonstrative adjectives, and the auxiliary verbs. All these followed their ancient usage, except that 'whom' had been scrapped as unnecessary, and the 'shall', 'should' tenses had been dropped, all their uses being covered by 'will' and 'would' . . .

The vexed question of grammar

Prescriptivists (people who like rules) believe you must know grammar in order to write good English. Others believe that learning grammar stifles creativity.

Look at these conflicting views and decide for yourself which (if either) is true. In order to do so, you need to know a little about grammar.

What is grammar?

Grammar is an umbrella term that covers two aspects of language:

1 the structure and function of individual words;
2 the arrangement of those words within a given sentence. (This second aspect is sometimes called *syntax*.)
   The grammatical exercises that prescriptivists want all students to do are called *parsing* and *clause analysis*. Parsing is based on the structure and function of individual words; clause analysis on the arrangement of words into clauses within a sentence.

Parsing

When we parse, we:

1 examine each word in a sentence;
2 put it into its own particular category of the 'parts of speech';
3 explain what its function is (i.e. how it relates to other words in the sentence).

The parts of speech

Every word in the English language belongs to one of the categories of the 'parts of speech'. There are eight of these categories: nouns, pronouns, adjectives, verbs, adverbs, prepositions, conjunctions, and the definite and indefinite articles *the* and *a*.

A word of advice

Don't be put off by these technical terms. You have been using the parts of speech since you were a toddler and you can handle them all with ease. All you have to do is learn their names.

A good way to learn the different parts of speech is to think of how we pick words up when we are small, beginning with the first kind of word we learn to use: the *noun*.

Nouns

Definition: A *noun* is a word that is used to name any person, animal, thing, idea, state, or quality.

The first words we learn to say are nouns – the names of people and of objects: *mummy*, *daddy*, *teddy*, *doggy*, *biccy* (biscuit), *jink* (drink) – simply because people and objects are the most important things in our lives. When we learn their names we acquire power over them to a certain extent: we can ask for things, call people's attention to us, generally start to function in society. The following are the different kinds of noun.

- **Common noun:** a name common to all members of a large class of people, animals, or things: *man*, *cat*, *table*, *town*, *friend*, *word*, *sentence*, *apple*, *fig*, *leaf*.
- **Proper noun:** the name peculiar to a particular person, place, or thing; it is given a capital letter to distinguish it: *Tiffany*, *New York*, *'The Catcher in the Rye'*, *the Empire State building*, *Friday*, *August*, *Concorde*.
- **Collective noun:** a name denoting a collection or group of people, animals, or things, regarded as a whole: *jury*, *committee*, *government*, *Cabinet*, *crowd*, *team*, *herd*.
- **Abstract noun:** the name of a quality, state of mind, physical condition, idea, or action: *attractiveness*, *intelligence*, *weariness*, *capitalism*, *belief*.

Activity

Pick out the thirty-six nouns in this extract, counting each only once.

Nouns used as adjectives

As he waited for his helping of blueberry pancakes with fresh cream and Wisconsin cheddar, the thought of dieting brushed feebly at his mind like an old remorse. He was aware that just eating a little of what he did not fancy would sooner or later do him good in the sexual chase. This idea had been brought sharply into focus at a fellow-publisher's party the previous year. Somebody's secretary had told him that what he wanted was all right with her on the understanding that he brought his block and tackle along. Five days later, sipping a half-cup of sugarless milkless tea to round off a luncheon of a lightly boiled egg with no salt, a decarbohydrated roll resembling fluff in plastic, and a small apple, he made up his mind for ever that, if it came to it, he could easily settle down to a regime of banquets and self-abuse. He sent his plate up now for a second helping of pancakes and put three chocolate mints into his mouth to tide him over. Outside every fat man there was an even fatter man trying to close in.

Kingsley Amis, *One Fat Englishman*

Pronouns

Definition: A *pronoun* is a word that stands in place of a noun, to save us saying the same noun twice: *she*, *he*, *they*, *it*, *we*, *you*.

Like nouns, certain pronouns are picked up early – *me* in particular, since our own needs and wants are the most important things in the world to us when we are small. However, some pronouns confuse two- and three-year-olds greatly: daddy, for instance, can be *I* when he's talking and *you* or *he* or *him* when mummy is. This is very puzzling, and is the reason why children come out with sentences like 'Him didn't go to work today' and 'I can see she's bed'. The difference between *I* (the subject case) and *me* (the object case) also takes some time to grasp. *Me* is used indiscriminately in the one- or two-word 'sentences' that all toddlers are capable of at first. Utterances such as 'Me!' or 'Me biscuit!' have to do duty for more complete constructions like 'I want a biscuit'. The following are the different kinds of pronoun.

- **Demonstrative:** *this, that, these, those, the former, the latter* (as in, 'I've had enough of this')
- **Distributive:** *each, either, neither* (as in, 'I would be happy with either')
- **Emphatic:** *myself, yourself, him/herself, ourselves*, etc. (as in, 'Do it yourself')
- **Reflexive:** *myself, yourself, him/herself, ourselves*, etc. (as in, 'He hurt himself')
- **Indefinite:** *one, some, any, someone, anybody, everybody*
- **Interrogative:** *who, which, what* (as in, 'Who are you talking about?')
- **Relative:** *who, which, what, that* (as in, 'The book which you ordered has arrived')
- **Personal:** *I, you, he/she, it, we, you, they*
- **Possessive:** *mine, yours, his, hers, ours, theirs*

Adjectives

Definition: An *adjective* is a word that describes (or qualifies) a noun or pronoun e.g. a *lucky* break; the *happy* hour.

Once children have mastered nouns, adjectives soon follow: they have strong feelings about the people and things they are surrounded by, and since adjectives can express their feelings, children pick them up quickly: 'Nice mummy', 'Good daddy', 'Naughty teddy', 'Bad dog'.

Note: nice, beautiful, and *good* are obviously descriptive words and most people would have little difficulty in assigning them to the category 'adjective'. Others, like the first five kinds of adjective listed below, are less easy to recognize because they don't pick out any obvious features. For example, 'I want that book, not this': here, *this* and *that* are clearly singling out/defining/describing which book is wanted and so can be only adjectives. The same is true of distributive, interrogative and numeral adjectives, shown below, all of which qualify or describe the nouns they precede. The following are the different kinds of adjective.

- **Demonstrative:** *this, that, these, those* (as in, 'I want that book')
- **Distributive:** *each, every, either, neither* (as in, 'Either knife will do')
- **Interrogative:** *which? what?* (as in, 'Which kind of book do you prefer?')
- **Numeral:** *one, two*, etc.
- **Indefinite:** *all, many, several*

- **Possessive:** *my, your, his, our, their*
- **Qualitative** (showing what kind): *male, English, middle-class*

Activity

Pick out the adjectives (sixteen, or seventeen if you include the number) in the following extract. Count each only once.

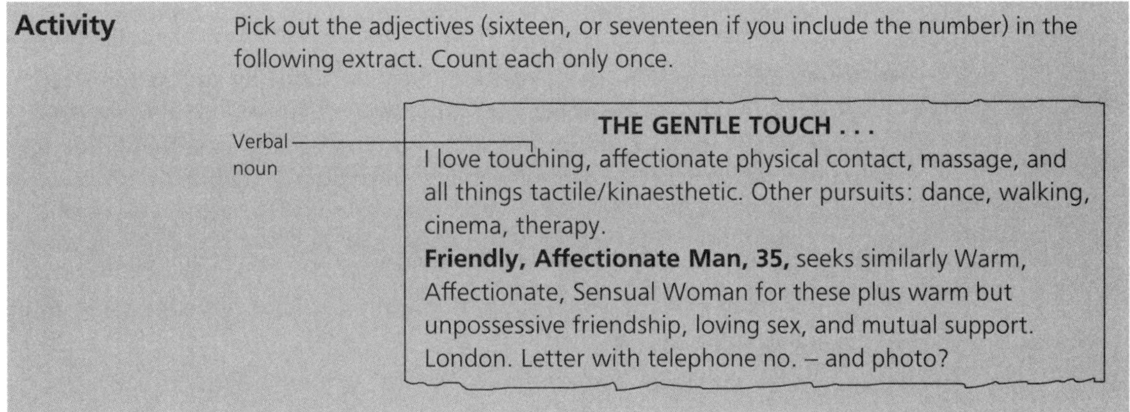

Verbal noun

THE GENTLE TOUCH . . .

I love touching, affectionate physical contact, massage, and all things tactile/kinaesthetic. Other pursuits: dance, walking, cinema, therapy.

Friendly, Affectionate Man, 35, seeks similarly Warm, Affectionate, Sensual Woman for these plus warm but unpossessive friendship, loving sex, and mutual support. London. Letter with telephone no. – and photo?

Verbs

Definition: A *verb* is a word that indicates an action or a mental or physical state, e.g.:

She *shot* him. She *was* drunk.

Verbs expressing action are another part of speech that children pick up early. Again, they learn them because there is something in it for them; verbs get them what they want: *wee-wee, go, want, give, get down* ('doing-words', as primary school teachers often call them) quickly become part of every toddler's vocabulary.

But not every verb is a 'doing-word'. In the group of sentences that follows, only the first expresses action:

She *shot* him.
She *wished* she had not. (*expresses feelings*)
She *felt* ill. (*expresses a mental and physical state*)
She *seemed* confused. (*expresses how she appeared to others*)

In addition, there is a category called auxiliary (i.e. helping) verbs, which some people have difficulty in accepting as verbs at all. These are the verbs *to be*, and *to have*, together with the incomplete verbs *shall, will, may, do*, e.g.:

I *have* seen, I *am* going, I *shall* go, she *will* go, we *may* call, *do* you want us to bring anything?

Children are slower to acquire non-action verbs like the above, and it is a clear sign of maturing intelligence when one appears in the vocabulary. One mother I know, chatting away as usual to her small son, asked him what he would like for lunch and was startled to hear him answer, 'I really don't mind'. She suddenly realized he was no longer a baby, but a person.

English verbs divide into two main classes: strong and weak.

- **Strong verbs** form their past tense and past participle by changing the vowel of the stem: *ride, rode, ridden*; *break, broke, broken*; *think, thought, thought*; *hide, hid, hidden*; *do, did, done*; *see, saw, seen*; *eat, ate, eaten*; *catch, caught, caught*; *spin, span, spun*; *bring, brought, brought*; *swim, swam, swum*, etc.
- **Weak verbs** form their past tense and past participle by adding the inflection *-ed* to the stem: *walk, walked, walked*; *prove, proved, proven*. Since weak verbs are far more common in English, toddlers frequently try to put weak endings on strong verbs: 'It hurted me'; 'He bited me'; 'I holded it'.

Verbs also have two voices: the active voice and the passive voice.

When the subject of the sentence is doing the action, the verb is said to be in the **active voice**:

Shug *sang* the blues.

When the subject of the sentence is having something done to him or her or it, the verb is said to be in the **passive voice**:

Squeak's songs *were sung* in a little tiny voice.

Small children cannot cope with the passive voice and may still be trying to sort it out when they are nine or ten.

Activity

Pick out the verbs in the following extract (fourteen main verbs and one participle):

> Socorro unhooked one of the white porcelain mugs from the underside of the cabinet shelf and poured it and turned the handle facing out and handed it to the old man and he took it and nodded and went back across the kitchen. He stopped at the table and spooned two huge scoops of sugar out of the bowl into his cup and left the room taking the sugarspoon with him. John Grady put his cup and plate on the sideboard and got his lunchbucket off the counter and went out.
>
> What's wrong with him? said JC.

Cormac McCarthy, *Cities of the Plain*, Picador, 1998

Adverbs

Definition: An *adverb* is a word that limits or modifies (i.e. tells us more about) the meaning of any part of speech except a noun or pronoun. Adverbs can therefore modify:

1. adjectives: *almost* eighteen; *very* nice; *fairly* cheap; *awfully* expensive; *rather* ill.
2. other adverbs: she jogs *quite* frequently; he *nearly* always goes with her.
3. prepositions: *close* by the lamp.

So, if you're not sure sometimes what part of speech you're dealing with, and it's got more than three letters, it's probably an adverb. The following are the different kinds of adverb.

- **Adverbs of time:** *now, then, soon, yesterday, recently, always, never, till*;
- **Adverbs of place:** *here, there, inside, outside, above, below, between*;
- **Adverbs of manner:** *slowly, quickly, angrily, calmly, eagerly, badly, well*;
- **Adverbs of degree:** *very, fairly, reasonably, almost, quite, too*;
- **Adverbs of number:** *once, twice, firstly, secondly* (etc.), *finally, again*;
- **Adverbs of certainty or uncertainty:** *certainly, surely, tentatively, perhaps, not*;
- **Interrogative adverbs:** *How? When? Where? Why?*

Adverbs of manner, degree, and certainty express complex mental judgements and so are too sophisticated for very young children to handle. Their minds are focused exclusively on physical things.

Activity

1 Discuss which of the above adverbs
   a you would not expect toddlers to use
   b you would expect to be in their vocabulary.
   Try to suggest reasons for this.

2 Pick out the adverbs in the following extract. There are twelve in all: eight modify verbs (one of which is in participle form), two modify other adverbs (one of these occurs three times), one (made up of three words) modifies an adjective, and one modifies a preposition. This last occurs at the end of the passage and may be the hardest to spot.

   (The *on* in *go on* and *move on* is taken to be part of the verb rather than a separate adverb.)

> Alice turned to the Dormouse and repeated her question. 'Why did they live at the bottom of a well?'
>
> The Dormouse again took a minute or two to think about it, and then said, 'It was a treacle-well.'
>
> 'There's no such thing!' Alice was beginning very angrily, but the Hatter and the March Hare went 'Sh! sh!' and the Dormouse sulkily remarked 'If you can't be civil, you'd better finish the story for yourself.'
>
> 'No, please go on!' Alice said very humbly. 'I won't interrupt you again. I dare say there may be one.'
>
> 'One indeed!' said the Dormouse indignantly. However, he consented to go on. 'And so these three little sisters – they were learning to draw, you know –'
>
> 'What did they draw?' said Alice, quite forgetting her promise.
>
> 'Treacle,' said the Dormouse, without considering at all this time.
>
> 'I want a clean cup,' interrupted the Hatter: 'let's all move one place on.'
>
> He moved on as he spoke, and the Dormouse followed him: the March Hare moved into the Dormouse's place, and Alice rather unwillingly took the place of the March Hare. The Hatter was the only one who got any advantage from the change: and Alice was a good deal worse off than before, as the March Hare had just upset the milk-jug into his plate.
>
> Alice did not want to offend the Dormouse again, so she began very cautiously: 'But I don't understand. Where did they draw the treacle from?'

> 'You can draw water out of a water-well,' said the Hatter; 'so I should think you could draw treacle out of a treacle-well – eh, stupid?'
>
> 'But they were in the well,' Alice said to the Dormouse, not choosing to notice this last remark.
>
> 'Of course they were,' said the Dormouse; '– well in.'
>
> Lewis Carroll, *Alice's Adventures in Wonderland*

Prepositions

Definition: a *preposition* is a word that shows the relationship between one noun and another noun or pronoun in a sentence. Prepositions are generally small words like *on, by, to, in, down, out, round*. Very young children find it difficult to handle most of them, and may even treat *on*, as in 'It's on the table' and *in*, as in 'Put it in the box' as verbs (e.g. 'In', said loudly as toys are put away in the box).

The technical definition of a preposition – 'a word that shows the relationship between two nouns (or pronouns) in a sentence' – doesn't seem to mean much as it stands. Translate it into terms of real life, however, and there's all the difference in the world between going *to* the pub and coming away *from* it; between being *below* or *above* something; between having a fascination *with* something and having fascination *for* someone.

Note: some prepositions consist of two prepositions, often combined to form one word, e.g.: *into, throughout, upon, from behind*.

By the time they are three, most children can handle nouns, pronouns, adjectives, verbs, and adverbs because they are what grammarians call *content words*: words that carry information about people and things and actions in real life; things that can be grasped with the senses. Children find it much harder to use prepositions, because prepositions refer to the grammatical relationships between words in a sentence. They are *structure words* as opposed to content words: small pieces of language like *to* and *on* that glue sentences together and help them to mean what they mean, without having any independent meaning of their own. For this reason, being new to grammar, you will probably find them harder to recognize too. Further information about the role of these two kinds of words in the construction of sentences will be given at the end of this section, under the heading 'The role of "glue" words in sentence construction' (page 137).

Not understanding prepositions, toddlers leave gaps where they should be: *Tom come me* or *Tom come my house* instead of *Tom come* **to** *my house*. They can cope with words that relate to physical things, but such abstract mental concepts as the relationship between them is still beyond their grasp. Andrew Wilson in *The Foundations of Language* explains why:

> Children deal with language by stripping it of inessentials, as we should do in writing a telegram.
>
> The child faced with *Daddy is eating cake* may produce, if he is at that stage, *Daddy eat cake*.
>
> To take an actual example, quoted by Brown and Bellugi (1964), a mother's sentence *No you can't write on Mr Cramer's shoe* was reduced by the child to *Write Cramer's shoe*.
>
> In both examples the child selects the grammatically important items, nouns, verbs, and adjectives, what are called 'content' words, because they carry high 'information' content. He leaves out, on the other hand, structure words – words whose grammatical function is more important than the meaning they carry – such as auxiliary verbs, determiners,* prepositions, and conjunctions. There is no object or process 'on' in his world.

Conjunctions

Definition: A *conjunction* is a word used to join single words, phrases, or sentences, e.g. bread *and* butter; he tried *but* he failed; she left home *then* came back.

Children have little trouble with simple conjunctions, using them to string sentences together in a continuous stream:

'And we had our dinner and then we washed up and then Mummy said I could go out and play and I played with Tracey and we played with our dollies . . .'

Grammarians divide conjunctions into two categories:

- **Co-ordinating conjunctions:** these join two or more main clauses: She was poor *but* she was honest.
- **Sub-ordinating conjunctions:** these join a dependent clause to a main clause: She was poor *because* she was honest.

Activity

In the extract from *The Foundations of Language* quoted above, prepositions (six in all) are unmarked.
Pick out these prepositions, counting each only once.

Articles

Definition: the *article* is a kind of adjective.

There are two articles: the definite and the indefinite.

* Auxiliary verbs are verbs like *have* and *might*, which help to form the tense of other verbs, e.g. *I might have broken my leg*, where the main verb is *broken*. Determiners are words like *the*, *a*, *some*; they determine that a noun is to follow.

- The **definite article**, *the*, is used to refer to some specific person or thing or event on which attention is being focused: Pass me *the* paper, please.
- The **indefinite article**, *a*, is used when any one of a group of objects, not some particular one, will do: e.g. Pass me *a* paper, please.

Like prepositions, these two little words are by-passed by children in the very early stages: verb plus object constructions (e.g. *Want drink*) are used in preference to verb plus article plus object (e.g. *Want a drink*). However, *a* is soon picked up, to be followed later by the more discriminating definite article, *the*.

Summary

Here is the information on the parts of speech again, in tabular form:

Nouns are the names	of people:	*Adam, Eve, man, woman*
	of animals:	*snake, worm*
	of places:	*garden, Paradise*
	of things:	*tree, fruit*
	of qualities:	*goodness, evil*
	of states of mind:	*innocence, guilt*
	of actions:	*temptation, eating.*

Pronouns are substitutes for nouns: *he, she, they, it, this, who.*

Adjectives describe nouns: *beautiful* garden, *subtle* serpent, *flaming* sword

Verbs express	actions:	they *ate*
	states of mind or being:	they *felt* guilty, they *suffered.*

Adverbs tell you more about:

1 verbs: the manner in which actions are performed: *beguilingly, quickly, angrily*

2 other adverbs: the degree of intensity of that manner: *fairly* quickly, *very* angrily, *most* beguilingly

3 adjectives: *quite* nice, *mildly* annoyed, *fairly* attractive

4 prepositions: *far* from Heaven, *close* to Hell.

Prepositions show relationship between two things in a sentence:
Adam was *in* the Garden.
Later he was driven *from* it.

Conjunctions join two words, two phrases, or two sentences: *and, or, but, then.*

The versatility of the parts of speech

Many words can function as several different parts of speech. Consider the word *fast*, for example, in the following sentences:

> Young men like to drive *fast.* (Adverb qualifying *drive*)
> *Fast* cars attract higher insurance premiums. (Adjective describing *cars*)
> Lent is a religious *fast.* (Noun)
> These days, few people bother to *fast.* (Verb)

In the same way, you can *back* a horse (verb), ride on a horse's *back* (noun), go *back* (adverb), and enter by the *back* door (adjective).

Activity

1 Write sentences in which the word *round* appears as each of the following: noun, adjective, verb, adverb, preposition.
2 Explain what part of speech the word *cans* is in the following sentence by the philosopher J. L. Austin: 'Are cans constitutionally iffy?'
3 Say what part of speech the word *more* is in the following sentences:
a Tell me more.
b I need more time.
c You couldn't have hurt him more if you had tried.

Shakespeare even turned the adverb *backward* into a noun:

in the dark backward and abysm of time.

Old sayings turn conjunctions into nouns and verbs:

If ifs and ands were pots and pans there'd be no need for tinkers.
Don't but me.
But me no buts.

Even pronouns can be turned into nouns in phrases like *her indoors* and *she who must be obeyed*.

Activity

Write down what you notice about the 'adjectives' in the two sets of headlines below:

a Roux cleans up in kitchen-sink drama
Britain loses £500m Tornado fighter deal
Yeltsin dispels ill-health rumour
Dons told exam row must end
Fireman dies in explosives van blast

b Explosives van warning
Explosives van warning inquiry
Explosives van warning inquiry report
Explosives van warning inquiry report denial

The prescriptivist approach to the parts of speech

Prescriptivists have to accept what has been done to the language in the past. They object, however, when we do the same kind of things today. Our habit of turning nouns into verbs at the drop of a hat annoys them greatly, not so much because the resulting structures are inelegant (though they are), but because they blur the clear outlines of the individual parts of speech. We must be guided by the grammar book if we want to keep English pure, they claim. Besides, if it is left in the hands of ordinary people, they perpetrate all kinds of foulness upon it, turning nouns into verbs in the crudest way:

'Bag it and bin it and we'll win it.' (Margaret Thatcher)
'Eyeball us today.' (notice outside garage)
'I waste-basketed it.' (secretary)
'Children must be enthused with a love of learning.' (Kenneth Baker)

'It will be televised next week.' (announcer)
'We are exiting the old year.' (chairman of ICI)
'Let me example that for you.' (Severn Water Authority official)
'Your wine is being room-temperatured.' (waiter)

Summary: what part of speech a word is is determined by its function in the sentence it happens to be in.

How parsing works

To show how parsing works when it is applied to an actual sentence, here is an example from Knight's *A Comprehensive English Course*.

Oh	**interjection**	expressing an emotion (here, surprise).
The old	**adjectives**	here describing or qualifying the noun 'postman'. 'The' is generally given the additional title of Definite Article.
postman	**noun**	here the name of a person.
very	**adverb**	here limiting or modifying another adverb, 'carelessly'.
carelessly	**adverb**	here modifying the verb 'dropped'.
dropped	**verb**	here describing an action, making an assertion.
some	**adjective**	here qualifying the noun 'letters'.
most	**adverb**	here modifying the adjective 'important'.
important	**adjective**	here describing the noun 'letters'.
letters	**noun**	here the name of a thing or object.
and	**conjunction**	here joining 'letters' and 'parcel'.
a	**adjective**	qualifying 'parcel'. 'A' or 'an' is usually given the additional title of Indefinite Article.
parcel	**noun**	here the name of a thing or object.
just	**adverb**	here modifying the preposition 'near'.
near	**preposition**	here showing relation between 'parcel' and 'you'.
you	**pronoun**	here used instead of noun 'man' or 'Smith', i.e. the person addressed by the speaker.

T. W. Knight, *A Comprehensive English Course*

Activity

1 To test your understanding of
 a the parts of speech
 b parsing
 write the following sentence vertically down the side of a page: 'The wretched Council very stupidly built some nasty houses and a really ugly school close by us.'

2 Opposite each word indicate:
 a what part of speech it is;
 b what work it's doing in the sentence.

Note: if you find any difficulty with this task, it will probably be with the prepositions and the adverbs, which are structure rather than content words, and so more difficult to grasp. If you can't decide what part of speech each word is, and it's comparatively short, it will probably be a preposition. If it's slightly longer, it's probably an adverb.

A knowledge of parsing is essential for clause analysis. Since the dependent clauses you would be asked to analyse have the same function as the single nouns, adjectives, and adverbs met in the parts of speech, it is obvious that you need to have done some parsing before going on to clause analysis.

However, true as this last argument may be, it begs an important question. Parsing may indeed be essential for clause analysis. The question is, 'Is clause analysis essential for the understanding and writing of good English?' Read what follows and make up your own mind.

Clause analysis

Clause analysis is the process of breaking down complex sentences into their constituent parts: the independent main clause, the dependent or subordinate clause, and the phrase.

 **Key words**

Independent main clause: a group of words that carries the main idea of a sentence. It always has a subject and a main verb.

Dependent clause: a group of words that adds extra information about the subject in the independent main clause. It also always has a subject and a main verb.

Phrase: a word or group of words that adds further information about the main clause or the dependent clause. Phrases either have no verb at all, or have a verb in the form of a present or past participle.

Before we can look at clause analysis proper we must discover what clauses are and what they do in a sentence. There are only two kinds of clause, and only one kind of phrase, so the task should not be too difficult.

The independent main clause or simple sentence

The structure that lies at the heart of every sentence we speak or write is known as the independent main clause.

When children first begin to talk they use one-word utterances: 'Mummy', 'Daddy', 'Teddy', and so on. Since these single words are ambiguous ('Daddy', after all, might mean either 'I want daddy' or 'I want daddy to go away'), they soon learn to add verbs to their nouns: 'Want Daddy', 'Smack Tommy', and so on. In other words, they learn to speak in sentences, for at their most basic, this is all that sentences are: nouns (or pronouns) and verbs. For example:

Manus broods. Yolland yearns. Maire hopes. Jimmy Jack dreams.

A subject-verb structure like these has two names: the **independent main clause** (imc) and the **simple sentence** (ss).

It is called *independent* because it can make sense without the help of another clause, e.g.:

Owen changes.

It is called *main* because when it forms a complex sentence with the help of a **dependent** or **subordinate clause** (dsc), it makes the main, or most important, statement, e.g.:

Manus changes [*imc*] when he learns what Lancey intends to do [*dsc*].

It is called a *simple sentence* because its structure is simple; it consists of only one clause.

Here are some further independent main clauses/simple sentences:

S	V	S	V	S	V
Owen	translates.	Yolland	is unhappy.	Something	will be eroded.
Doalty	larked about.	Bridget	laughed.	The English	were puzzled.

Not all independent main clauses are as short as this, of course. Most have objects or other groups of words that extend their meaning. We can call these *completers* for convenience. Below are some examples:

Subject	**Verb**	**Object**
Yolland	loves	Maire.

Subject	**Verb**	**Object**
Maire	forgets	Manus.

Subject	**Verb**	**Completer**	**Object**
Manus	tries	to insult	Yolland.

Even when they have completers like these, however, simple sentences still consist of only one clause, because they have only one subject and only one verb.

The punctuation of simple sentences

Some people have difficulty in recognizing where a simple sentence ends, particularly in examples like the following:

1 Paul went home. He entered the house silently.

They argue that *he* should be included in the first sentence here by putting a comma rather than a full-stop after *home.* Readers, they claim, won't know what the pronoun *he* refers to if it's put into a separate sentence from the noun it stands for – *Paul.*

In fact, readers **will** know who *he* refers to because the preceding sentence – *Paul went home* – will have told them. The second sentence doesn't exist in a vacuum, cut off from what has gone before.

2 William wanted to bring Gyp home. Mrs Morel said she should come at Christmas.

In example 2, people again argue for a comma rather than a full-stop. Having been taught in primary school to start a new sentence only when they change the subject, they refuse to start a new one here. The pronoun *she* in the second clause, they point out, refers to *Gyp* in the first. The subject is therefore the same, and so the two statements should be linked by a comma rather than separated by a full-stop.

Here, those who argue for a comma have misinterpreted the description of a sentence as a 'complete statement'. They interpret 'complete' to mean 'containing everything that is said about the subject', when what it really means is 'grammatically complete in containing a subject and a verb'. If we took these two arguments to their logical conclusion, no one would ever be able to start a sentence with a pronoun, which is clearly absurd.

Note: putting a comma rather than a full-stop between sentences is the most common punctuation error. If you have this habit, try to stop it now.

Activity

Insert full stops between the simple sentences below.

1 Annie and Leonard are friends as well as lovers their marriage is a very happy one.
2 The physical attraction between Arthur and Beatie is very strong they get carried away one night.
3 Clara was unhappy in her marriage to Baxter Dawes she was unhappy with Paul for another reason.

Key words

Simple sentence: a sentence made up of one independent main clause.

Compound sentence: a sentence made up of two independent main clauses, usually joined by a conjunction.

Complex sentence: a sentence consisting of at least one independent main clause and one dependent clause.

Simple/compound sentences

When two or more simple sentences are joined together by the co-ordinating conjunctions *and*, *so*, *but*, and *then*, the resulting structure is known as a **compound sentence**. (*Co-ordinating conjunctions* are so called because they join two clauses of equal value.) For example:

Mrs Morel washed up and [she] put the children to bed.
Walter ate his dinner then [he] got washed and [he] went out.

When we use the term 'simple sentence' in future, therefore, you should understand it to include compound sentences also, since they are nothing but simple sentences joined together.

Activity

Read the following paragraph and follow the instructions below.

Hugh knows what is going on. He ignores it. He is self-indulgent. He is the ablest man in Ballybeg. He is to blame for his people's plight.

1. Re-write these five simple sentences as two longer ones, using only the co-ordinating conjunctions *but* (twice) and *so* (once). You may use an *and* before the *so* if you wish. You will need to change the order of the third and fourth sentences.
2. Explain why the two longer sentences are to be preferred to the five shorter ones. You should have three reasons, concerning:
   - **a** the psychological effect it has on you (the way you feel about it);
   - **b** the logic of what is said (how does joining the sentences help to convey the meaning?);
   - **c** the style.

The semi-colon in compound sentences

Strings of independent main clauses joined by co-ordinating conjunctions are simplistic in style and monotonous to the ear. One or two are acceptable in a sentence; more than this should be avoided by the use of the semi-colon. The semi-colon is a stop that lets you have your cake and eat it. It marks the end of an independent main clause/simple sentence, but it saves you from having to bring the sentence to an end. You can therefore join two simple sentences on the same subject into one longer compound sentence, which has the additional advantage of preventing your style from being too abrupt. For example:

> Hugh is an educated man; he speaks Irish, Latin, English, and Greek.

To join two sentences that were not on the same subject with a semi-colon would be as illogical as joining them with a conjunction. For example:

> Hugh is an educated man; Maire wants to go to America.
> Hugh is an educated man and/but Maire wants to go to America.

Semi-colons wouldn't suit the rambling style of a child's story, but they add force and sophistication to writing on more serious themes. For example:

> At last Mrs Morel despised her husband. She turned to the child; she turned from the father. He had begun to neglect her; the novelty of his own home was gone.

Activity

Read the pairs of sentences below, then answer the questions below:

1. **a** Paul cannot give himself completely to Clara but Baxter can.
   b Paul cannot give himself completely to Clara; Baxter can.
2. **a** Clara wants Paul's body and she also wants his mind and heart.
   b Clara wants Paul's body; she also wants his mind and heart.

3 a The episode involving the swing tells us about Paul and Miriam's attitudes towards life and sexuality and so is highly symbolic.

b The episode involving the swing is highly symbolic; it tells us about Paul and Miriam's attitudes towards life and sex.

1 Which of the statements in the above pairs seems to you to carry the greatest authority and weight?

2 Why do you think this is so?

A classic pattern for the semi-colon

There is a classic pattern for the use of the semi-colon, indicated below:

Noun in the first imc/ss	Semi-colon	Pronoun in the second imc/ss
Clara is passionately in love with Paul	;	*she* pursues him around the factory.
Miriam despises Paul's relationship with Clara	;	*she* thinks he debases himself by indulging in a purely physical relationship.
Paul is frightened of both his women	;	*they* want to possess him, body and soul.

Activity

Join the following imc's/ss's into compound sentences *where appropriate*:

1 Mrs Leivers is very religious. She elevates ordinary things on to a very high plane.
2 Paul loves painting. He hopes to be a famous artist one day.
3 Clara is a feminist. She feels bitter towards men.
4 Paul worked in a hosiery factory. The countryside was beautiful.
5 Miriam hated maths. Her mother was very intense.

Uses of the simple sentence

Simple sentences figure largely in instructions.

Activity

Read the alternative sets of instructions below, then carry out the activities that follow.

A Before you start to light the boiler, the electricity should be switched off. When this has been done, the thermostat should be checked to see if it is at the right setting to bring the heating on when the boiler is lit. Next, the control knob should be turned to 'pilot' and fully depressed. A match can now be inserted into the special holder provided and applied to the burner while you count to 30. When 30 seconds have passed the knob can be released and turned to 'On', after which the electricity can be switched on again. All that remains to be done then is for the thermostat to be adjusted to the desired temperature.

B Switch off the electricity at the socket. Set the room thermostat to high. Turn the control to 'pilot', depress fully, and apply a match to the burner. Check that the pilot is lit and count to 30. Turn control knob to 'On'. Switch on the electricity and adjust the thermostat.

1 Say which set you found clearer and easier to understand.

2 Explain why, being careful to mention:

a the transformation of dependent clauses into independent main clauses;

b the change from the passive to the active voice of the verbs. (If you don't remember what the passive voice is, see under the heading 'Verbs' on page 108.)

Because they tell people quickly and clearly what they mean, simple sentences are good attention-grabbers. People who want to persuade us to buy their products know this, too. An advertiser buying space in a newspaper, for example, has to make a big impact in a small space. So he or she chooses short simple sentences.

Letraset was invented on a train.

John Dankworth composes music on trains.

Peter Barkworth reads scripts on a train.

This advertisement was conceived on a train.

The only thing ever created in cars is a jam.

British Rail advertisement

The complex sentence

Complex sentences are those that contain two different kinds of clause:

1 an independent main clause that makes the main statement;
2 a dependent/subordinate clause that adds something extra to that statement.

They are called *complex* because their structure is more complex than that of independent main clauses.

The dependent or subordinate clause

There are two important facts to note about the dependent/subordinate clause:

1 It **resembles** the independent main clause in one respect: it, too, always has a subject and a main or finite verb (one that is not a participle ending in *-ing* or *-en*, or an infinitive i.e. the verb stem plus *to*: *to write, to think*, etc.)

2 It **differs from** the independent main clause in one respect: it is always introduced by a subordinating conjunction such as *although*, *because*, *if*, *when*, *until*, *unless*. For example:

Although Clara loved Paul [*dsc*], she went back to her husband [*imc*].

Remove *although* from the head of the dependent/subordinate clause and place it at the beginning of the independent main clause, and you will cause them to exchange their functions: the dependent/subordinate clause is now the independent main clause and vice versa:

Clara loved Paul, although she went back to her husband.

A second difference, related to the first, should now be apparent: any clause introduced by a subordinating conjunction must necessarily be incomplete, and is therefore

a *dependent* on the independent main clause for the completion of its meaning, and
b *subordinate* to it in value or importance.

Activity

Distinguish the dependent/subordinate clauses from the independent main clauses in the following sentences:

Maire refuses to marry Manus, unless he will get a proper job.
Because he prefers the past, Hugh ignores the real world.
Hugh drinks so that he can escape reality.
When Manus teaches her to speak, Sarah finds her identity.
She has hope until he abandons her.
Although he knows the language well, Manus refuses to speak English.

The function of dependent/subordinate clauses

Independent main clauses/simple sentences are used to make unqualified assertions and statements. Dependent/subordinate clauses allow us to say much more about the circumstances surrounding the statements made in the independent main clause. With their help we can talk about:

- **when** events happened:
  After Paul fell in love with Miriam, he neglected his mother.
- **why**:
  Paul gave Miriam up *because* he wanted to reassure his mother.
- **how**:
  Paul behaved towards Miriam *as if* she were a stranger.
- **what** concessions are being made:
  Paul treated Miriam as if she were a stranger, *although* his conscience pricked him sorely at times.
- **what** limits are being set:
  Paul held himself aloof from Miriam *until* her attraction for him proved too strong.

◆ **what** conditions are being imposed:
Paul threatened to break off with Miriam *unless* she gave herself physically to him/*if* she did not agree to give herself physically to him.

The three different categories of dependent clause

Clause analysis does not ask you simply to distinguish between independent main and dependent clauses. It asks you also to assign each dependent clause to the particular category to which it belongs: *Noun*, *Adjectival*, or *Adverbial*.

Note: you are not expected to learn the difference between the three kinds of dependent clause (unless, of course, you would like to). This is because knowing whether you were writing a noun, adjectival, or adverbial clause would help you neither to write well yourself nor to appreciate the prose style of anybody else. You are, however, asked to learn the difference between independent main clauses, dependent/subordinate clauses, and the phrase, because knowing this will help you to do both.

1 The noun clause

The *noun clause* has just the same function as the single noun: it acts as the subject or object of a verb. For example:

Single noun: Yolland told Maire of his *love*.
Noun clause: Yolland told Maire *that he loved her*.
Single noun: Jimmy Jack's *madness* is obvious.
Noun clause: It is obvious *that Jimmy Jack is mad*.

In both cases here the noun clause is equivalent to the noun: *that he loved her* is the thing he told her; it is just as much the object of the verb *told* as *love* is in the first example. In the same way, *that Jimmy Jack is mad* is equivalent to a fact; it is as much the subject of the verb *is* as the single noun *madness* is in the first example. Both clauses are equivalent to *things*.

There are four different kinds of noun clause:

i Noun clause as subject
This usually precedes the independent main clause, e.g.:

That Albert loved Shug was obvious.
What Celie wanted was love.

ii Noun clause as object
This usually follows verbs like *say*, *think*, *wonder*, *know*, *ask*, *hear*; they are introduced by conjunctions like *that*, *what*, *how*, *where*.

Celie said *that Albert had changed*.
Shug asked *how Celie liked the song*.

iii Noun clause as complement
This completes verbs of incomplete predication, such as *seem*, and the verb *to be*:

It seems *that Albert had been hiding Nettie's letters*.
That was *what Shug discovered*.

iv Noun clause in apposition

This is almost always introduced by *that*, and can be recognized by the fact that it spells out what the noun in the imc means:

Shug's idea *that God was a 'It'* was radical.

that God was a 'It' is the *idea*. The noun and the noun clause mean the same thing and have the same relationship to the rest of the sentence.

Note: a verb of incomplete predication is simply one that is unfinished until a statement (or complement) is added to it. For example:

It was (verb of incomplete predication) *a wet morning* (complement).

In practice, life is too short to worry about distinctions such as these (although sorting out the various kinds does give more scope for logical thinking than most English exercises).

Activity

Pick out

1 the independent main clauses,
2 the noun clauses in the following sentences. (If you can distinguish those of subject, object, complement, and apposition you will be showing double brilliance, but to recognize the noun clause is the important thing.)

a Sugar knew what was in Celie's mind.
b Harpo believed that Sofia was a bad wife.
c Celie didn't know where Nettie had gone.
d His behaviour to Shug was what Celie disliked.
e Celie didn't ask Mr if she could leave.
f What Sofia said about Harpo's bullying was true.
g That Harpo loved Sofia was obvious.
h Women had to learn the rule that they must not talk back to men.
i The beating was what she had expected.

Note: if you are doubtful about a noun clause, ask yourself if it could be replaced by a single noun. You will find that it often can, as in (a) and (c), for instance.

2 The adjectival clause

This has the same function as the single adjective: to describe the subject or object of the sentence. For example:

Single adjective: Sugar was an *independent* woman.
Adjectival clause: Nobody controlled Sugar, *who went her own way.*
Single adjective: Celie's Pa was an *evil man.*
Adjectival clause: Celie's Pa was a man *who abused his children.*

Activity Pick out

1 the imcs,
2 the adjectival clauses in the following sentences:
- **a** Squeak had the kind of skin that looked yellow.
- **b** Albert's Pa hated Sugar, who was coal-black.
- **c** Albert cleaned up his house, which had been filthy for months.
- **d** They went to Shug's room, where they could be alone.
- **e** The frog that Albert gave Celie was green.
- **f** Nettie was a child who managed to escape.
- **g** Sofia had several sisters, who were called the 'Amazons'.

3 The adverbial clause

Like the single adverb, this can modify adjectives and other adverbs as well as verbs. Adverbial clauses are easy to recognize, however, because they always begin with one of the following subordinating conjunctions:

- *as, because, since* (introducing adverbial clauses of **cause**):
  As/because/since she loved Harpo, Sofia waited for him.
- *as . . . as, than* (introducing adverbial clauses of **comparison** or **degree**):
  Harpo ate *as much as he could.*
  Harpo ate *more than two men ate.*
- *although, however* (introducing adverbial clauses of **concession**):
  Although he couldn't make Sofia 'mind' him, Harpo loved her.
  Harpo couldn't make Sofia 'mind' him, *however hard he tried.*
- *if, unless* (introducing adverbial clauses of **condition**):
  A man was not a man *if he could not rule his wife.*
  A man was not a man *unless he could rule his wife.*
- *as, as if* (introducing adverbial clauses of **manner**):
  Albert warned Celie to do *as he told her.*
  He treated her *as if she were a slave.*
- *where, wherever* (introducing adverbial clauses of **place**):
  Celie could not go *where she pleased.*
  (Compare with the noun clause:
  Celie did not know *where Nettie had gone.*
  The adjectival clause describes the kind of places Celie cannot go to; the noun clause tells us what piece of information she doesn't know.)
- *so that* (introducing adverbial clauses of **purpose**):
  Celie made herself wood *so that she wouldn't feel pain.*
- *so that, so . . . that* (introducing adverbial clauses of **result**):
  The rock injured her forehead, *so that it bled.*
  Celie controlled her emotions *so well that she seemed indifferent to pain.*
- *when, whenever, since* (introducing adverbial clauses of **time**):
  When Celie saw Shug's picture, she felt a gleam of hope.
  Whenever she looked at Shug she became aware of her own ugliness.
  Celie had thought of nothing but Shug *since she came.*

Note: some people have difficulty in recognizing independent main clauses in complex sentences like these because they are often so short that they don't seem to make much sense on their own. *It is obvious, Yolland told Maire,* and *He treated her,* for example, don't seem to do what independent main clauses are supposed to do – make sense on their own. To overcome this problem, remember that:

1 such clauses are **grammatically complete** (they have a subject and a verb), and
2 they are as long as they need to be to do their job in these particular sentences.

Activity

The advertisement on the following page contains eighteen clauses, four of which are adverbial and fourteen adjectival. List them under appropriate headings. (Remember that some adverbial clauses are headed by two subordinating conjunctions which may be separated from each other by other words, e.g. *as good as.*)

The punctuation of complex sentences

The stop to use between an independent main clause and a dependent clause is the comma. That is, if you need a stop at all, for the trend in writing today is towards lighter punctuation, with fewer stops. Consider the following examples:

A Until he met Miriam Paul was happy.
Because she loved him she was jealous.
B Paul was happy until he met Miriam.
She was jealous because she loved him.

Most people would put a comma between the main and dependent clauses in the sentences in A, but not in B. But even in A it is not really necessary, unless you feel that a comma would add emphasis to or alter the movement of your sentence.

Activity

1 Write out each pair of sentences, putting a comma in the ones in A and leaving the ones in B without one.
2 Now do the same thing in reverse.
3 Discuss the difference made to
a the movement,
b the emphasis of each sentence.

For most purposes it might be best to adopt the rule: 'Use a comma only where failure to do so might alter completely the meaning of the sentence, or make it very confusing to read' – as in the following examples:

a If a pregnant woman smokes her baby may suffer damage of some kind.
b However you may feel I'm wrong.
c One day we decided we would visit another town in the mountains.
d The passengers who were in the front of the train were seriously injured.
e All the students who had been in the examination hall at the time were interviewed by the police.

*These are the pans that were used for
the meal that was made from the
recipe that featured a cream sauce
that dried on the plates that went
into the washer that has a powerful
triple spray that gets things so sparkling
clean that it doesn't matter how
dirty the pots and pans are that
go into the exceptionally quiet
machine that has five fully
automatic programmes that
include two for economy that
makes running costs so low
that it's no more expensive
than washing by hand that
is a feature of the dishwashers
that come with a Free Five
Year Parts Guarantee and
Free Installation Check
that give such peace
of mind that it's no
wonder people say . . .*

"Thank you Hotpoint"

Activity

1 Write out each of these sentences twice, putting in a comma the second time. What difference does this make to each of the sentences?

2 If a comma were to be placed after the word 'Campbell' in the sentence below, what difference would this make to the trio's living arrangements?
Designer Colin Davenport, former lover of actress Janie Campbell who now lives with Hollywood director Stewart Baker, has issued a summons in the West Land County Court.

More complex complex sentences

So far, the complex sentences we have looked at have had only one independent main clause and only one dependent clause. They can however have more than one of each. *Multiple complex sentences* consist of **one** independent main clause and several dependent clauses, each of which is dependent on the one that came before. For example:

> Sugar said [*imc*] that God would be pissed off [*dnc*] if someone didn't notice the colour purple [*d.adv.c*] when walking in the fields [*d.adv.c*].

Composite sentences consist of **two** independent main clauses and one or more dependent clauses. The independent main clauses may come together at the beginning of a sentence –

> Shug loved Celie [*imc*] but she also loved Germaine, a young man [*imc*] who had nice buns [*d.adj.c*].

The handling of complex and composite sentences

It is complex and composite sentences like these that sometimes make writing hard to read. If writers do not make the connection between their main and their dependent clauses clear, their readers may be confused. This is particularly likely when one clause cuts across another, as in the example below:

> (Shug loved Celie) but (she also loved Germaine, a young man) (who [she said] had nice buns).

Here, yet another main clause – 'she said' – comes between the two parts of the adjectival clause 'who had nice buns', complicating the sentence considerably.

In sophisticated writing, clauses often cut across each other like this. A dependent adverbial clause, for instance, is often put between the subject and the verb of the independent main clause, like this:

> Harpo, *when he forgot about being boss*, was very happy with his wife.
> The Queen Honey Bee, *because she was emotionally frail*, depended on Celie.
> Albert, *when he realized Celie's true worth*, wanted to marry her again, 'in spirit'.

The phrase

Both complex and simple sentences may well contain one or more phrases as well as dependent clauses. Phrases can consist of one word – *however, nevertheless, recently, fortunately, today*, etc. – or several: *of course, on the other hand, in contemporary society, on a good day, on the whole, little by little*, etc. You should be able to see that phrases differ in one important respect from independent clauses: they do not have a main (or finite) verb, as in *Paul* **gave** *Miriam up*. What phrases sometimes have instead are *participles*: either *present* participles ending in *-ing*, like the ones below –

> talking about poetry, making haycocks, cooking chicken, burning bread, breaking off relationships, eating cherries

– or *past* participles ending in *-ed*, *-en*, or *-t*, like those that follow:

> the umbrella broken, the wages collected, the bread burnt, the chicken cooked, the meal eaten.

Other past participles can also be formed from a combination of the two kinds above:

> having painted the picture, having won the prize, having looked at the rose bush, having burned the bread

The phrase and economy

Phrases use fewer words than clauses and move at a faster pace – qualities that make them valuable to journalists who need to cram much detail into a small space. For example:

> Blond-haired Betty, mother of Wayne, two, and Darren, four, a keen dancer and part-time Avon lady, said today . . .

Activity

1 Compare the alternative versions of the same ideas that follow.

Although he was repentant, he was jailed for five years.
Although repentant, he was jailed for five years.

Wilson, who is a member of the hard left, has been defeated in the Council elections.
Wilson, a member of the hard left, has been defeated in the Council elections.

The glass making firm of Carterton Brothers, who are based in Birmingham, is gearing up to mount a fierce defence against the £1.16 billion take-over bid which has been made by the industrial conglomerate ORT. They will preface this defence with the early publication, in just over a week, of their pre-tax profits, which are sharply higher for the six months to the end of September.

Birmingham glass maker Carterton Brothers is gearing up to mount a fierce defence against the £1.16 billion take-over bid from industrial conglomerate ORT. They will preface this defence with the early publication, in just over a week, of sharply higher pre-tax profits for the six months to end September.

2 a Re-write the following paragraph using phrases instead of clauses wherever possible.

(You will have to alter the sentence structure and leave out words where necessary.)

Paul Leonard Newman was born sixty-one years ago in Cleveland. He was the son of a Jewish sporting-goods store owner, and was raised in the affluent suburb of Shaker Heights. He has appeared in forty-seven films and directed five. He has been nominated for an Oscar six times, and last year was awarded an honorary one recognizing his career and his 'personal integrity and dedication to his craft'. He lives with Joanne Woodward, to whom he has been married for twenty-eight years, in a 200-year-old carriage house in Westport, Connecticut. He is a champion racing-driver. He has also founded a successful food business. He is a political activist, and he is noted for his philanthropy.

b Assess whether your alterations have improved or worsened the quality of the piece as journalism.

Misuse of participles in phrases

Beware of *dangling* or *unattached participles* that have no proper subject to go with, and so attach themselves to the wrong one. For example:

Crossing the road, a bus ran him over.
(As he was . . .)

Aged seven, both his parents died.
(When he was seven . . .)
Being a little girl of eight, her father ran off with another woman.
(When she was a little girl . . .)

Activity

Pick out the phrases in the following extract from *Sons and Lovers*:

'You brazen imp!' she exclaimed, rushing and scuffling for the comb, which he had under his knees. As she wrestled with him, pulling at his smooth, tight-covered knees, he laughed till he lay back on the sofa shaking with laughter. The cigarette fell from his mouth, almost singeing his throat. Under his delicate tan the blood flushed up, and he laughed till his blue eyes were blinded, his throat swollen almost to choking. Then he sat up. Beatrice was putting in her comb.

D.H. Lawrence, *Sons and Lovers*

Why clause analysis went out of fashion

Students used to hate analysing clauses for two main reasons:

1 Dependent clauses were sometimes hard to distinguish from one another. Consider for example the following dependent clauses, all beginning with the same subordinating conjunction, *where*:

a Sugar went *where she pleased.*
b Celie often didn't know *where she was.*
c Celie took Shug to the house *where she was born.*

In (a) the clause is modifying the verb *went* – Where did she go? Where she chose – and so is an **adverbial clause**.
In (b), the clause is acting as the equivalent of a noun: it is an object, the thing that Celie didn't know, and is therefore a **noun clause**.
In (c), the clause is describing or identifying the particular house where Celie was born – Which house did they visit? The one where she was born – and so is an **adjectival clause**.

2 There seemed to be no real point in the exercise. What good did it do to identify clauses as noun, adjectival, or adverbial, they asked, and when they left school and became teachers themselves, they decided to have nothing more to do with it. The result was a conflict over the teaching of English that has raged ever since.

Activity Try to identity the different clauses in the following sentences, all involving the subordinating conjunction *that*:
a Celie told Albert that he looked like a frog.
b She liked the purple frog that he made for her.
c He changed, so that she grew to like him.

The usefulness of parsing and clause analysis

How far do grammatical exercises in parsing and clause analysis help students:

a to understand complicated sentences written by other people,
b to write well themselves?

Breaking a sentence down into the different kinds of clause it contains will tell us something about its construction but little about its meaning. For that, a more practical approach is needed, as Wydick demonstrates below.

Look at the following example of the kind of writing that gives us difficulty in real life:

> In a trial by jury, the court may, when the convenience of witnesses or the ends of justice would be promoted thereby, on motion of a party, after notice and hearing, make an order, no later than the close of the pretrial conference in cases in which such pretrial conference is to be held, or in other cases, no later than ten days before the trial date, that the trial of the issue of liability shall precede the trial of any other issue in the case.

The subject matter of that passage is not profound or complicated, but the passage is hard to understand. It consists of a single sentence, eighty-six words long, containing five pieces of information. It tells us that:

1 in a jury case, the liability issue may be tried before any other issue
2 the judge may order this if it will serve the convenience of witnesses or the ends of justice;
3 the order may be made on a party's motion after notice and hearing;
4 in a case with a pretrial conference, the order must be made before the end of the conference; and
5 in a case with no pretrial conference, the order must be made at least ten days before the trial date.

The passage is hard to understand for two reasons. First, the single-sentence format caused the author to distort the logical order of the five pieces of information. The first thing the readers want to know is what the passage is about. It is about the trial of the liability issue before the other issues. But the readers do not discover that until they have climbed through a thicket of subsidiary ideas and arrived at the last twenty words of the sentence. Second, the single-sentence format strains the readers' memories. The subject of the sentence ('court') appears at word seven. At word thirty-two, the verb 'make' finally shows up. Part of the object ('an order') comes next, but the critical part remains hidden until the readers arrive, breathless, at word sixty-eight. By then they have forgotten the verb and must search back in the sentence to find it. The remedy is simple. Instead of one long sentence containing five thoughts, use five sentences, each containing one thought. Here is one way the passage could be rewritten:

> In a jury case, the court may order the liability issue to be tried before any other issue. This may be done if the court finds that it would serve the convenience of witnesses or the ends of justice.
>
> The order may be made on motion of a party, after notice and hearing. In cases where a pretrial conference is held, the order must be made before the end of the conference. In other cases, the order must be made at least ten days before the trial date.

Wydick, *Plain English for Lawyers*

Activity

Rewrite the two passages below by using Wydick's method of breaking one long sentence down into several shorter ones. Remember to arrange your sentences in logical order. (You will need to add words here and there, and cut out others which are no longer needed.)

a By establishing a technique whereby the claims of many individuals can be resolved at the same time, class actions serve an important function in our judicial system in eliminating the possibility of repetitious litigation and providing claimants with a method of obtaining enforcements of claims which would otherwise be too small to warrant individual litigation.

b While there are instances in which consumer abuse and exploitation result from advertising which is false, misleading, or irrelevant, it does not necessarily follow that these cases need to be remedied by governmental intervention into the market place because it is possible for consumers' interests to be protected through resort to the courts, either by consumers themselves or by those competing sellers who see their market shares decline in the face of inroads based on such advertising.

Wydick, *Plain English for Lawyers*

It should be clear to you by now that, as in any clash of extreme opinions, the truth lies somewhere in the middle ground. Grammar exercises *per se* help us neither to write well ourselves nor to comment sensibly on the writing of other people. A working knowledge of the different kinds of clauses and their arrangement within sentences will however help us with both.

The grammar every student should know

The parts of speech: Nouns, pronouns, adjectives, verbs, adverbs, prepositions, conjunctions, the definite and indefinite articles.

The main or finite verb: A finite verb is one that shows number (singular or plural), person (*I*, *you*, *she*, etc.), and tense (present or past – *think*, *thinks*, *thought*).

The present participle: The part of the verb that ends in *-ing*, e.g. *eating*, *drinking*, *sleeping*, *waking*.

The past participle: The part of the verb that ends in *-en*, *-t*, *-ed* e.g. *forgotten*, *broken*, *learnt*, *destroyed*.

The independent main clause: A group of words that contains a subject and a main verb and so can make a complete statement without the help of another clause. Independent main clauses are also known as simple sentences.

The dependent clause: A group of words that gives further information about the main clause; it contains a main verb but cannot stand alone because it is introduced by a subordinating conjunction.

The phrase: A group of words that adds information to a sentence. It often does not contain a verb at all, but when it does, it is always in the form of a present or past participle.

The simple sentence: A sentence that consists of a single independent main clause.

The compound sentence: A sentence that consists of two or more simple sentences joined together, usually by conjunctions such as *and*, *but*, *so*, *then*.

The complex sentence: A sentence that consists of one or more independent main clauses, and one or more dependent clauses.

The subject of a sentence: The person (or thing) by whom the action of the verb in the main clause is performed.

The object of a sentence: The person (or thing) for, or to, or on whom the action of the verb in the main clause is performed.

Knowledge of all of these is important, but knowledge of the independent clause, the dependent clause, and the phrase is essential. The skilful handling of these three structures is what gives informative writing its clarity and force, and literary writing its style. We shall look at this next.

Grammatical characteristics of good writing

The length of clauses within sentences

Consider the two sentences below:

1 Most experts agree that for conveying complex factual information, particularly to the general public or to young people, short sentences are best.
2 Most experts agree that short sentences are best for conveying complex factual material (a) to the general public, (b) to young people.

Talking point Which of these two structures did you find easier to read? Why?

Many authorities on writing claim that short sentences are best for conveying factual information. 'We preach that a good average sentence length in public information documents is fifteen to twenty words', the British *Plain English Campaign* declares, and its American counterpart agrees: 'Write short sentences with an average of no more than twenty words.' This advice is backed up by an even higher authority: an official booklet issued to the staff of the Cabinet Office: 'Use short sentences. For writing to civil servants, aim to average fifteen to twenty-five words. For the public, average fifteen to twenty.'

To test the readability of a piece of prose, the American Campaign for Plain English uses the *Flesch Reading Ease Test*. They take a representative sample of 100 words from the piece, then assess it mathematically.

Activity

1 Read the following passage from an A Level textbook, then run the Flesch test on it. (The instructions are given below.)

Acceptability is concerned with the attitudes of native users of the English language to particular forms of usage if one form of usage is 'acceptable' to substantial numbers of such users, then the grammatical description of the language must take that into account. For example, 'I don't want nothing' is acceptable to large numbers of people as a very emphatic statement of what somebody does not want. Such an emphatic use of double negatives must feature in a description of English grammar, although 'prescriptive' grammarians might argue that such double negatives ought not to be used, since they are illogical.

Step 1 Count the words in the piece of writing.
Step 2 Count all the syllables in the words.
Step 3 Count the sentences. Count as a sentence each full unit of speech marked off by a full-stop, colon, semi-colon, dash, question mark or exclamation mark.

Step 4 Calculate the average number of syllables per word, dividing the number of syllables by the number of words.

Step 5 Calculate the average number of words per sentence, dividing the number of words by the number of sentences.

Step 6 Find your readability score as follows:

- Multiply the average sentence length by 1.015.
- Multiply the average word length by 84.6.
- Add the two numbers together.
- Subtract this sum from 206.835. The balance is your readability score, on a scale from 0 to 100.
  To be considered plain English, a text must score a minimum of 60. The higher the score, the more readable the passage will be.

2 How accessible for A Level students do you find the extract?

The same criterion of brevity is also cited by journalist Peregrine Worsthorne:

> As a general rule, when considering post-war non-fiction texts, the grammarians say this about the number of words per sentence:
> 0–14: staccato, or 'sergeant-major' English
> 15–24: good English
> 25–37: long-winded
> 38 upwards: intolerably verbose, legalese.

He is dismayed to find that, judged by these criteria, two of his favourite writers, Bernard Levin and Auberon Waugh, have average sentence lengths of 26 and 36 respectively, putting them into the 'long-winded' category. How can this be, he wonders, when they write so well? The answer is that length in itself has very little to do with whether a sentence is good or bad. A sentence may contain well over fifty words, yet be easily understood at a first reading. Even lawyer Richard Wydick, who believes that long sentences make legal writing difficult to read, has no objection to them *per se*. He offers a qualified guide to clarity:

> **1** In most sentences, put only one main thought.
> **2** Keep the average sentence length below twenty-five words.
>
> *Do not misinterpret this guide.* The first part says that *most* sentences should contain only one main thought. It does not say that *every* sentence should contain only one main thought. The second part says that the *average* length of your sentences should be below twenty-five words. It does not say that *every* sentence should be twenty-five words or less. A succession of short, simple sentences sounds choppy:
>
> Defence counsel objected to the question. She argued that it called for hearsay. The Court overruled the objection, and the witness was allowed to answer.

> You need an occasional longer sentence in which two or more main thoughts are joined:
>
> Defence counsel objected to the question, arguing that it called for hearsay; the Court overruled the objection, and the witness was allowed to answer.
>
> Wydick, *Plain English for Lawyers*

For writing that seeks to convey anything more than facts, even more allowance needs to be made. When talking about such things as ideas and feelings, attitudes, values, and beliefs, writers must be free to qualify or enlarge upon their statements with as many subordinate clauses as they feel necessary. As long as the connection between the clauses is clear, so will be the meaning of the sentences.

The clear arrangement of clauses within complex sentences

The key to good writing in general therefore lies not so much in brevity as in the skilful handling of clauses *within* long sentences. If

a the meaning of the main clause is well expressed,
b the connection between the main clause(s) and any dependent clauses and phrases is clear,
c the relation of each dependent clause and phrase to all other dependent clauses and phrases is clear,

then it is a good sentence, regardless of its length. Take, for example, the following sentences from a piece by Bernard Levin:

> But Stoppard fills the pool with a flood of laughter apparently conceived for its own sake, and only when his audience has drowned in the pool, weak with a total surrender to joy, does he permit the hideous creatures from the deep to come crawling to the surface. Freezing an audience's laughter with a stroke of horror is a familiar playwright's device, and not a particularly difficult one for a technically accomplished writer to handle, but Stoppard goes further; he shifts the whole structure bodily into the horror, and so deftly that we do not even realize we are moving until we are there.

These sentences are obviously well over the twenty-word limit, yet are easily grasped at first sight. Now compare Levin's sentences with those of another well-known journalist, Alastair Forbes:

> I am pretty sure that the mere 2,000-plus other, mostly West End and Grub Street, consumers to whom John Murray has made available the present 125,000 words long specimen of Frank Giles's journalism (boasting a Good Housekeeping Seal from that most admirable of Gray's Inn Road literary editors, the late lamented Jack Lambert) will suffer no such cardiac

> arrhythmia,* not even on the early page where the avowedly colour-blind autobiographer asserts that the naked near-albino Duke of Windsor (for whom, and his 'quiet, dignified, and composed . . . never anything but stately wife', he then felt an 'infatuation') had absolutely no hair on his body, even in the places where one would most expect it to be.

What makes the Forbes passage so difficult to read? The solitary main clause, *I am pretty sure*, has five dependent clauses and three lengthy phrases hanging on to it, yet it is not the number of the clauses but the lack of clear connection between them that confuses the reader. Dependent clauses and phrases grow out of one another as each new thought strikes the writer. The result is that they cut across one another, blurring the train of thought. For example, the writer begins by saying, 'I am pretty sure that the mere 2,000-plus other, mostly West End and Grub Street, consumers', then doesn't complete his statement by adding the verb – 'will suffer no such cardiac arrhythmia' – for another thirty-seven words. Instead he introduces a lengthy adjectival clause – 'to whom John Murray has made available the present 125,000 words long specimen of Frank Giles's journalism' – and a lengthy phrase in brackets – '(boasting a Good Housekeeping Seal from that most admirable of Gray's Inn Road literary editors, the late lamented Jack Lambert)'.

So thirty-seven words come between the subject ('consumers') and its verb, and by the time readers have ploughed through the thicket of dependent clause and phrase, they've lost the thread of what the sentence was about.

Talking point Can you find a similar splitting apart of subject and verb later in the passage?

Activity

1. Run the Flesch test on the two passages above and record their scores.
2. Basing your answer on the Forbes passage, what advice would you give to inexperienced writers on the handling of dependent clauses? (Children, by the way, prefer the main statement of a sentence to come first: 'Pat your tummy then rub your nose', not 'Before rubbing your nose, pat your tummy'.)

The match between complex vocabulary and complex sentences

Generally speaking, the longer a writer's sentences are, the more elaborate and obscure his or her vocabulary is likely to be. You can prove the truth of this statement by working a calculation based on what is called the Fog Index. As with the Flesch test, a sample of prose of as near as possible 100 words is chosen, starting at the beginning of a sentence and finishing at the end. The following steps are then taken:

* Cardiac arrhythmia is a term used to describe any deviation from the normal rhythm of the heart.

Step 1 Count the exact number of words and divide by the number of sentences.

Step 2 Add to the total the number of words of three or more syllables. Do not count proper names, compounds (e.g. shock-horror) and suffixed words (e.g. publish[ing]).

Step 3 Multiply the grand total by 0.4. The resulting score is the Fog Index.
Readability levels indicated by Index scores:
1–10: readable by any school-leaver
14–16: readable by the average sixth-former
18 upwards: too hard for most people to read.

Activity Calculate the Fog Index of the Levin and Forbes extracts.

The role of 'glue' words in sentence construction

According to Wydick,

> . . . in every English sentence there are two kinds of words: working words and glue words.* The working words carry the meaning of the sentence. In the preceding sentence the working words are these: *working*, *words*, *carry*, *meaning*, and *sentence*. The others are glue words: *the*, *the*, *of*, and *the*. The glue words do serve a purpose: they hold the working words together to form a proper English sentence. But when you find too many glue words, it is a sign that the sentence is badly constructed.

To see what Wydick is getting at, consider the following sentence:

Please send clean clothes and money to me at the Palace Hotel Bath.

The content or working words here are *send*, *clothes*, *money*, *Palace Hotel*, *Bath*. Strip the sentence down to these content words, as you would when sending a telegram, and it will still communicate its meaning clearly:

Send clothes money Palace Hotel Bath.

If a sentence cannot communicate as clearly as this when reduced to its content words, then, Wydick suggests, it must be badly written. To verify the point, consider the following:

If you want to write well, the thing to aim at is to use as few structure words as possible.

Reduced to its content words this would never make an intelligible telegram:

You want write well thing aim use few structure words possible

* Referred to as 'content' and 'structure' words in the section on Prepositions, page 110, and in the rest of this section.

It could be rewritten more succinctly:

> To write well, use few structure words.

Activity

Rewrite the sentence below using as few structure words as possible/fewer structure words. (As you can see, it's easy to use six words where three will do). Since sentences that contain large numbers of words will be long ones, make this your subject and begin, 'Long sentences . . .

The fact that there is a large number of words in a sentence does not necessarily mean that it will be difficult to read.

Constructions that create structure words

Three constructions in particular can lead to the build-up of unnecessary structure words in a sentence. They are:

1 the false subject
2 the use of abstract nouns
3 the passive voice.

1 The false subject

Consider the following sentences:

a The thing that makes sentences difficult to read is the number of long constructions that they contain.

This is not a long sentence, but it contains almost as many structure as content words. The writer's mistake was to begin the sentence with a false subject: *The thing*. Having done so, he or she is forced to use three clauses stuffed with structure words to finish it off:

> . . . that makes sentences difficult to read
> is the number of long constructions
> that they contain.

Had the writer begun the sentence with the true subject –

> Long constructions . . .

and followed it immediately with its verb and object –

> make sentences . . .

then the rest of the sentence –

> difficult to read

would have fallen naturally into place, and the sentence would have been both shorter and crisper to read.

b In the case of teachers, they are very badly paid.

In this example the opening phrase, *In the case of*, is again redundant. The subject – *teachers* – should come first, tightening the sentence up:

Teachers are very badly paid.

Activity

Rewrite the following sentences, using fewer structure words. Remember to throw out false subjects such as *it* or *there is*, and to put the true subject first:

1. It has been twice that I have telephoned the shop to complain.
2. In older people, drink changes their personalities.
3. She was pregnant, and it was not very far away that her baby was due.
4. In a recent survey it shows that crime is on the increase.
5. There are two factors that have contributed to this rise in crime: poverty and unemployment.
6. There is a lack of wisdom in the way some people spend their money.
7. Sentences are not necessarily verbose just because they contain a lot of words.

2 The use of abstract nouns

Good writers use concrete subjects and active verbs: their sentences are full of **people**, **doing** things.

Poor writers use abstract nouns instead of people, causing structure words to proliferate. Wydick explains:

Base verbs v derivative nouns and adjectives*

At its core, the law is not abstract; it is part of a real world full of people who live and move and do things to other people. Car drivers *collide*. Plaintiffs *complain*. Judges *decide*. Defendants *pay*. To express this life and motion, a writer must use verbs – action words. The purest verb form is the base verb, like *collide*, *complain*, *decide*, and *pay*. Base verbs are simple creatures. They cannot tolerate adornment. If you try to dress them up, you squash their life and motion. Unfortunately, that is done all too easily. The base verb *collide* can be decked out as a derivative noun, *collision*. Likewise, *complain* becomes *complaint*, *decide* becomes *decision*, and *pay* becomes *payment*. Lawyers love to ruin base verbs. Lawyers don't *act* – they *take action*. They don't *assume* – they *make assumptions*. They don't *conclude* – they *draw conclusions*. With too much of this, legal writing becomes a lifeless vapour. When a base verb is replaced by a derivative noun or adjective, surplus words begin to swarm like gnats. 'Please *state why you object* to the question' comes out like this: 'Please *make a statement of why you are interposing an objection* to the question.' The base verb *state* can do the work all alone. But to get the same work out of *statement*, you need a supporting verb (*make*), an article (*a*), and a preposition (*of*). The derivative noun *objection* attracts a similar cloud of surplus words.

* By *base verb* Wydick means the main stem of the verb, to which endings are added; the infinitive, without the *to*, e.g.: *(to) write, talk, think, feel,* etc.

> Do not conclude from this that derivative nouns and adjectives are always bad; sometimes you need them. But do not overuse them in place of base verbs. You can spot the common ones by their endings: *-ment*, *-ion*, *-ance*, *-ence*, *-ancy*, *-ency*, *-ant*, and *-ent*. When you spot one, stop to see if you can make your sentence stronger and shorter by using a base verb instead.
>
> Wydick, *Plain English for Lawyers*

3 The passive voice

The *active voice* is a grammatical term to indicate that the subject of a verb is actually doing the action:

> The lawyer [subject of this sentence] *believed* his client [the object of this sentence].

The *passive voice* on the other hand is used to show that the subject of a verb is suffering the action – i.e. having it done **to** him:

> The client [subject of this sentence] *was believed* by his lawyer [the object of this sentence].

Again, Wydick has an interesting note on this:

> *The active voice v the passive voice*
>
> When you use the active voice, the subject of the sentence acts: 'The union filed a complaint.' When you use the passive voice, the subject of the sentence is acted upon: 'A complaint was filed by the union.'
>
> The passive voice has two disadvantages. First, it takes more words. When you say 'the union filed a complaint', *filed* does the work by itself. But when you say, 'a complaint was filed by the union', the verb *filed* requires a supporting verb (*was*) and a preposition (*by*).
>
> The second disadvantage of the passive voice is its detached abstraction. With the active voice, the reader can usually see who is doing what to whom. But the passive voice often leaves that unclear:
>
> > It is feared that adequate steps will not be taken to mitigate the damages that are being caused.
>
> Who is doing the fearing? Who is taking the steps? Who is causing the damages? We cannot tell because the actor in each case is hidden in the fog of the passive voice.
>
> The passive voice has its proper uses. First, you can use it when the thing done is important, and the one who did it is not:
>
> > The summons and complaint were served on 19th January.
>
> Second, you can use it where the actor is unknown or indefinite:
>
> > The ledgers were mysteriously destroyed.

Third, you can use it to place a strong element at the end of a sentence for emphasis:

In the defendant's closet was found the bloody coat.

Fourth, you can use it on those rare occasions when detached abstraction is appropriate:

All people were created with a thirst for knowledge.

But elsewhere, use the active voice; it will make your writing stronger, briefer, and clearer.

Activity

Rewrite the following sentences

1 replacing abstract nouns with people and things;
2 using the active voice.

The first is done for you as a guide:

a The general opinion was that the money should be spent on the improvement of the leisure centre. (8 structure, 7 content words)
Most people wanted to spend the money on improving the leisure centre. (8 structure, 4 content words)
b It should be noted that the closing date for entries is 1st April.
c A request was made by many of the students for a ban on smoking in the refectory.
d It is hoped that it will be possible for us to finish the work by Easter.
e A government inquiry should be made into the running of old people's homes.
f Early application is advisable.
g It is the opinion of many critics that Shakespeare is the greatest writer who ever lived.
h Literary criticism was held by F. R. Leavis to be a branch of moral philosophy.

Summary

To keep your sentence constructions clear, forceful, and brief:

- Use phrases instead of clauses wherever possible: *Having written the book she sent it to the publisher*, rather than, *After she had written the book she sent it to the publisher*.
- Avoid putting lengthy clauses or phrases between the two halves of another clause or phrase.
- Avoid false subjects.
- Use the active voice of verbs.
- Use concrete subjects instead of abstract nouns: *Most people want*, instead of *There is a general desire for*.
- Use one word instead of several wherever possible: *because* instead of *due to the fact that*; *if* instead of *in the event of*; *about* instead of *with reference to*.

- Avoid what Wydick calls 'throat-clearing' – pompous little phrases that add nothing to the sentence but superfluous words:
  it is important to add that
  there is little doubt that
  it is obvious that/obviously
  it is clear that/clearly
  it may be recalled that
  it is interesting to point out
  actually
  in point of fact

The appropriate versus the correct

There are people who cannot bear to hear English spoken 'incorrectly' and who write to the BBC to tell them so. Their complaints about grammar focus on the following points:

1. When to use *I* or *me* in phrases such as *you and I*, or *you and me*.
2. Whether words like *none* and *a number* should take a singular or a plural verb.
3. Whether or not we should split infinitives, i.e. say *to boldly go* rather than *boldly to go* or *to go boldly*. (Infinitives in Latin could not be split because they were a single word rather than the two used in English: *amare*, for example, as opposed to *to love*. Grammarians who were keen on Latin therefore ruled that infinitives shouldn't be split in English – the sort of thing that gets grammar a bad name.)
4. Whether we should say *different than*, *different to*, or *different from*.
5. Whether we should say *I wish I was* (the indicative mood used for making definite statements of fact), or *I wish I were* (the subjunctive mood used for expressing wishes and hopes).
6. Whether it is correct to end a sentence with a preposition: should it be *Who did you give it to?*, or *To whom did you give it?*
7. When to use *who* and *whom* in sentences such as *Who were you talking to last night?* Is *who* correct here, or should it be *whom*?
8. When to use *shall* and when to use *will*.
9. Whether it is acceptable to use sentences without verbs; newscasters, for example, will often say something like, '*And now over to Michael Fish at the London Weather Centre*', instead of, '*And now we are going over to Michael Fish at the London Weather Centre*'.

In the 1940s, complaints like these might have been taken seriously. Announcers read the news in 'cut-glass accents' like that of the Queen today and wore evening dress to do so, even on the radio. In an age when 'common' accents are used as a matter of course in the media and four-letter words have found their way even into poetry, such formality is not only dated, but doomed.

That does not mean that all rules and conventions have been abandoned, of course. It is taken for granted that essays, scholarly articles and books, serious journalism, and so on should continue to be written in formally correct, conventional English. (Think of the difficulties foreign readers would have if they were not.) Creative writers, advertising copy-writers, TV and radio script-writers on the other hand are allowed to break the rules whenever they want to on the grounds that it is sometimes necessary to do something 'wrong' in order to get it 'right'. Copy-writers can happily use incomplete sentences in their advertisements, serious novelists can use unconventional sentence structure, punctuation, and spelling to get the effect they want. The phrase to remember is 'appropriate for the purpose'.

Breaking the rules in advertising

Consider the following advertisement. It breaks two writing conventions:

1 It breaks one complete sentence into fragments, treating each fragment as if it were a sentence in its own right, e.g.:
 A belt-drive semi-automatic turntable;

2 It treats each of these non-sentences as a separate paragraph, defying the convention that all points on the same subject should be grouped together to form one coherent whole.

> There's a Compact Disc Player with front-loading motorized disc tray, track select and skip function.
> (1 in either direction.)
> A belt-drive semi-automatic turntable.
> A twin cassette deck with auto tape switching and Dolby noise reduction.
> A 3-band synthesized digital timer with 21 pre-sets, no less.
> And, (wait for it) a ferocious 35 watts RMS per channel amplifier feeding high quality two-way speakers with flat, square bass drivers.

Activity

1 Write out the advertisement in one long, formally correct sentence.
2 Explain what, if anything, has been lost by doing so.
3 How far do you think that acceptance of the paragraphing used in such advertisements might damage:
a a writer's ability to present a carefully worked out argument;
b the general public's ability to read one?

Advertisers also fracture conventional sentence structure with their treatment of the dependent/subordinate clause. In the Volkswagen advertisement on page 144, for instance, the copy-writers deliberately ignore the rule that a dependent clause cannot stand alone. They detach it from its independent main clause by a full stop and leave it to masquerade as a sentence in its own right. For example:

> Will we never learn that cars are virility symbols? That spoilers, for instance, should jut out the back looking mucho macho?

Trust Volkswagen to put a spoiler where no one can see it.

Will we never learn that cars are male virility symbols?

That spoilers, for instance, should jut out the back looking mucho macho?

Believe us, if that's where they worked best that's where we'd put them.

But our engineers insist that on the Golf they work better closer to the road.

Underneath the car where they deflect the turbulent airflow away from the axles.

Thereby easing drag so the Golf has the best aerodynamics in its class, cd 0.34.

Which, in turn, helps the Golf go faster and further on less fuel.

Which, in turn, means it needs, and gets, better direct-acting servo brakes.

Which we hope shows why we make such a fuss over a little thing like a spoiler.

Everything on a Volkswagen has to work. Everytime.

Again and again.

Frankly, gentlemen, isn't that what the ladies really look for in a virility symbol?

THE NEW GOLF PRICES FROM £4,597 MODEL ILLUSTRATED GL £6,696, EXCLUDING NUMBER PLATES AND DELIVERY. FURTHER INFORMATION FROM VOLKSWAGEN SALES ENQUIRIES, YEOMANS DRIVE, BLAKELANDS, MILTON KEYNES, MK14 5AN. TELEPHONE: (0908) 679121. EXPORT AND FLEET SALES, 95 BAKER STREET, LONDON W1M 1FB. TELEPHONE: 01-486 8411

Activity

Consider the treatment of sentence structure in the rest of the advertisement and carry out the activities suggested below.

1. What convention regarding conjunctions are the copy-writers breaking in line 7? Are they justified in doing so?
2. Lines 9–10 and lines 11–12 consist of a phrase followed by a dependent adverbial clause. What is 'incorrect' about these 'sentences'?
3. Find three further examples of dependent clauses being used 'incorrectly' as complete sentences.
4. Find one example of a phrase being used as a sentence in its own right.
5. Explain what the copy-writers are satirizing in the first two sentences. Why do they drop into fake Spanish?
6. What reason do they give for Volkswagen's refusal to follow this trend?
7. Explain the appeal being made to male readers in the use of the phrase 'virility symbol' in the last sentence (it has a double meaning).
8. How does this relate to the mocking of such things in the first two sentences?
9. Re-write the advertisement in conventionally constructed sentences.
10. Compare your version of the advertisement with the copy-writers' and say how far you think the original version's unconventional sentence structure is justified by results.

Breaking the rules in literary writing

Creative writers (from whom copy-writers probably stole their ideas in the first place) had begun to shatter language conventions early in the century. Lawrence's novel *Lady Chatterley's Lover*, first published in 1928 (though not in England), used language obscene enough for the book to merit prosecution in 1961. Earlier, in 1922, James Joyce's *Ulysses* upset readers as much by the originality of its style as by the explicit nature of its content – vivid descriptions of every aspect of life from eating through going to the lavatory to masturbating and making love. Sometimes the words would flow in an unbroken torrent, with no full-stop for several pages: at others they would be arranged in sentence fragments, with full-stops everywhere they should not be.

Activity

In the two extracts that follow, the writers are trying to capture the way in which thoughts grasshopper through our minds. Something we see or hear reminds us of something else, which sparks off another memory or thought, which makes us think of still another. Read the extracts and then carry out the activities suggested below.

a Yes because he's always asking what I'm at when he's off all day pretending to be useful mooching about in everybody's way more likely it's Paddy Malloy he has making up to me I'm sure the thin one from Corkhill not the stout one from Bantree just because he's divorced now no children thank God so he's as free as a bird as they say his wife the poor thing couldn't conceive supposing I fell for another now sure it would be a miracle after all these years wouldn't that shake him out of his high and mightiness though always trying to make himself interesting to anyone will listen to him it's bad enough the fool he makes of himself in O'Leary's without him thinking he's love's young dream with girls not old enough to be his daughter was anyone in creation ever plagued with such a man . . .

b What's that? Starlings. Flying in to roost. What was it Yeats called them? Stares. More rhymes than starling. They like the warmth of the lamps. Cheery little beggars. Carry psittacosis though, or is that just parrots? Still, birds the symbol of the soul. Philomena for instance. Metempsychosis. From woman to nightingale. I wonder does it work the other way around? There's the beam from the Howth light. Nine seconds between. Has to flash or they'll think it's a house. Remember when Milly frightened of the dark. Light a reassurance. A dark hole waiting for us all one day I suppose. No escape from that. Paddy Dignam now, as decent a little fellow as ever drew breath. Heart was it I wonder. That and the whiskey. A lot of money he spent getting his nose that red. What was it the priest said? Asleep in paradise. Has to say that about every body of course. The nature of the job.

The first passage is a glimpse into the mind of a woman as she lies drowsily in bed; the second depicts the thoughts that go through the mind of a man as he walks in the streets at dusk. Discuss how far the sentence structure and punctuation of each passage is appropriate,

a for describing the kind of thoughts that go through our minds when we're alone,

b for revealing the thinker's gender. (The stereotypical view pictures women as emotional, spontaneous, and impulsive; men as more rational, controlled, and detached.)

Depicting character in this way has been called the *stream of consciousness* technique, because all we are given is the flow of the characters' thoughts and feelings as they live from minute to minute. Later writers have found other ways of breaking the rules.

Below is an extract from Russell Hoban's novel, *Riddley Walker*. In this passage, Riddley and his friend Lissener, more intuitive and sensitive than most of their fellows, visit a ruined nuclear power station:

The lite wer coming from behynt some girt mouns of rubbl unner where the over head ben barmt out. It cudntve ben no moren a cuppl of candls or lanterns jus a feabl glimmer and the jynt shadders wivvering on the stanning walls and broakin stoan and rubbl and what ever over head wer lef. The jynt shadders wer from girt machines o they wer guvner big things and crouching all broakin but not dead they cudnt dy there wer too much Power inthem . . .

Lissener hispert me, 'What is it? Be they terning be they moving?' I hispert back, 'It's broakin machines they ain't moving.' It wernt nothing like

> when you dig up old rottin machines ourt of the roun these wer in ther parper working place nor nothing rottin they wer some kynd of iron dint rot it wer all shyning all catching that shaky glimmer . . . Tears begun streaming down my face and my froat akit. Lissener hispert, 'What's the matter?'
>
> I hispert back, 'O what we ben! And what we com to!' Boath of us wer sniffling and snuffling then. Me looking at them jynt machines and him lissening ther sylents.

Hoban never actually tells us that his characters are living in a world left desolate by nuclear war, but the language he gives them to speak quite clearly shows that civilization and knowledge as we understand them have broken down. Does his book offer any support for the idea that correct writing is the basis of a civilized society?

Finally, 'incorrect' grammar can be used to create convincing characters. Here is an extract from Alice Walker's novel *The Color Purple*, which contains the following solecisms:

- the omission of the *-s* from the ending of the third person singular ('Sofia say' instead of 'Sofia says'),
- the omission of the main verbs from many sentences ('What that?' instead of 'What is that?');
- the omission of the *-ed* ending of the past tense of the verb ('We kill them off' instead of 'We killed them off');
- the omission of the *-en* ending of the past participle ('she beat' instead of 'she was beaten');
- the omission of the subject from many sentences ('look like her old self' instead of 'she look like her old self');
- the use of the object or accusative case of the pronoun instead of the subject or nominative case ('Us outnumbered' instead of 'We (were) outnumbered'):

> Sofia say to me today, I just can't understand it.
>
> What that? I ast.
>
> Why we ain't already kill them off.
>
> Three years after she beat* she out of the wash house, got her color and her weight back, look like her old self, just all time think bout killing somebody.
>
> Too many to kill off, I say. Us outnumbered from the start. I speck we knock over one or two, though, here and there, through the years, I say.
>
> (*beaten)

The uninflected use of the verb *to be* is the other major grammatical 'error' that runs through the book: *I/she/they/us be*, rather than *I am*, *she is*, *they are*, etc.

Activity

1. Write out the passage in conventionally correct grammar.
2. Explain what has been lost in your translation.

It is easy to justify 'bad' writing like the above: it gives authenticity to both character and situation. It is also possible to defend 'bad' writing by advertisers: cleverly done, it entertains, and it helps the economy by persuading us to buy.

There is a hidden paradox here, however: if writers are to be free to experiment with the language like this, must the rest of us be content to follow the norms? Perhaps originality can flourish only where there are rules still left to break. If colloquialisms, obscenities, and slang were in general use, how could writers use them to make their points? If Standard English (with slight variations) had not been the norm in America and England, how could Alice Walker have created Miss Celie, or Russell Hoban his Riddley Walker? If everyone wrote in sentence fragments, how could Joyce have achieved his stream of consciousness technique or advertisers their hard sell? The concept of appropriateness may itself be an argument for teaching 'correct' English, for everyone in a society as developed as ours must be able to use the vocabulary and grammatical structures appropriate to formal contexts – even if only to talk to the DSS. People who cannot speak or write in formal terms and structures find it hard to function in formal situations. Their ability to use language appropriately is therefore limited and they are disadvantaged.

Activity

Read the passage below, then discuss the question that follows.

> Modern scientific language study has rendered the notion of one correct English untenable. We are used to wearing different clothes for different occasions, and with language many of us are used to doing something similar. The little boy in a Liverpool playground who says to his assailants 'Geroff, youse' (a perfectly grammatically regular plural of 'you' in his speech) is using language likely to work there. If he had said something with a distinctively Standard English flavour it would have been counter-productive. There is no one correct language; there is only language appropriate or inappropriate to particular circumstances, and education should aim to produce language users likely to select and use such language effectively.

How far do you agree with the ideas expressed by the writer of this piece? In your opinion, should Standard English and dialect forms be given equal treatment in schools? (Note that failure to 'talk proper' is still a rich source of humour in British plays, films, and television sitcoms.)

Semantics

Semantics is the study of the meaning of words. It is a subject fraught with difficulty: the word *meaning* was itself found to have 16 different meanings by Ogden and Richards (*The Meaning of Meaning,* 1923), and the word *word* was also found to be problematic, since it could be applied only to single units like *die* and not to idiomatic phrases like *cash in one's chips.* This is the reason why semanticists now prefer the terms *lexeme* and *lexical items* to *word.* Here are some of the meanings of *meaning.*

John means to write	'intends'
A green light means go	'indicates'
Health means everything	'has importance for'
His look was full of meaning	'special import'
What is the meaning of life?	'point, purpose'
What does 'capitalist' mean to you?	'convey'
What does 'cornea' mean?	'refer to in the world'

Old-fashioned approaches to discovering meaning

1 One approach to meaning was to treat words as the names of objects and people in the external world:

Word **Referent** (thing referred to)

tree

chair

man woman

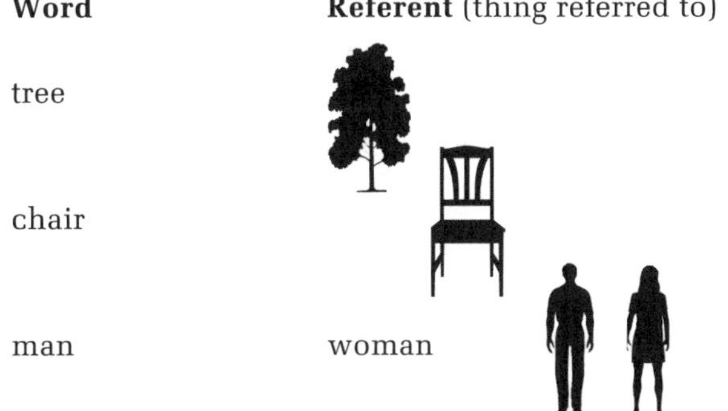

Even on this physical level, however, words do not succeed in representing things as they are. *It's a tree,* we tell a child, and the child, not yet understanding how language works, is left to guess what *tree* refers to: its leaves? its colour? the way it moves in the wind? Later, he or she will learn that language is a closed system referring to things within itself rather than the outside world; that the meaning of a word lies in the sense we give it when we speak.

The majority of the things we wish to talk about, however, do not even exist on the physical plane, or at least not in any direct sense. Rather they exist in the form of mental concepts. We organize our world by grouping individual things together in categories: trees become forests; chairs become items of furniture; men and women become people, or the English or any other nationality, or a sub-group of some kind such as Chelsea supporters, or the largest group of all, human beings. None of these categories has a real-life, physical existence. Look at a 'forest' and all you will see are thousands of trees; a furniture shop window can't show you 'furniture', only individual items like tables, chairs, settees and beds; and when you look at groups of people, individuals are all you can see. Collective nouns like these, in other words, have no direct referents of their own; to ascertain their meaning they have to be chased back to the individual items with direct referents that make them up.

Word	**Referent**
furniture (which does not exist)	individual items (which do)

Tell people 'the English' don't exist and they will think you're mad; yet clearly we are not a homogeneous mass, thinking, eating, dressing, speaking and behaving alike. We're not even all the same colour. Using language as if we were encourages us to think in terms of stereotypes, and the consequences can be unfortunate (see 'Affective meaning', page 156).

Another drawback of treating words as if they simply label things is that some of the 'things' they have to label exist only inside our heads. People refer to *intelligence*, for instance, as if it were a lump of something solid. They assess it in interviews and examinations; they even purport to be able to measure it in terms of IQ. But is what they're measuring 'intelligence', or simply the ability to answer certain questions, or solve certain problems in a way that suits the assessors?

Talking point What do you understand by the terms (a) intelligence (b) morality?

2 Another approach to the problem of meaning was exemplified in Ogden and Richards's 'semiotic triangle'.

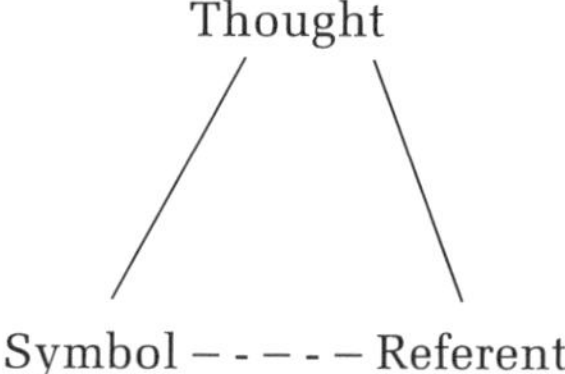

According to the authors, every word has an idea associated with it in the speaker's mind. This doesn't seem to help much, since (a) we don't need to have a visual image of something like a chair in order to talk about it – in fact it might be argued that the whole point of words is to do away with the need to represent objects at all – and (b) when it comes to concepts like 'intelligence', most people can't be said to have any clear idea in mind of what they mean, and certainly no visual picture.

3 A third approach to the meaning of words is described by David Crystal *(The Cambridge Encyclopaedia of Language)*. According to Behaviourists like Bloomfield:

meaning is something that can be deduced solely from a study of the situation in which speech is used – the stimulus (S) that led someone to speak (r), and the response (R) that resulted from this speech (s). He draws this as follows:

S ——————→ r . . . . s ——————→ R

In Bloomfield's example, Jill is hungry, sees an apple (S) and asks Jack to get it for her (r); this linguistic stimulus (s) leads to Jack getting the apple (R). Bloomfield argues that you can tell what the meaning of r . . . s must be just by observing the events that accompanied it. However, in very many situations it is difficult to demonstrate what the relevant features of the stimulus/response are – a real problem when events are not clearly visible in physical terms (as in the expression of feelings). And it proves even more difficult to handle cases where people do not act in the 'predicted' way (if Jack did not fetch the apple, perhaps because of a quarrel with Jill at Monte Carlo two years before).

Modern approaches to the discovery of meaning

Most semanticists now believe that the word *meaning*, like *intelligence* and similar abstract nouns, does not denote some physical entity distinct from language. Just as we cannot find *intelligence* anywhere but in the kind of behaviour which might be described by using that term, so we can find *meaning* only in the way in which words are used within utterances. *The meaning of a word is its use in the language,* as Wittgenstein remarked. Or, to quote G.H.R. Parkinson's paraphrase of Gilbert Ryle *(The Theory of Meaning,* OUP, 1968), *Language is a set of moderately permanent possibilities of carrying out particular momentary communicative acts.* To quote Crystal again:

> The primary focus of the modern subject [Semantics] is on the way people relate words to each other within the framework of their language – on their 'sense', rather than their reference.

The way to teach someone how a lexeme or lexical item is used, Parkinson suggests, is to give them an expression they already know which can be substituted for it without unduly altering the sense. The way to teach someone how to use an unfamiliar lexeme themselves is to give them an expression they already know for which it could be substituted. This does raise the question, 'How far can you explain how a word is being used without defining what it means?'

Nevertheless, the focus is still on sense rather than reference, and this is felt to be a more useful approach than trying to define meaning with reference to things.

Humpty Dumpty and the meaning of words

Lewis Carroll's Humpty Dumpty boasts that when he uses a word, it means just what he chooses it to mean – neither more nor less. At first sight, this may seem close to the position of Wittgenstein and other philosophers, who argue that the meaning of a word is its use. The egoistical Egg, however, is overlooking a very important point also made by Wittgenstein: general agreement about that use is necessary if communication is to occur. Hanfling explains the point:

> [Wittgenstein] certainly isn't saying that at some stage people sat down and made a convention, or came to an agreement, to use ordinary language in the way we do. Nor is he saying that it's open to us to choose and change our basic concepts by making a *new* convention. And again, when he says [language] is '*founded* on convention', he doesn't mean that there is after all something outside language – namely a convention – which provides an independent foundation for what we *do* in language. The position is rather that the convention, or agreement, that is meant here, *is* just the fact that we all use words – ordinary words like 'red' and 'green', 'wet' and 'cold' and so on – in the same kind of way. Without such agreement, language wouldn't exist. But what is meant by autonomy, convention and the like, is that the agreement is an agreement *in* the way we use language, and not something beyond or behind language.
>
> *Philosophy in the Open*, ed. Godfrey Vesey (Open University Press, 1974)

If everyone were to use words in Humpty's idiosyncratic way, Crystal comments, 'the result would be communication anarchy'.

Activity

Outline the arguments underlying the position of each of the characters in the discussion of idiom below, indicating which one you support.

(Ben has just given Gus some matches)
Ben: Go on, go and light it.
Gus: Eh?
Ben: Go and light it.
Gus: Light what?
Ben: The kettle.
Gus: You mean the gas.
Ben: Who does?
Gus: You do.
Ben *(his eyes narrowing)*: What do you mean, I mean the gas?
Gus: Well, that's what you mean, don't you? The gas.
Ben *(powerfully)*: If I say go and light the kettle I mean go and light the kettle.
Gus: How can you light a kettle?
Ben: It's a figure of speech! Light the kettle. It's a figure of speech!
Gus: I've never heard it.
Ben: Light the kettle! It's common usage!

Gus: I think you've got it wrong.
Ben *(menacing)*: What do you mean?
Gus: They say put on the kettle.
Ben *(taut)*: Who says? *(They stare at each other, breathing hard)*

Harold Pinter, *Plays One* (Faber and Faber, 1999)

Associative meaning

A fruitful way of exploring lexical meaning is to look at the way in which lexemes relate to one another by various kinds of associations. They say you can tell a lot about people by the company they keep, and the same is true of words. *Forehand, smash,* and *volley,* for instance, belong to the **semantic field** of tennis; *metre, rhyme,* and *couplet* to the semantic field of poetry. Other types of association include:

1 **Syntagmatic relations**, in which certain lexemes trigger others in automatic sequence: e.g. the adjective *diplomatic* seems automatically to select lexemes like *speech, gesture, incident,* etc;
2 **Paradigmatic relationships**, in which lexemes are grouped together by virtue of the fact that one can be substituted for another. These include:
   - *synonyms*, which although never exact equivalents can be used to mean much the same as one another: e.g. *impartial* for *disinterested*;
   - *antonyms*, which have opposite meanings to one another: e.g. *young–old*;
   - *hyponyms*, which carry the idea of inclusion: *tabby* is a hyponym of *cat*; *cod* of *fish*.
3 **Collocative meaning** has some similarity to syntagmatic relations; it consists of the associations that rub off on a word through contact with the meanings of other words tending to occur in its vicinity. *Pretty* and *handsome*, for example, both share the sense 'good-looking', but are likely to co-occur or collocate with a different range of nouns.

Activity

Write *Pretty* and *Handsome* at the top of two different columns. Choose from the list below the words with which each collocates, and write them under the appropriate heading.

computer garden village woman car dustjacket man overcoat flower colour girl inscription

Sentence meaning

Crystal distinguishes five different types of sentence meaning, the most important of which are the **prosodic**, the **pragmatic** and the **propositional**.

Prosodic meaning

Sentences can be given different meaning according to where we place the main stress. Consider the following examples:

I'm not doing THAT!	(how dare you suggest such a thing)
I'M not doing that!	(you or somebody else will have to)
I'm not DOING that!	(and that's final)

Pragmatic meaning

Pragmatic meaning results from the interaction of an utterance with the context in which it is uttered. *There's a window open* may be a factual statement when uttered by someone trying to break into a house, but an indirect command when uttered to another person in the same room by someone sitting in a draught. Trask (*Key Concepts in Language and Linguistics*, Routledge, 1999) illustrates the point well:

> Consider the sentence *Susie is a heavy smoker.* In all circumstances, this sentence carries with it its intrinsic meaning: Susie smokes a large quantity of tobacco every day. This meaning is intrinsic and inseparable. But now consider what happens when this sentence is uttered as a response to three different utterances produced by Jessica in three different contexts.
>
> First [Jessica is trying to have smoking banned in offices]:
>
> *Can you ask Susie to sign this petition?*
>
> Second [Jessica is trying to arrange a blind date for Dave, a non-smoker who hates cigarette smoke]:
>
> *Would Susie like to go out with Dave?*
>
> Third [Jessica, a medical researcher, is looking for smokers to take part in some medical tests]:
>
> *Do you know of anybody I could ask?*
>
> In each case, you will agree, something very different is being communicated. In the first case: Susie is unlikely to sign the petition, so there's no point in asking her. In the second: Dave and Susie won't get on, so there's no point in fixing them up. Third: Susie will be a suitable person for your study.
>
> Now, it is not possible to maintain that this single unvarying sentence actually *means* all of these different things. Rather, these three meanings have been communicated as a consequence of the interaction between what was said and the *context* in which it was said. Every time the context changes, what is communicated changes as well. And it is this variable, context-bound relation between what is said and what is communicated that is the subject-matter of pragmatics.

Propositional meaning

Propositions are the statements made by declarative sentences: e.g. *God exists.*

Semanticists borrow the techniques of philosophy to examine the meaning of such sentences. They break such sentences down into their underlying propositions, then test these propositions for truth or falsity in relation to the real world. The process is illustrated by the following discussion between the philosopher Bertrand Russell and the Jesuit historian Frederick Copleston. Russell will accept only analytic propositions, i.e. those that are true by reference to meaning alone, independent of fact or experience: e.g. *bachelors are unmarried men*; Copleston wants to make synthetic propositions, i.e. ones that are based on the fact of experience in the world, such as *God exists*, without the support of physical evidence.

> **C** You may say that the world has no cause; but I fail to see how you can say that the proposition that the cause of the world exists is meaningless. Put it in the form of a question: 'Has the world a cause?' or 'Does a cause of the world exist?' Most people would surely understand the question, even if they don't agree about the answer.
>
> **R** Certainly the question 'Does a cause of the world exist?' is a question that has meaning. But if you say 'Yes, God is the cause of the world', you are using God as a proper name; then 'God exists' will not be a statement that has meaning because it will follow that it cannot be an analytic proposition ever to say that this or that exists.
>
> *Philosophy in the Open*, ed. Godfrey Vesey (Open University Press, 1974)

Words and penumbral meaning

Even when speakers conform to the semantic norms, however, meaning may not get across to their hearers in quite the way intended. Words do not simply **denote**, i.e. convey factual information; they also **connote**, i.e. suggest ideas and associations above and beyond their literal meaning. Words are not clean, crisp, pristine things that come fresh every time from a speaker's mouth. They bring chequered histories with them, and carry layers of associations that affect different people in different ways. They have, in other words, a rich **penumbra** of meaning around their denotive core, like the hazy penumbra or outer ring of mist that surrounds the moon.

Activity

Draw two circles denoting the full moon, and label them (a) and (b). Write inside each the word 'England' and the facts denoted by the word. Draw a penumbra around each circle. Now write in the penumbral rings

a the associations the word 'England' might have for people who read literature and attend the Proms

b the associations it might carry for people who support the English football team and do not read much at all.

Now do the same with the word *march*,

a for most English people

b for Orangemen in Northern Ireland.

When the writing in the penumbral ring occupies more space than the denotive, we are in the territory of emotion.

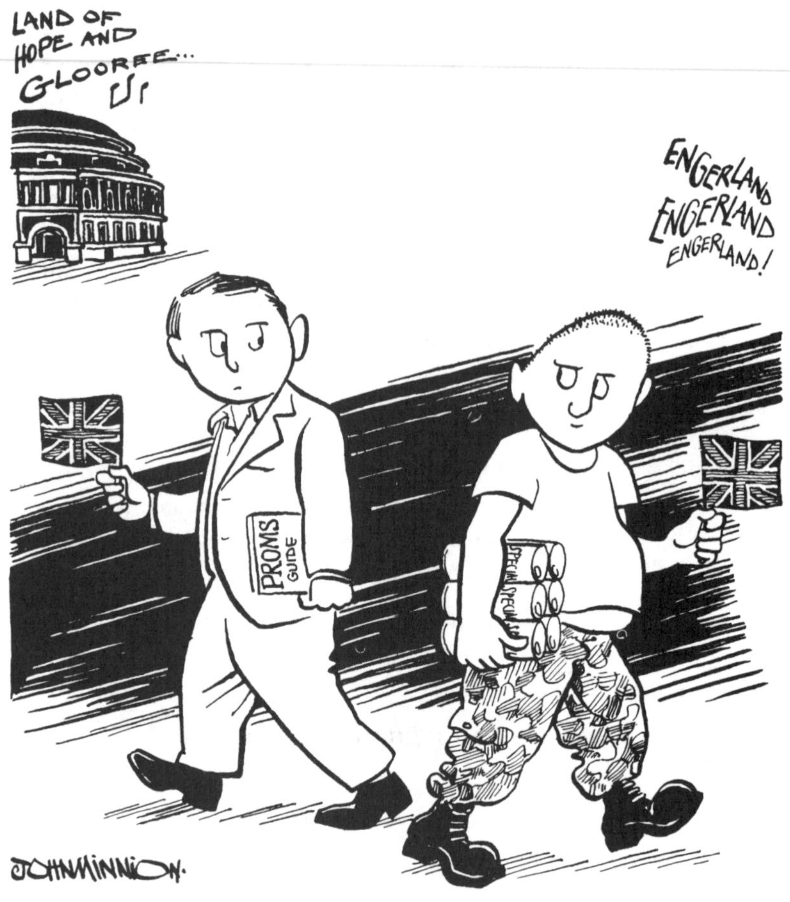

Affective meaning

Speakers can express their feelings towards a subject in a variety of ways:

1 through tone of voice – sarcastic when being overtly polite, for instance: *Would you mind awfully being quiet for a few minutes?* or friendly when being rude to a friend: *Shut it, man.*

2 through the use of pejorative adjectives attached to collective nouns – the technique is to bundle together thousands of individuals who have some feature in common (their race, gender, colour, sexual orientation, and so on – Jews, women, blacks, queers) then attach to them an unpleasant descriptive label: *filthy* Jews, *man-hating* feminists, *shiftless* blacks, *degenerate* queers and so on. Once individuals are lost in the collective noun they can more easily be attacked and damaged. It's easier to hate a faceless group than individual men and women. *Bogus asylum seekers* is a recent example of the technique – every individual wishing to enter Britain is bundled into the same category, whatever the merits of his or her case, and smeared with the implication of dishonesty.

Talking point Discuss the possible uses of the term 'bogus asylum seekers'.

Summary

The more semanticists probe into meaning, the more elusive it seems to become, presumably because the only tool we have to explore language with is language itself. Even the most stringently logical approach hasn't got us very far. As Professor J.N. Findlay once remarked:

> There can be nothing really 'clinching' in philosophy: 'proofs' and 'disproofs' hold only for those who adopt certain premisses, who are willing to follow certain rules of argument, and who use their terms in certain definite ways. And every proof or disproof can be readily evaded, if one questions the truth of its premisses, or the validity of its type of inference, or if one finds new senses in which its terms may be used.
>
> *Philosophy in the Open,* ed. Godfrey Vesey (Open University Press, 1974)

Perhaps we exaggerate the importance of language anyway, as Tom Stoppard has his philosopher, Anderson, suggest in *Professional Foul:*

> . . . I would only like to offer Professor Stone the observation that language is not the only level of human communication, and perhaps not the most important level. Whereof we cannot speak, thereof we are by no means silent.
>
> Verbal language is a technical refinement of our capacity for communication, rather than the *fons et origo* of that capacity. The likelihood is that language develops in an ad hoc way, so there is no reason to expect its development to be logical. *(A thought strikes him.)* The importance of language is overrated. It allows me and Professor Stone to show off a bit, and it is very useful for communicating detail – but the important truths are simple and monolithic. The essentials of a given situation speak for themselves, and language is as capable of obscuring the truth as of revealing it.

Section B: **Language and the Social Context**

3 Language and Society

The language of gender

Women make up roughly half the population and over forty per cent of the work-force. They have an appreciable effect on the country's economy, yet their work is given little public recognition and they are often paid less for doing the same jobs as men.

Even women do not show as much respect to women as they do to men in public life. When women students were given two sets of booklets containing the same article, one bearing the name of a male, the other of a female author, they found the writing of John T. McKay superior to that of Joan T. McKay in all areas (Goldberg, 1974, quoted in Spender, *Man Made Language*) .

Why is this? One reason may have to do with our use of language.

Gender and grammar

When we look at the world around us we perceive it in two ways:

1 with our physical eyes;
2 through the distorting lens of language – the language of our society.

As they learn to speak, children absorb the values, assumptions, and expectations of the adults who surround them *through the words they are given to learn*. Language therefore shapes our view of reality: there is no such thing as a culture-free view of the world.

It follows that if the language children learn in our society is biased towards men and against women, even girls will grow up to take for granted the superiority of the male over the female sex.

Is there evidence of such an inbuilt linguistic bias? Consider the following facts and make up your own mind:

1 In 1553 the grammarian Wilson ruled that the man should precede the woman in pairs such as *male/female*; *husband/wife*; *brother/sister*; *son/daughter*. It was 'more natural'. (Nobody disagreed with him.)
2 In 1646 the grammarian Joshua Poole ruled that the male should precede the female because this was both more 'natural', and more 'proper', since men were the 'worthier' sex. (Other men seemed happy to agree.)
3 The grammarian John Kirkby ruled that the male gender was 'more comprehensive' than the female, which was therefore to be included in it.
4 Nineteenth-century grammarians reinforced the resulting idea of male superiority by condemning the use of the neutral pronoun *they* and *their* in such statements as, 'Anyone can do it if they try'. Their reasoning was that

anyone and *everyone*, being singular, could not properly be followed by plural pronouns.

The male-as-the-norm syndrome

In any book which deals with human beings in general, the nouns that recur are *men*, *man*, and *mankind*. The pronoun that inevitably follows these nouns is of course *he*. The result is that women are not linguistically represented. As the American writer, Julia Stanley, puts it, they occupy 'negative semantic space'.

Women are also rendered invisible in the language when the masculine pronoun *he* is used to follow gender-free nouns like *writer*, *critic*, *novelist*, *politician*, *speaker*, etc.

Writers who are asked why they follow this practice are often bewildered by the question. It seems they had always taken it for granted that *man*, *mankind*, *men*, and *he*, automatically included the idea of women in utterances such as *Men have always worshipped gods*, and *Men fear death as children fear to go in the dark*. And the use of the masculine pronoun after such nouns was simply a matter of convenience, a way of avoiding the long-winded *he or she*, the clumsy *s/he*, or the ungrammatical *they*. (*Man* and *mankind* are both singular collective nouns and so should properly be followed by a singular pronoun.)

I believe these claims are often sincere, having followed words like *writer*, *novelist*, and *poet* with *he* quite unconsciously myself in the first draft of this book. But the fact that there is no *conscious* bias here is beside the point. The real question at issue is, how far does such writing succeed in:

a making women invisible in large and important areas of life;
b brainwashing younger generations into believing that man is the more important and superior sex?

Anthropologist Elaine Morgan suggests that it might have such effects in the preface to her book on the evolution of man (sorry, the human species), *The Descent of Woman*. Using the masculine noun–pronoun forms *man . . . he* in a book about the human race in general can have unforeseen effects:

> . . . before you are half-way through the first chapter a mental image of this evolving creature begins to form in your mind. It will be a male image and he will be the hero of the story; everything and everyone else in the story will relate to him . . .
>
> A very high proportion of . . . thinking is androcentric (male centred) in the same way as pre-Copernican thinking was geocentric. It's just as hard for man to break the habit of thinking of himself as central to the species as it was to break the habit of thinking of himself as central to the universe. He sees himself quite unconsciously as the main line of evolution with a

> female satellite revolving around him as the moon revolves around the earth.
>
> The longer I went on reading his own books about himself, the more I longed to find a volume that would begin: 'When the first ancestor of the human race descended from the trees, she had not yet developed the mighty brain that was to distinguish her so sharply from other species'.

Talking point

1 How far does the use of *man* at the expense of *human beings* instil and support the idea that men are more important than women?

2 Male readers of such books presumably form pictures, if not directly of themselves, at least of other men with whom they can associate themselves. What pictures do you suppose women see?

Activity

1 Which of the following statements are readily acceptable? Explain why you think so.
   - **a** Man devotes more than forty hours a week to housework.
   - **b** Man, being a mammal, breast-feeds his young.
   - **c** Man is the only animal that commits rape.

2 Re-write these sentences where necessary.

3 What conclusions do you draw from the above statements, as originally written?

4 Analyse the following statements taken from books about the development of the human species and draw your own conclusions:
   - **a** . . . man's vital interests are life, food, access to females, etc. . . . (Erich Fromm)
   - **b** . . . his back aches, he ruptures easily, his women have difficulty in childbirth . . . (Loren Eisely)

Here is another example of unconscious bias. In his informative book *Advertising*, Frank Jeffkins describes the work of each member of an advertising agency's team. Here is his account of the copy-writer:

> . . . His writing style is unlike any other. He seldom writes complete grammatical sentences, but uses words and punctuation and their typographical presentation like [sic] a painter uses colours and shapes. He can write a one-word one-sentence paragraph that grips the reader's interest and desire. He can virtually mutilate the English language for effect. He can write a thousand words and make every word count. He can sell . . .

These repeated, insistent *he*s fill us with admiration for such outstanding male talent – yet wasn't Fay Weldon one of the best copy-writers of her generation, creator of such brilliant slogans as *Go to work on an egg*? Why does Jeffkins mention only *he*? And what effect might reading this have on young women eager for a career in advertising? Only one member of the team gets the *or she* addition after the *he* – the Account Executive – the inescapable conclusion being that this is the only aspect of advertising at which a woman might succeed. Is this what Jeffkins meant? Or did he remember for one fleeting moment that women, too, exist in the world of work?

Activity

1 **a** Go to a library and look at books on any of the following topics: anthropology; the origins of man; childbirth or child-rearing; sociology (the chapter on education); sport; hotel management; training to be a chef.
b Make notes on the gender of the nouns and pronouns used.
c Explain what Spender means by the following:
'She' represents a woman but 'he' is mankind. If 'she' enters mankind 'she' loses herself in 'he'.

2 Until recently, girls and women were never mentioned in maths textbooks. Get hold of as many maths textbooks as you can and see if
a girls and women are mentioned,
b they are given different occupations and/or activities from the boys and men.

3 **a** Go to the children's section of your library and look at as many story books for each of the different age groups as you can.
b Record the gender of the chief character(s). (It does not matter whether they are human or animal, since animals are given the same characteristics as human beings.)
c Record the kind of things the characters are made to do.
d Read through your notes and assess honestly whether you have any evidence of gender prejudice (male or female characters being made to appear more important and interesting than those of the opposite sex) or role stereotyping (male characters being given exciting and adventurous things to do, and female ones being confined to doing more domestic things or following timidly behind).
e Write your research up in report form, adding your conclusions as to the possible effects of such stories on the boys and girls who read them.

Is all this talk of female invisibility merely the nit-picking of embittered feminists? Two pieces of evidence suggest that it is not:

1 Men themselves have recognized the consequences of leaving women out of the language used to describe all the most important areas of public life:

> . . . that our language employs the words *man* and *mankind* as terms for the whole human race demonstrates that male dominance, the *idea* of masculine superiority, is programmed, institutional, and rooted at the deepest level of our historical experience.
>
> Richard Gilman, *Life* magazine

2 Men are themselves bitterly hurt and distressed when they are made

invisible by language in this way. Spender relates how in the 1960s, when most primary schoolteachers were female, articles referring to them habitually followed the gender-free noun *primary schoolteacher* with the feminine pronoun *she*. One of the few males in the profession wrote a letter to protest:

> The interests of neither the women, nor of the men, in our profession, are served by grammatical usage which conjures up an anachronistic image of the nineteenth-century schoolmarm . . .

He preferred the male pronoun to be used instead, on the 'objective' and 'correct' grounds that the women would be understood to be included in *he*. Women would still be in the majority within the profession, but it was 'neither incorrect nor improper to exclude them linguistically' (Miller & Swift, *Words and Women: New Language in New Times*.)

Talking point Men consider it improper to refer to individuals within mixed groups as *she*, but not as *he*. Why do you suppose this is?

Activity

1
 a Assemble a group containing both males and females.
 b Give the members of the group an extract from a textbook (e.g. on nursing) that uses the feminine pronoun *she* throughout.
 c Ask the group to replace *she* with *he* throughout.
 d Record any comments.
 e Now give them an extract that uses *he* throughout and ask them to replace all the *he*s with *she*s.
 f Record any comments.
 g Write up:
 - the responses of the members of the group,
 - your own reactions to the experiment.

2
 a Assemble an unsuspecting all-male group and get them to discuss the topic 'What I think about women'. Record the discussion.
 b Now do the same thing with an all-female group on the topic 'What I think about men'. Record the discussion.
 c Analyse the way in which the two sexes talk about each other to see how well it accords with the material you read in this section.

3 Report the conclusions you have formed on male and female attitudes towards gender and language as a result of these experiments. You can do this in the form of an article for your school or college magazine or a woman's magazine, or a letter to the editor of a daily newspaper.

Gender, titles, and naming

Marriage

Just as the use of masculine nouns and pronouns helps to render women invisible in public life, so, it is claimed, the practice of giving up their own name and taking on their husbands' name robs women of a public identity of their own. In so far as they have an identity, it is one shared with their husbands. The individual Gertrude Coppard, for instance, becomes Mrs Walter Morel, part of that new creation, 'the Morels'. ('Have you heard the Morels have got a son?/lost their eldest boy?') In *Man Made Language*, Spender points out that the only real names belong to men, since these are handed down from father to son. Without a male heir, a family dies out.

Talking point

1 How far does changing her name make it difficult for a woman to preserve an identity for herself outside the home?
2 Why do famous actresses, singers, dancers, and others choose to keep their 'maiden' names?
3 How would a visitor returning to the town where she grew up set about tracing her old school-friends? What might make it difficult?
4 How far do you think the practice of giving up their names on marriage reinforces the idea that women are the property of their husbands?
5 In *Sons and Lovers* Gertrude Morel's ambitions, aspirations, and social status were limited by her husband's job and attitude towards her. How far is this still true of the average woman today? Does her access to the wider life of society still depend upon her husband?
6 Why is it important that women should reveal their marital status (calling themselves 'Mrs', wearing a ring on the third finger of their left hands), but not men?

Work

Women who enter the professions are not always given the same gender-free title as their male counterparts: *doctor*, *lawyer*, *solicitor*, *constable*. The appropriate noun is used, but it is sometimes prefaced by *lady* or *woman*. In the same way, women are not given job titles such as *waiter*, *steward*, or *drum major*. The diminutive *-ette* or *-ess* is added, signalling, it is claimed, that they are somehow 'not the real thing' in not being male.

Talking point

Does it diminish the dignity and importance of a woman who writes poetry to call her a poetess? Or to call a woman who acts an actress? Explain your point of view.

Social life and personal relationships

Ask any group of women – including those happily married to, or living happily with, men – and they will agree unanimously on one point: many men patronize, insult, and control women by calling them offensive names.

Patronizing terms include *dear*, *love*, and *pet*. They are patronizing when used by a man to a girl or woman he does not know simply because they imply that

a it is his right as a man to speak to them like this, and
b any right-minded female will welcome it.

The test for patronage is easy: would he use the same terms to a man he didn't know? Calling grown women *girls* is another patronizing ploy used to make women feel inferior. When it was used against women at the 1983 Labour Party Conference (male socialists aren't all democratic enough to treat women fairly), they retaliated by referring to Comrade Chairboy and the boys. Not very witty, admittedly, but the best they could do at the time.

Talking point

1 If a man calls a woman *dear*, *pet*, or *love*, is he necessarily patronizing her, or simply being friendly?
2 Women on City & Guilds Catering Courses have been known to complain because their college lecturers address them as 'dear' and the male students as 'chef'. Is their complaint justified? Explain your answer.

The **insulting** and **controlling** aspects of male language can be dealt with together, since the insults are the means of control. Julia Stanley has shown not only that there are more words available to describe men than women, but also that more of these words show men in a favourable light. In the large vocabulary of words used to describe men, only twenty-six words implying sexual promiscuity were found, and of these many – such as *stallion* and *stud* – were felt to be complimentary. It is simply not possible to call a man the equivalent of *slut*. In the much smaller list of words used to describe women, by contrast, 220 terms signalling sexual promiscuity were found. All were of a degrading nature. (Some degree of confusion in male thinking is shown by the fact that a woman is damned if she shows too much interest in sex and damned if she does not show enough: derogatory words like *tight bitch* then come into play.)

In her book on sexuality and adolescent girls, *Losing Out*, Sue Lees argues that men control female sexual behaviour by the use of such derogatory terms – in particular, the word *slag*. This is used, not necessarily of girls who actually sleep with boys they love before marriage, but of girls who want to make the running in sexual relationships; who actively pursue boys and show their interest in them; who treat boys, in fact, as boys treat girls. These it seems are the real *slags*, whether they actually do it or not. Nice girls wait for boys to make the first move.

Since the male equivalent of *slag* is *stud*, and *stud* is a term that confers prestige, the language men use to discuss sexuality seems biased rather heavily in their favour.

Talking point

1 Which of the following once equal pairs of words now have negative or unpleasant associations?

spinster/bachelor	baronet/dame	master/mistress
king/queen	old master/old mistress	old man/old woman

2 Can you call a group of girls 'you guys'?
Can you call a group of boys 'you girls'?
Can you call a girl a 'bachelor'?
Can you call a boy a 'spinster' or an 'old maid'?

3 Which is the possibly ambiguous statement here:
he's a professional; she's a professional?

4 Consult at least five other people of either sex and list as many derogatory words as you can find to describe
a women, **b** men.

5 Now do the same for words that describe the conversation or talk of
a women, **b** men.

Activity

1 Write an essay, newspaper or magazine article, or script for a TV or radio show on the topic of Gender and Language. Jazz up the title as you wish.

2 Argue the case for or against reforming the practices described in the first section, 'Gender and Grammar'.

The language of the media

As Bell points out, 'communicators who work in the mass media are always in some sense trying to win audience approval' (*The Language of News Media*, Blackwell, 1991). Their intention may be to inform, persuade, provoke, or entertain, but unless they can attract their readers' or listeners' interest they are wasting their time.

The main method they use to attract this interest is what Bell calls **audience design**: speakers or writers call up a mental picture of the audience they want to impress, then tailor their material and style to suit. Audiences (the term is used loosely to include readers) have their expectations too; if they don't find a reflection of their own attitudes, values, and ideas in what they read, they will buy something else instead. Liverpool readers, for instance, refused to buy the *Sun* for months after it unfairly blackened the reputation of fans caught up in the Hillsborough disaster.

How then do newspapers present themselves to make the greatest impact on their readers?

Audience design in newspapers: visual style

1 Layout

Newspapers make their content attractive to readers by the way they arrange it on the page. As Ingrid Marhd points out (*Headlines: On the Grammar of English Front-page Headlines*, Gleerup, Lund, 1980), the natural movement of the eye for Western readers is from top left to bottom right: items of the greatest interest are therefore usually, though not always, arranged in descending order from top left to bottom right. (The 'fallow corners' left empty by this technique are generally filled with pictures and/or less important, smaller headlines.)

2 Typography

Editors also grab our attention by the size and boldness of their headlines. As Bell remarks, 'Large headlines in striking black print are the written equivalent of an excited shout.' They are also reader-friendly in that they and the white space around them break down the body copy into smaller chunks. (The **body copy** is the technical term for the columns of writing below the headlines.) Nothing puts inexperienced readers off like long columns of close print. 'All that reading!' said one tabloid fan faced with a copy of *The Guardian*.

The greater the news value of a headline, the larger the type it is printed in: readers can judge its importance visually before they see what is being said. When something really important happens, the inevitable result is that headlines become so big they swallow up most of the front page, as the *Sun*'s **GOTCHA!** did on the sinking of the *Belgrano* in the Falklands War. This is especially true of the tabloids, which in any case habitually give more space to their headlines than the broadsheets: 40% in the *Daily Mirror* as opposed to 20% in *The Times*, although Ingrid Marhd shows that the latter has doubled the space given over to headlines over the past fifty years.

Sub-headlines in smaller, heavy black type are similarly used to break up the body copy within an article. These often consist of one word hinting at what is to come in the next paragraph: e.g. *Attacker*; *Knife*; *Arrested*.

Activity

1 Compare and contrast the layout, style and content of the *Sun*, the *Daily Mail* and *The Times* and describe the kind of reader each of these papers aims to appeal to.
2 Do the same for one day's output of the five main television channels.
3 Read the following extracts from the sports pages.
Which kind of paper might each extract be taken from?

PISTOL PETE'S WHIPPING UP A STORM

By JOHN CROSS

PISTOL Pete Sampras fired a Wimbledon warning yesterday as he looked every inch a record-breaking champion. Top seed Sampras whipped Czech outsider Jiri Vanek with an awesome 6–4 6–4 6–2 straight sets victory which proved his long-running back injury is behind him.

Sampras, 28, chasing a record 13th Grand Slam win, appeared invincible as he cruised to an easy victory without even breaking sweat on Centre Court . . .

The quiet American tiptoes through

Pete Sampras begins a march on history with a minimum of fuss

Frank Keating at Wimbledon

Pete Sampras began his assault on history yesterday with a muted, reserved, even shy, first-round defeat of a game Wimbledon debutant from Prague, Jiri Vanek, by 6-4, 6-4, 6-2.

Last year the American posted a sixth Wimbledon title, a record for the last century, and another championship victory in 12 days' time would overtake Roy Emerson's long-standing dozen grand slam titles. But this was no imposing and warlike emperor clanging on the gates of destiny yesterday . . .

Audience design: The use of language in newspapers

Diction

Journalists make their material easier to read by using short, concrete, mainly Anglo-Saxon words wherever possible. There are three main reasons for this:

i they take up less space, having fewer syllables;
ii they can be immediately understood by a wide range of readers;
iii they have a forceful quality that makes an immediate impact.

Thus in broadsheets and tabloids alike, words like *probe* are used for 'in-depth investigation', *slam* for 'criticize severely', *slash* for 'make sweeping or random cuts', '*is set to*' for 'is preparing to' and so on. Nicholas Bagnall (*Newspaper Language*, Focal Press, 1993) calls words like these *buzzwords*, to convey the impression of urgent and exciting activity they create.

The red-top tabloids make further concessions to their readers by using colloquial language and outright slang in their reporting of serious social concerns, as in the article printed below.

BOOZE IS 'RUIN OF BRITAIN'

HEAVY boozing is taking a whopping £3.3 billion toll on Britain.

Sozzled employees unable to work properly – or who go sick – cost **INDUSTRY** £2.8 billion.

> Treating alcohol-related illnesses leaves the **NHS** with a £200 million hangover. Meanwhile the bill for **CRIME** and **ROAD ACCIDENTS** fuelled by drink is £257 million, Alcohol Concern revealed yesterday.
>
> The *Sun*, 11 May 2000

The tabloids go further than this in their lighter features, however, choosing a cheesy vocabulary of 'snogging, canoodling' or 'bonking' with 'stunning blondes' or 'vivacious redheads' in 'secluded love-nests' where 'sizzling sex-romps' take place. The result is a generally coarse, matey style and a knowing tone of voice.

Word play

Headline writers also use rhetorical devices to catch our attention. Alliteration is common, especially in the red-tops:

MILE HIGH MANDY GETS RANDY ON BRANDY (The *Sun*)

So are puns and associated word play:

TIME BAFTA TIME (*Sun* journalist reporting the Bafta awards)

IMPERFECT PASTS ARE THE BEST PRESENTS FOR PINTER
(Theatre critic in the *Mail on Sunday*)

The Times and *Guardian* are happy to join in with headlines like **Time to Roam While The Fiddle Burns** (on the visit of a famous violinist to Italy) and **The Joys of Fourplay** (on new recordings by a famous chamber quartet).

Metaphor can also be found, though not always with any aesthetic intent: **HOP OFF, YOU FROGS** was an insult aimed at the French during a trade dispute.

The red-top tabloids have two further tricks up their sleeves to grab and hold readers' attention: sensationalism and the use of emotive clichés.

Sensationalism

The attempt here is to heighten already disturbing facts by the use of exaggeration. It is usually reserved for terrorists and sex-murderers, and runs the danger of over-kill. In the space of one article the following terms were used to describe the man accused: *psycho sex monster, lust-crazed, frenzied sex-fiend, caged, madman.*

Instead of being aroused, readers' emotions may be overwhelmed by the sheer weight of language hurled at them.

Emotive clichés

As Nicholas Bagnall points out, there is a ritualistic feel to the writing of the red-tops, where women, if young, are always stunning or sizzling, men are always hunks, the bereaved are always tragic, etc. Why? Because tabloid readers want stories that fit with their conceptions of what life is like, not ones that turn their ideas about the world upside down.

Clichés – statements that have been repeated so often that we take their truth for granted – are obviously part of this comforting ritual. The two most potent and frequently used are *brave* as in *brave Jill Morell* and *tiny*, as in *the parents followed the tiny coffin*, or *tiny Leo slept peacefully throughout.* Other clichés Bagnall notices are *horrors, terror, mysteries, bitterness*, and *massive.*

Taken together, the buzzwords, the slang, and the clichés create a misguided impression of poor writing in the tabloids, yet their editorials often offer clearer and more cogent expressions of complex issues than writers in the broadsheets can achieve. And the broadsheets themselves frequently resort to clichés in reporting the scenes of disasters and fires: *fire appliances, at the scene, battling, blaze, engulfed, threatened*, etc.

Personalization

Another technique used to stimulate interest is **personalization**. Conflict in the abstract hardly stirs the blood, but conflict between people does. Compare 'Major differences of opinion over Europe were revealed in the Commons yesterday' with 'Hague clashes violently with Blair in Commons'.

Claire Lundgren Lerman, in *Language, Image, Media* (edited by Walton and Davis, 1983), suggests that 'sports and entertainment provide the thematic model' for news reporting of this kind: 'Political campaigns and issues of public policy are reduced to personality conflict, sporting contests, or battles. The focus is "who's winning?"' Not surprisingly, therefore, 'metaphors of warfare and to a lesser extent sport are prevalent', and even complex issues are presented in terms of conflict between two opposing sides.

Walton and Davis make much the same point:

> In practice, social descriptions are polarised and tend to operate with binary distinctions: for example, workers/non-workers, dropouts; peaceful/violent; organised/disorganised; moderate/extreme; democracy/civil war, anarchy. This gives rise to the tendency to reduce a complex system of social relationships to simple opposites.

Connotation versus denotation

If political issues are presented in terms of conflict between two opposing sides, one aggressive (the workers), one passively resisting (the management), it is easy to see how accusations of subjective writing can be levelled at the journalists reporting them. When a journalist writes, for instance, *The mob swept across the car park, crushing Mr Blank against the fence*, he or she may simply be writing objectively what was seen (denotation); there may be no intention to vilify the 'mob' or present the person crushed as victim (connotation). 'Mob' is simply a more exciting word than 'crowd', and more accurate, in that a mob's actions are more violent and unpredictable than those of the more ordinary 'crowd'. It is not so much the language that is at fault here as the fact that the reporter has neither the time nor space to give an in-depth explanation of the reasons behind the 'mob's' behaviour.

On the other hand, reporters do have prejudices, too, like the rest of us, and when these are awakened their writing may become overtly emotive: *The angry mob swept violently across the car park, crushing their helpless victim against the fence.* The adjectives *angry* and *helpless* and the adverb *violently* leave us in no doubt where the writer's sympathies lie.

Speech verbs also help to colour newspaper reports. *Say* and *tell* give a personal note; *announce*, *declare* and *refuse* are neutral, while *claim* is altogether more ambiguous in tone, and may be used to cast doubt on the truth of what is being said: *Mr Aitken claimed that his wife, and not he, had paid the bill in question.*

Verbs such as *threaten, insist*, and *denounce* show us events through the filter of the reporter's eyes; they create news action.

Walton and Davis (*Language, Image, Media*) distinguish two main aspects of connotative/subjective reporting: **inclusion** and **exclusion**.

Inclusive reporting uses terms which 'linguistically express the consensus [of civilized society]', from which those who are perceived as hostile in some way are excluded. Examples are 'the overwhelming majority', 'the people', 'ordinary citizens', 'the majority of decent people', 'right-thinking people'.

Exclusive reporting can be signalled in at least three different ways.

- **i** By the use of punctuation: the placing of inverted commas around the name of the excluded group, e.g. the 'Tamil Tigers'.
- **ii** By the use of qualifiers: the placing of 'self-styled' or 'so-called' before the name of the excluded group.
- **iii** By the direct use of connotative terms carrying heavy implications of disgust: *criminals, killers, murderers, criminal psychopaths, left-wing extremists, urban terrorists, violent anarchists, political killers, Marxist revolutionaries*, etc.

In the same way, direct quotations in inverted commas allow journalists to report on controversial issues while preserving an impartial stance, as in:

Lecturer 'robbed of career' after she miscarried.

Activity

1. Scan one tabloid and one broadsheet for nouns or verbs that signal conflict.
2. Find copies of *Hansard* for the years when Margaret Thatcher was battling with what she called 'the enemy within' (the miners), and examine the speeches reported there for the language of conflict. Analyse what this reveals of attitudes within society during the 1980s.

Stereotyping

Journalists often simplify complex social and political issues by presenting them in terms of stereotypes. Stereotypes are fixed ideas of individuals or groups that endow them with particular attributes, values, attitudes and ideas: *radical feminists*; *a male chauvinist pig*; *the New Man*; *New Labour*; *the Far Right*. Once people have been slotted neatly into such stereotypes, they can be brought into conflict with one another without any of the niggling details or qualifications that might otherwise spoil the broad sweep of the story.

Activity

Read at least one tabloid and one broadsheet, looking for articles about particular groups of people: political groupings, ethnic minorities, the unemployed, homosexuals, etc.

1. Examine the language used in relation to these for evidence of stereotyping.
2. Examine the language used in relation to these for evidence of prejudice on the writer's part.

Audience design: The grammar of newspaper reporting

All newspaper reports are written in good grammatical English. The tabloids make some concession to their readers, however:

1. by using shorter sentences with fewer dependent clauses;
2. by using simple concrete nouns instead of abstract ones;
3. by writing one-sentence paragraphs.

> **Drive 'em down**
>
> **BUYING a new car in Britain is the biggest rip-off of all.**
>
> Motorists pay thousands over the price charged in other European countries.
>
> Now the Government is to force the cost down.
>
> *This is not just a victory for buyers of new cars but for all consumers.*
>
> *The Mirror*, 11 April 2000

Compression of appositional phrases

Journalists use this technique to save space and add pace to an article. Before the 1950s it was usual to place the name of the person in the news first – e.g. 'Mrs Mary Message' – and the appositional phrase afterwards, e.g. 'a widow of 30 Bow Terrace London . . .'

Today, appositional phrases are largely replaced by modifiers which are placed before the names, resulting in the shorter, racier version below. The standard form of name apposition in many media is now as follows:

1or 2 pre-modifiers	**+ Noun acting as title**	**+ First & last names**
Notorious Tory	Rebel	Alan Clark
Former	SpiceGirl	Gerri Halliwell

Talking point

It has been claimed that appositional phrases of this kind can function as pseudo-titles, conferring undeserved fame on people who simply happen to be in the news.
How far do you agree?

Further compression can be seen in the writing of headlines, which are forced to break with conventional sentence structure for reasons of space. They use what Strauman in 1935 called **block language**, and Halliday in 1967 **economy language** – the kind of abbreviated writing we find in diaries, recipes, and advertisements.

Most headlines, therefore, consist of dependent clauses or phrases below the level of a sentence:

WORLD WEATHER
MORE HUMBUG THAN FUDGE
THE CAR YOU WIGGLE
THE HOME COMPUTERS ONLINE IN AN INSTANT

Block or economy language concentrates on words that carry the heaviest charge of meaning, leaving out the function words that carry little information – such as definite and indefinite articles (*the* and *a*) and finite forms of the verb *to be*, like *is* and *are*. The result is a kind of 'telegraphese' that can be understood only by reading the article beneath it. Perhaps this is the reason they are made ambiguous in the first place. Consider for example the headline **EXPLOSION PLOT ALLEGED**. Without a definite article we cannot tell whether the plot is fact or fiction; without finite verbs like *is*, *was*, or *has been*, the time-scale of events is totally vague.

The ambiguity deepens when heavily modified noun phrases are used as headlines:

HISTORY MAN TRIAL
HISTORY MAN TRIAL ACCUSATION
HISTORY MAN TRIAL ACCUSATION DENIAL etc.

Several different interpretations are possible, and unless we have been following previous reports of the case, we can have no idea which is correct.

The language of magazines

Magazines lure their readers as newspapers do, with a combination of words and pictures. Since most magazines are bought on impulse, however, the appeal of the cover is all-important and makes an enormous impact on sales.

In this country, more than 100 magazines are published specifically for women (men mainly buy magazines devoted to hobbies), and since the 1980s these have shown an increasing tendency to concentrate on beauty (how to look and feel good) and sex (how to improve it).

Women's magazines welcome their readers into an empathetic, supportive environment where problems can be shared and inadequacies, whether physical or emotional, can be overcome. Add colour and glamour to this warmth (articles about film stars and celebrities, full-page colour ads for clothes and make-up), and readers are grateful:

> As a *Red* subscriber I'm writing to say 'thanks' for your lovely and inspiring magazine. As a young, house-bound disabled woman it enables me to gain access to a more glamorous world from which I am often excluded . . .

Editorials addressed to readers establish the predominant tone of a particular magazine. Compare the confiding 'we're-all-in-the-same-boat' tone and tentative sentence structure of Terry Tavner (lots of questions), with the forcefully assertive, self-congratulatory tone of Kate Carr and Deirdre Vine (lots of crisp statements) below:

> It's difficult enough dating the first time round, isn't it? All that worrying about what to wear, whether your make-up's right, does your bum look big and so on. But when you have to start all over again and you've got kids as well, it can be a bit of a nightmare. Not only are you aware that you might not look quite as good as you did before you had them, the little darlings are standing there watching you get ready to go out . . .See p48 to see how other mums cope with dating.
>
> Terry Tavner, *Woman's Own*, 8 May 2000
>
> We were the ones who read *Honey*, wore loons and Biba T-shirts, screamed at the Monkees, had the Che Guevara poster . . .
> We were groovy. We still are. Ours has always been the most provocative generation. We thought we would change the world and we certainly bounced it around a bit.
> No surprise then that as we enter our Jaffa Cake years – the juiciest bits in the centre of our lives – we're ploughing up the myths of middle-age. We have no role models; we are the role models. So here's *Aura*, a magazine to reflect our influence, energy, emotions – and sense of fun.
>
> Kate Carr and Deirdre Vine, *Aura*, May 2000

Note the very different tone achieved by the use of 'you' in the first address and the much more sharply deictic 'we' in the second. 'You', meaning women in general, draws readers together, sharing the experiences of the sisterhood as a whole. 'We' is exclusive, used to distinguish a particular, elitist band of women – the editor's targeted readership – from those with lesser talents, drive and energy It's the old advertising ploy of flattering the people you want to sell to.

Sometimes an editor tries for a wider readership, leading to uncertainty of tone and style. Introducing the magazine's contents, the editor of *Red* writes:

> He [Tony Blair] believes passionately in the family, both personally and politically, so when he talks about a radical reform of the adoption laws, he's speaking straight from the heart . . . Even as a very young man he had a passionate belief in social reform and equality and, while critics label him a control freak, that's just another phrase for passion. Driving difficult policies through the labyrinthine coils of government requires unswerving belief. We may, or may not, agree with those policies, but nobody can say our prime minister lacks conviction.
>
> Sally Brampton, *Red*, June 2000

So far so conventional, but then Sally Brampton feels she must jazz things up a little, suiting her style to the trendier topics in the magazine before readers have the chance to get bored. The article on the death of political correctness, she tells us,

> is well worth a read. So is Suzanne Moore's article, *A Woman's Place Is In The Wrong.* What is it with women now we're taking the rap again? Check out what Suzanne has to say. She's not exactly a writer who pulls her punches.
>
> A point of view – that's another thing we like . . . We aim to tell it like it is . . . take a look at all that's hip and happening in the arts, books and movies . . . All in all, it's a great new look for *Red*.

Since much of the slang used here already has a dated feel, it's difficult to assess whether it will repel as many readers as it attracts.

Magazine style

Like the newspapers, magazines are written in good, grammatically accurate English. Articles begin with a paragraph that catches the reader's attention in some way (sex in some form or other is always a good attention grabber, as is humour, or a vivid account of personal experience). The middle part of the article contains some new information of general interest, and this leads to a well-shaped ending. Here, for instance, is the opening paragraph of Ed Haliwell's account of the life and work of fashion designer Paul Smith:

> Of all the painful moments in an adult male's life, few are as excruciating as when your mother dusts off old family photo albums for the benefit of a new girlfriend. Never mind the shame of hearing Mum tell her favourite anecdote about your bed-wetting exploits, or the frustration of seeing your bedmate's gaze shift from uncontrollable desire to bland, sexless affection as she coos over endless pictures of you as a toddler. The real stomach-churner is the fact that, for the rest of the relationship, the lady will be able to puncture your self-respect simply by referring to the orange paisley shirt or purple bell-bottoms you were spied wearing so proudly in former years.
>
> Judging by the photographs of a young Paul Smith held in the designer's archive in Nottingham, he has never risked this ritual humiliation . . .
>
> *FHM*, Spring/Summer 2000

Magazine style and gender

It might be thought that women's magazines are written in a consciously 'girly' style, and men's in an obviously macho one.

In fact, when discussing neutral subjects a writer's gender is very difficult to assess. When writing specifically for their own sex, however, or invited to display their own tastes and personalities, differences of style do emerge. No man would dare risk the hyperbole, rhetoric, and emotive language used by editor of *Cosmopolitan*, Mandi Norwood, below:

> The editorial combination we've established here at Cosmo – a mix of knowledge, inspiration, empathy and encouragement – is a powerful one. It makes things happen. It changes lives. It turns ordinary women into goddesses. Fuelled by these four tools, you can't be bullied or bamboozled. You can make anything you want happen. Wildest dreams can come true.

In the same way, few men would risk the bathos implicit in the following piece by Nigella Lawson. Addressing her women readers she announces: 'I have done something, on your behalf, that has changed my life and may change yours. I went and had the hair on my legs removed by laser.'

Writing on such a theme by a man would have been written in mock heroic style; Lawson plays it straight, although she does admit 'we're not talking front line here'.

It's not that men consistently use a different vocabulary from women, or use fewer adjectives, or write in shorter sentences, or in a more forceful style, or in a brusquer tone. Compare the passages below for proof of this.

A I've spent most of my thirties in a state of self-disgust – but I haven't changed my diet one jot. I have lain in the bath and watched the flab ruck up around my nipples; I have wondered why my girlfriend's breasts are smaller than my own; I have rigged up a system of mirrors to inspect my dimpled love handles (who says men don't get cellulite?). Yet I still drink beer, steal pizza from my kids, and gorge myself on kebabs . . .

Andrew Purvis, *Red*, June 2000

B Women now know that their lives are more about muddling through than having it all. We are more realistic about the choices we make, and the decisions we are taking show quite clearly that young women today have no desire to turn back the clock.

That doesn't mean that each of us isn't going to have days when we wonder if we are doing the right thing. We know life isn't perfect. But the next time you find yourself in a 'Women, know your limits' sketch, remember this:

Women, know your enemy. If you are not for us, then you are against us. Blaming us for everything does not make us feel guilty, it just makes us angry. And we are not going to go away.

Suzanne Moore, *Red*, June 2000

C Headquartered at the University of Arizona in Tucson, my adopted hometown, the Wildchairs are a source of frustration, wry amusement and perverse underdog pride, both to the players and the few of us who support them. They have the skills, you understand, they have the potential. They play a fluid, open, ambitious, free-passing game and, when it comes together, it's a thing of grace and beauty. But all too often, just as they're starting to take charge or get back into the game, a key pass goes astray and then another and the team loses confidence and momentum . . .

Richard Grant, *Arena*, June 2000

What does emerge from these different extracts is the more emotionally in-your-face, felt quality of female writing. The approach of both **A** and **C** is cooler, more objective, less immediately personal. They merely mention self-disgust and frustration; the writer of **B** takes us behind these emotions and makes us share them.

How are these effects created?

1 Women use more emotive language; male writers tend to make plain statements of fact, less coloured by emotion.

2 Women also make more use of the personal pronouns *I*, *my* and *we*, which has the effect of drawing us closer to the writer and identifying to some extent with her.

Activity

Consider the extracts below, and discuss what the style reveals about each writer's attitude to his or her subject.

A What I wanted was elusive. I wanted wit – a car with a sense of humour and a touch of irony. Could one off-the-wall manufacturer have managed to conceive a car that could make you laugh, warm your cockles, take the piss out of itself and still have power steering and a dash of pizazz? Well, what do you think? I had almost decided to throw in the towel when a well-wisher gave me an obscure specialist car-import magazine. I flicked. I fell in love – or at least, something dangerously like it.

It was small and spherical, bosom shaped to be precise. Fifties in spirit and style, it was a convertible – with a white leather roof, seats and dashboard, retro headlamps, bedecked in metal fleur de lys. What's more, it was available in the prettiest pastels – pistachio ice-cream green, slightly fogy LA-sky blue, and an edible cross between oyster and cream. Better still, the gorgeous little creature came complete with all mod cons including air conditioning, power steering and CD player . . .

B Horsepower isn't the thing in the 911 Turbo, although 420 is a handsome amount; no, this car is all about torque (the engines's muscle), delivered deep and crisp and even right across the rev range . . .

In the end, this is quite simply the most impressive car I've ever experienced. Its straight-line speed is awesome, its build quality exemplary, it's remarkably refined all the way to 150 mph, and it'll even deliver a barely believable 30 mpg if you drive it with a modicum of environmental friendliness. But to really understand it, you need to tackle a few corners. It glues itself to the road. Go faster. It goes faster. Even more adhesion. Packed with computers that divert power to whichever of the four wheels need it most – in whatever combination – your internal organs (battered by multiplying G-forces) begin waving the white flag long before the 911 Turbo does.

I can't remember the last time a car gave me indigestion.

Jason Barlow, *GQ*, June 2000

Magazine style and the youth market

Magazines that sell to teens – even those like *YM* and *Cosmo Girl*, published in the States – write their informative features in standard, grammatically correct English. When writing direct answers to readers' questions, however, they switch to what they take to be current teen slang. *YM* in particular is full of Black American street-talk:

Q Is it true that you can't get pregnant if you have sex during that time of the month?

A Listen up, baby! Your monthly crimson companion is no substitute for birth control. That's because your ovaries can release an egg at any time even when you have your period, explains Yvonne S. Thornton, M.D., a gynaecologist in Morristown, NJ. To add to the risk, sperm can stay present up to seven days after you have sex. Bottom line: You're never *totally* off the pregnancy hook when you hook up.

ask anything in *YM*, May 2000

Cosmo Girl is blander in style, hitting a less extreme, mid-Atlantic note. English magazines like *Bliss* and *J-17* are written in far more conventional style, the main concession to 'cool' being abbreviations like 'cause and 'rents (parents). A faint echo of American style on the fashion advice page is all that remains: 'This is the major prob that every shopping sista has to face Leanna. . . . Designer gear is gorge but, as you've discovered, it's way expensive' (*Bliss*, May 2000).

The language of radio and television

Study the media and you quickly become aware of how they feed off one another: radio and television review the newspapers; newspapers print radio and television schedules, trail important programmes and review them after transmission; actors in soap operas appear on morning television to discuss issues raised in the story lines (teenage pregnancy in *Coronation Street*, for example); magazines run full-length features on the lives of the sporting heroes, fashion models and film stars who are currently featured on television or in the press.

Radio and television channels even to some extent imitate the content and style of the different newspapers. Radio 4, for instance, has something of the earnest tone, conventional style and worthy preoccupations of the *Daily Telegraph*, and like that newspaper, speaks for middle-aged, middle-class England (programmes like *I'm Sorry I Haven't a Clue*, containing the filthiest and funniest innuendo to be heard on air, are the exception that proves the rule). Radio 5 has the livelier tone and more populist approach of the *Daily Mail* (but without its moral stuffiness), involving listeners in a dialogue by reading out their e-mailed comments on the news, while London Live goes for the more blatant in-your-face tone and style of tabloids like the *Sun*.

Audience design in broadcasting: Radio

Mode of address

Consider the breakfast shows put out by the different radio stations. Radio 4's *Today* begins with the news read in a remote, authoritative style by a staff newsreader, and the rather impersonal announcement:

You're listening to *Today*, with James Naughtie and Sue McGregor.

Radio 5 Live chooses a more personal, conversational style, the less formal tone being helped by the fact that the presenters themselves read the news: 'Good morning. I'm Julian Warriker, it's Tuesday, 6 o'clock, here are the headlines.'

London Live goes for mateyness:

> GOOOOD MORNING, LONDON! It's 6 o'clock, it's Wednesday the 8th of June and you are listening to the breakfast show on the BBC programme for London, London Live, 94.9, with me, Paul Ross, and me [*woman's voice*] Claire McDonald.

Pitch and intonation

Pitch and intonation match the style of address: level tones for Radio 4, more varied for Radio 5 Live; positively exaggerated for London Live. The 'good' of 'Good Morning' here, for instance, as well as being uttered at the top of the presenter's voice, is drawn out to emphasize the impression of bonhomie the programme wants to create.

Accent

Accent also plays a part. Radio 4's presenters speak in cleanly articulated, flawless RP (Received Pronunciation), albeit in James Naughtie's case with a slight Scots accent; the presenters on Radio 5 Live use a slightly modified RP, still obviously educated middle-class, but with consonants that are less crisp and vowels that are slightly more vague; the accent of London Live's presenters is frankly Estuary, with glottal stops and vowels not found in the Universal Phonetic Alphabet. They make fun of RP speakers (as, to be fair, do some of the presenters on Radio 5 Live), and are confident enough to send themselves up (deprecate themselves) for their general lack of education and polish: 'A sad and bowed-down middle-aged oik' (Ross), and 'A cheap-looking Essex girl' (McDonald). Since both are obviously sharp and successful, the aim must be to match the idiom of the audience that the programme is targeting: intelligent and aware, but not highly educated.

Diction

The choice of language on each programme is geared to audience and content. Radio 5 will happily use expressions like *posh, up for grabs, hell of a lot* and *a bit of a kerfuffle*. Although for the most part its idiom is conventionally correct, expressions such as *Now get this* are used to introduce really interesting items. *OK* is used throughout. London Live will use a slang idiom even in interviews with prize-winning authors: 'What you goin' to do with your 30 grand?', Caroline Johnston demanded of the winner of the Orange award for best book by a woman writer. The two main presenters mix words like *credibility* and *gullibility* in with their *blimey*s. Radio 4 rarely stoops to either slang or colloquialisms: 'I'll have to shut you both up now' is about as far as James Naughtie allows himself to go, and it just isn't Sue McGregor's style.

Humour

Humour is another area in which the programmes differ. The male/female pairs on Radio 5 and London Live work much more closely than those on Radio 4, often making jokes about each other, or commenting on what a regular sport or travel or weather reporter has to say. When Radio 4's presenters descend to joking, it feels exactly like two old-fashioned school teachers unbending in front of their pupils, self-consciously enjoying a joke.

Jingles

Listen to *Today* and many other programmes on Radio 4 and you will hear long unbroken stretches of monologue or discussion, demanding the same concentration as unbroken columns of print in *The Telegraph* or *Guardian*. Listen to Radio 5 or London Live, however, and repeated jingles break up the talk, acting like the sub-headlines that break up body copy in the tabloids. They also give a sense of urgency and excitement to the programme: 'it's all happening here', they tell the listeners, 'this is where it's at'. Radio 4 has no such jingles, although it does use the 'bongs' of Big Ben to create an air of authority and importance.

Playing to the audience

Bell has pointed out (in *The Language of News Media*) the importance of audience design: gear your material to your audience, or they will switch off. Broadcasters play to their audiences in a variety of ways:

1 They build up a pseudo-personal relationship with their audience by using second-person pronouns ('In case you think I'm exaggerating . . .') and vocatives (nouns used in addressing people, e.g. 'Hello to Rupe in York').
2 They use what Bell calls **responsive design**, creating a mental image of their targeted audience and matching content and style to it (particularly in news broadcasts and informative programmes).
3 They use the opposite technique called **initiative design**, where they use language alien to their audience to make a point, or to interest or entertain (as in, for example, the patter of various DJs).
4 They use **upward** or **downward divergence of speech**, shifting their speech towards RP and conventionally correct English or towards local or regional dialect forms (particularly in phone-ins and gardening programmes).
5 Bell also distinguishes something he calls **referee design**. At the back of a speaker's mind, he claims, is the image of a group with great prestige and importance; a group he identifies with and refers back to mentally all the time. Bell further distinguishes two aspects of referee design: **in-group** and **out-group referee design.**

In **in-group referee design**, whether addressing members of their own referee group (in-group addressees), or people outside the group (out-group addressees), speakers use a heightened form of their usual style of speech. In the first case, speakers are appealing to solidarity with their own kind. In the second, they are asserting their difference from the audience actually present in order to claim identity with their own absent group. Bell gives the example of a Welsh bilingual speaker addressing a monolingual English audience in his own language. The adoption of an exaggerated accent or a vocabulary heavy with dialect words might be a more useful example when examining broadcast speech.

In **out-group referee design**, speakers may adopt the characteristic speech patterns of groups to which they do not belong. They may speak like people from another class, another ethnic or age group, another region or country, or from another historical period. Comedy programmes are rich in this particular usage: see for instance *Ab Fab, Keeping up Appearances* and *Ali G.*

The most skilful broadcasters are those who move most easily between these various speech styles. Radio 5's Nicky Campbell, for example, moves from exaggerated in-group referee design – 'What is the burden of your song?' (spoken to a visiting expert on his talk show) to out-group in seconds: 'Alex in Newcastle, what do you reckon?' Terry Wogan is also adept at style switching, and can hold an audience for hours.

Activity

Listen to Chris Tarrant or Chris Evans or any other DJ or presenter, and analyse the appeal of the programme with the help of the following guidelines:

1. What audience is being targeted? Explain your reasons for thinking so.
2. Discuss the style of presentation. Are the listeners addressed directly? If so, in what terms?
3. Discuss the DJ's characteristic diction.
4. Describe the characteristic pitch and intonation employed by the DJ.
5. Discuss any use of jingles.
6. Discuss the DJ's language skills in the light of points 1 to 5 above.

Television

The most striking change in radio and television has been the move from an authoritarian style to one of conversational ease. Instead of delivering monologues in clipped, impersonal tones *de haut en bas*, television sets up a dialogue with its viewers: continuity announcers 'hope you enjoyed that episode' of whatever we've just been watching, while presenters address their remarks to the unseen 'you', use the inclusive 'we' to make us feel part of what's going on and invite our opinions on what they're discussing.

Even true interaction is common now on radio and television, thanks to the introduction of phone-ins, discussion programmes and talk shows. These set the agenda for ordinary people's concerns and offer them a forum (public debating space) in which to air them. The talk is lively, often argumentative and controversial, with experts or authority figures challenged to defend their views by members of the public or by media presenters questioning them on our behalf.

The range of language to be found on television is broadly similar to that found on radio. Perhaps because it accompanies pictures, however, it tends to be less innovative and creative: compare Radio 5's morning phone-in or any *Late Night Live* discussion with BBC 1's *Question Time* introduced by David Dimbleby, where the formal language of presenter and panel matches the formal set and tightly controlled format.

Talk shows

Daytime talk shows differ from most other programmes in having a studio audience. Sometimes they get to speak, sometimes not, but through their body language and their use of phatic communication (non-verbal noises of encouragement or derision), they always participate.

Jane Shuttuck (*The Talking Cure*, Routledge, 1997) sees talk shows as the equivalent to tabloid newspapers, citing American talk-show host Phil Donahue in evidence: 'We are tabloid – I'm happy to wear the label.' Both focus on stories of human interest: sex and violence, deviancy and suffering told in simple words and uncomplicated sentence structures. Both use sensationalism – 'subject-matter, style, language, or artistic expression intended to shock, startle, excite or arouse intense interest' – in order to stir the senses of their audience.

Because they deal primarily with emotional problems and their repercussions on relationships, talk shows are labelled as dealing with 'women's issues', in spite of the fact that the percentage of male and female viewers is much the same.

Some sociologists take a political view of these shows, claiming that they allow women to overcome their alienation through talking about their particular experience as women in society, and American talk-show host Oprah Winfrey has herself proclaimed 'We do programme these shows to empower women'. The real reason for the popularity of talk shows, however, lies in the talk:

> The audience in the studio and at home are encouraged to tell their own stories, agree or disagree, confirm or contradict, confront or support the speaker, generating a polyphony of narratives on and beyond the small screen.
>
> Livingstone and Lunt, *Talk on Television*, Routledge, 1994

The talk-show host has to tread a fine line between encouraging her guests' emotional expression and limiting it so that other people may speak and the main lines of the discussion are not blurred. Other tasks are to sum up her guests' sometimes incoherent responses and to support or clarify any contributions by experts that may be difficult to understand.

Activity

Record a daytime talk show and analyse it a) in the light of what you have read about the language of the media, b) in the light of the unspoken rules that govern conversation.

The language of advertising

As Vestergaard and Schroder point out (*The Language of Advertising*, Basil Blackwell Ltd), advertising has certain things in common with the arts. Like novels, plays and films, like radio and television, advertising is a form of one-way communication with an anonymous audience. Like them, it creates ways of drawing that audience into what appears to be a two-way relationship.

Purpose

Advertisers have one purpose only: to make us buy one product over all its (usually very similar) competitors on the market.

Approach

Advertisers use a psychological approach – an implied promise to supply us with the things we want the most: sex (including attractiveness), status (including money), and power (including money). Most ads can be chased down to one of these three categories, however unlikely. Cleaning agents that practically work by themselves, for instance, promise less effort and greater leisure, the prerogatives of the wealthy upper class. As they readily admit, what advertisers really sell is hope.

Method

Like scriptwriters in the movies, advertisers construct fictional scenarios. According to Vestergaard and Schroder, a typical scenario depicts the audience as the **subject** or **receiver** of the action (which is some kind of problem that is troubling us), the product as the **helper** that solves the problem, and the **object** as some desirable quality.

Context

The success of any ad depends on the effectiveness of its verbal and non-verbal elements, and this in turn depends upon the advertiser's grasp of context. This includes:

- the specific features of the social situation in which the communicative interaction takes place, and
- the wider social, political and historical circumstances within which it is made meaningful.

Copy-writers must consider both the physical context (where the ad will appear, the spending power of the audience targeted) and the mental context (the degree to which the members of that audience share the copy-writers' knowledge of the wider cultural context). Ads featuring a cowboy would be unlikely to work in women's magazines, for example; the Carling ad showing the coming of football to England couldn't work without some knowledge of history. Recognition that what we're looking at is an ad is also an important part of context, since such knowledge shapes our perception of the material it contains.

Direct address advertising

The simplest form of advertising is direct and impersonal. It avoids the second-person pronoun 'you', using deictic words like *here*, *this*, *now*, and imperatives like *look*, *see*, *watch*, referring to visible features of the product advertised. Direct address advertisements have two main participants: the addressor (the advertiser) and the addressee (the audience).

Indirect address advertising

Indirect address ads introduce one or two secondary participants who act as vehicles for the advertiser's message. The simplest form of indirect address advertising has one speaker (usually a satisfied consumer or a supposed 'expert') who uses the first person 'I' or 'we' to create the impression of events happening in real life. The copy-writers' ability to handle register is vital here: it must be appropriate to the speaker's situation, social class, age, and sex, or it will sound like what it's trying to avoid – direct address copy.

The same difficulty presents itself in scenarios that introduce two secondary participants: how to make their dialogue sound convincing. The copy-writers' task is to dramatize a scene from ordinary domestic life – husband and wife, mother and child, householder and plumber, etc. – using ordinary language, and at the same time to praise the virtues of a product whose name can hardly be mentioned in case the whole thing sounds ridiculously artificial. The usual technique is to rely on colloquial language and slang, partly to make the participants sound convincing, and partly to make the audience relate easily to them.

Activity

Consider the husband seen cleaning the kitchen and bathroom in Flash advertisements and discuss the accent and language he's given to use in the light of the above, and the brand name of the cleaner.

Advertising stereotypes

The people portrayed in advertisements are stereotypes rather than individuals: housewives are always happy, well dressed and cheerful, they preside over homes that are orderly, clean and tidy, and even when they are glad to save on the cost of an item, they never seem pushed for cash. Husbands and other males are immaculately dressed and obviously middle class, unless brought in to advise on the right soap powder to use, when they can be either a scientific boffin in a stereotypical white coat or a salt-of-the-earth blue-collar worker. The great thing about stereotypes is that they contain a grain of truth and never offend the paying public – which is the last thing advertisers can afford to do.

A vein of British whimsy stretching back to *The Wind in the Willows* is tapped and up-dated in some advertisements, notably that for Budweiser, where mafia boss-type lizards hire professional hit-ferrets to clean out the opposition.

Activity

1 Find an example of :
   a monologue, and
   b dialogue in separate TV ads. Examine each for its skill in handling language, and its effectiveness in promoting the product.

2 Find a cartoon strip advertising PG Tips in a national broadsheet, and discuss the appeal its visual and verbal elements make, or attempt to make, to consumers.

Verbal and visual interaction in advertising

Visual images may be the first things that catch the eye in advertisements, but for them to have their fullest effect, they need the help of words. It's sometimes difficult to tell what product an ad is promoting until the caption or slogan appears at the end. Consider the image of a sheet of purple silk, its beauty marred by a central slit. Being, like all images, polysemic, it is open to interpretation in many ways; write the words 'Silk Cut' above or below, however, and its meaning in this particular context becomes clear.

The relation between text and image in cases like this is known as **anchorage**. The word anchors the image to the context.

Words are also needed to anchor an image in time. Most utterances indicate time by the use of the past or present tenses, but images by their nature are unable to do this. Vestergaard gives the example of the present tense used to anchor the image of a diamond in the text 'A diamond is forever'.

The diction of advertising

Advertisers use certain emotive words more freely than others: adjectives like *new, good, better, best, free, fresh, great, delicious, full, wonderful, bright*; and evaluative ones like *sure, clean, special, crisp, fine, real, easy, extra, rich, safe, delicate, perfect, expert, glamorous, lovely*.

Extra force is added by turning some adjectives into compound ones: *undreamed-of, country-fresh, creamy-mild, shining-clean*, etc.

Since the advertiser's task is to make us act, most verbs are in the imperative mood. Certain verbs are repeated time and again; like those favoured by the tabloids they are short, crisp and forceful:

make set give have see get come go know keep look
need love use feel like take start taste call hurry let
send for use ask for

Get is used far more often than *buy* for psychological reasons. *Buy* is a word that has one major meaning: the spending of money. It denotes what for most people is an unpleasant action. *Get* on the other hand is a word with wider and vaguer associations. It connotes acquiring, and makes the spending less obvious. Other verbs on the list, like *choose*, are also ways of avoiding *buy*, as are *make [Blank] your way to start the day; give someone you love a [Blank].*

Negated interrogatives are also common: *Isn't it time you* (did something or other), *Why not* (do something or other). These of course are just disguised imperatives.

Sometimes the nudge to buy is given in the form of advice: *If* (something or other is a problem) *you should try [Blank].*

Finally, the least obviously directive is the apparently objective remark: *You'll find [Blank] at all good stores; You can use [Blank] in the kitchen or the bathroom.*

The grammar of advertising

Advertising language is grammatically simple. The use of an imperative without a subject is particularly common.

Advertising copy is written in disjunctive rather than discursive grammar, closer to the block style of headline writing than to conventional prose. Dependent clauses and phrases are used in their own right, without the support of a main clause, particularly in TV advertising:

Introducing the outstanding toploader
Toploader's new album out now

Sometimes the grammatical unit consists of a single word:

Tesco. *Every little helps*

The shorter units of disjunctive grammar make a more immediate impact on idle listeners than discursive sentences, and fewer demands on their concentration.

In some ads they can also create the kind of brusquely masculine effect that goes with hard physical labour:

The all new transit
Job done

Advertisers also break the rules of grammar with unconventional spelling. Sometimes the violation is used to enhance an effect, as in *Krisp*, where *k* gives an apparently harder edge to the sound than *c* could do, or in *creem*, where doubling the vowel may help to intensify a rhyme. Sometimes the changes in spelling seem to have no purpose other than to attract attention by looking different, as in *Whiskas Glocoat.* Playing games with the normal distribution of upper- and lower-case letters is another attention-seeking device.

The creative use of language in advertising

Since products vary very little from one another or from month to month, advertisers try to inject originality into the copy used to promote them. They use neologisms (newly coined words) like *peelability, temptational, outsparkle*, and phrases like *unzipp a banana.*

They turn commonsense and conventional meaning on their heads in coinings like 'In the best circles washing machine is pronounced Parnell'. Part of the appeal here depends on the echo of the cliché, *a pronounced success.*

They use figurative language also to subvert conventional sense in paradoxical phrases like:

eating sunshine *smiling colour* *purposeful shape*

and assertions like

Flowers from Interflora speak from the heart

Copywriters also give the kiss of life to old clichés:

Are you a Cadbury's fruit and nut case?

Sometimes they use outright puns:

When it rains, it pours! (Morton's salt)

Sometimes, however, originality appears in language of a terse and simple kind:

It is. Are you? (*The Independent*)
I think, therefore IBM (adapting the famous statement of Descartes).

The use of pattern in advertisements

If the judgement of the Advertising Hall of Fame's panel is anything to go by, the thing that really makes an ad stick in our minds, sometimes for years, is the repetition of linguistic patterns. Even the *Sun*, not normally interested in language studies, ran a full page on advertisements under the headline:

10 BEST SLOGANZ WE'VE EVER 'AD

– testimony to the significant part that advertising plays in most people's lives today.

Many of the most popular ads picked out by the panel work on devices borrowed from poetry: alliteration, assonance, metre, rhyme, and onomatopeia.

If you want to get ahead, get a hat
Hello Tosh, gotta Toshiba
Happiness is a cigar called Hamlet
Don't be vague, ask for Haig

My goodness, my Guinness
Snap! Crackle! Pop!
A newspaper, not a snoozepaper
Ariston and on and on
A Mars a day helps you work, rest and play
Plop, plop, fizz, fizz, oh what a relief it is
a US slogan advertising Alka-seltzer; in the UK it became:
Plink, plink, fizz, fizz, oh what a relief it is

(See *www.adslogans.co.uk* for further information.)

A more recent example that makes a similar appeal is Tesco's poster

From mouse to house

advertising its Internet shopping service.

Activity

1. Analyse the use of language in any five of the above advertising slogans.
2. Find five recent ads that use the same devices, and analyse their appeal.

Parallelism, arranging equivalent pieces of text close to one another to create a formal pattern, is another device used by advertisers:

It's new! It's crisper! It's lighter!
It's the new Ryvita!

Beginning a number of equivalent clauses with the name of the product achieves the same effect.

One ad stood out above all others in the popularity poll. Why? Because it contained just about every device in the list above. Here it is in full:

˘ / ˘ / ˘ / ˘ /
A million housewives every day

/ ˘ ˘ / ˘ / ˘ /
Pick up a tin of beans and say

/
Beanz

/
Meanz

/
Heinz.

Notice:

- the almost perfectly regular iambic metre;
- the rhyme on *say* and *day*;
- the internal rhyme or assonance of *beanz, meanz*, and *heinz*,
- the alliteration of the *p* in *pick up* and the voiced consonant *z* at the end of the last three lines.

Notice also how the lines build up to a climax, allowing for three separate nuclear stresses on the three final monosyllables. No wonder once heard it could never be forgotten.

Activity

1 Consider the following ad from the point of view of (i) metre, (ii) assonance.
   Mum rollette protects you best
2 Find an example of a recent ad that uses metrical patterning.
3 Assess the appeal of the Pepsi ad below. It may help to copy it out without any of the apostrophes. What kind of consumers do you think it targets?
   Lipsmackin'thirstquenchin'
   acetastin'motivatin'
   goodbuzzin'cooltalkin'
   highwalkin'fastlivin'evergivin'
   coolfizzinPepsi

The language of the electronic media

As Marshall McLuhan pointed out in 1962, 'The medium is the message'. The methods by which we communicate not only affect the way we speak and write, but may also influence the way we think and act.

E-mails are a case in point. Notorious for misspellings, misplaced words and missing punctuation, they compare badly with hand-written letters sent by the same writers through the post. Under the headline, 'Is e-mail killing literacy?' the education correspondent of the *Daily Mail* worries about the effects of the new medium.

> Aficionados of all things high tech and computerised claim that e-mailing should be regarded as more akin to talking, rather than writing. Just as we converse with each other in bursts of informal, unedited speech, they insist, the e-mail should be free and easy, unfettered by grammatical rules.

Such an argument is fair enough, she concedes, but not only is sloppy writing an insult to the receiver:

> . . . the danger is that, with e-mailing becoming more and more commonplace, within a generation people will no longer be able to write in any other way . . .

And a further problem will then follow:

> . . . if the e-mail culture continues to spread, bringing with it a deterioration of literary skills, there will not be anyone left who can write the books that people want to read.

It is the medium itself that is to blame:

> As speed is the prime attraction of the e-mailing process, the whole point is to whack it off into the ether as soon as possible.
>
> The time-consuming niceties of literary composition sit uneasily in our pace-obsessed era.

Talking point How far do you think e-mails are capable of destroying people's ability to read and write conventional English?

GSM and SMS

In 1992, the telephone engineers of the EU set up a form of radio communication called the Global System for Mobile Communication – GSM for short. To enable users to communicate with the Internet via their phones, they built in a facility to send bits of text. SMS – the Short Message Service, or text-messaging as it is commonly known – was born.

Like e-mail, text messaging has had a strong influence on how we communicate. It's cheap (10p sends a message anywhere); it's simple (no manual needed); it's discreet (no ring to be heard); it's convenient (you can read it anytime, anywhere), it's more personal than e-mails on your pc, yet impersonal enough to let you send messages you might not risk committing yourself to via voicemail. '[Text] messages have got that kind of flirty thing . . .' according to one female TV researcher.

Young people use SMS the most, creating a whole new shorthand language for themselves in the process. *Thx! UR A* * is cooler, pacier and more fun than *Thank you. You're wonderful.*

Will text messages have any lasting effect on the language? Richard Benson speculates in *The Guardian Weekend*:

> Cd vwls dspr frm th lng'ge altgthr? Or could we end up with a two-tier language system, in which everyday English wd b abbreviated, + cd include numbers + l8rs 2gthr? . . . It's impossible to know what effect emails and text messages will have on us, but it is clear that they have instigated the biggest boom in 'letter' writing for 200 years; and while we don't, yet, have a text-message novel, the tight, subjectless sentences and the reproduced emails in Bridget Jones' [sic] Diary have at least a touch of the digital missives.
>
> Mike Short, the chairman of the GSM Association's Mobile Data Taskforce, believes that text-messaging is part of an epoch-making shift in the way we communicate with one another, a 'move from a verbal to a visual culture', as he puts it. That seems a rather grand claim to make on its behalf, but

then, if you're not sure what's happening, you might as well try to sound excited about it.

The rest of us . . . will carry on using SMS because, of all the clever services and bits of information the techies find to give us, our favourites are the ones that let us talk to each other and make each other laugh. And because, as all good text-maniacs know, when you're dialling, the whole world :-)s with you.

A TXT MSGING GLSSRY

B	Be
BCNU	Be seeing you
Bwd	Backward
B4	Before
C	See
CU L8R	See you later
F2T	Free to talk
Fwd	Forward
Gr8	Great
H8	Hate
L8r	Later
Mob	Mobile
Msg	Message
NE	Any
NE1	Anyone
NO1	No one
OIC	Oh, I see
Pls	Please
Ppl	People
R	Are
RUOK	Are you OK?
Some1	Someone
THNQ	Thank you
Thx	Thanks
UR	You are
Wan2	Want to
W/	With
Wknd	Weekend
X	Kiss
Yr	Your
2	To, too
2day	Today
2moro	Tomorrow
2nite	Tonight
4	For

:-)	smiley face
;-)	winking face
:-o	surprised face
:-(	sad face
d:)	baseball-cap face
:@)	pig's face

Activity

1 Translate the opening sentence of any novel and the first verse of any poem into text-message form.
2 Discuss any differences in tone, style, and meaning that result.

The language of literature

Sentence structure, meaning, and style

In the work of good writers the structure of a sentence is an integral part of its meaning; it underpins and emphasizes what is being said. Consider for example this sentence from *David Copperfield* describing the death of Barkis:

> And, it being low water, he went out with the tide.

The rise of the voice towards the comma and its falling away from it afterwards reflect both the rise and fall of the tides and Barkis's movement towards death, creating at the same time a mood of gentle melancholy. Reverse the order of the clauses and you ruin the effect:

> He went out with the tide, it being low water.

As writers re-create experience (real or imagined) they reach instinctively for the particular words and structures that will bring it to life. Thus in the following extract Dickens, having chosen the steam engine as his symbol for the destructive greed of an increasingly mechanized society, calls up its sounds and rhythms in his head and re-creates them in the structures of his sentences. Read carefully and you will hear in the first sentence exactly where the train settles down to run smoothly on a level gradient, and in the second, the actual moment when it goes through the points, changing rhythm before settling down again to a new, rapid, even pace:

> Away, with a shriek, and a roar, and a rattle, from the town, burrowing among the dwellings of men and making the streets hum, flashing out into the meadows for a moment, mining in through the damp earth, booming on in darkness and heavy air, bursting out again into the sunny day so bright and wide; away, with a shriek, and a roar, and a rattle, through the fields, through the woods, through the corn, through the hay, through the chalk, through the mould, through the clay, through the rock, among objects close at hand and almost in the grasp, ever flying from the traveller, and a deceitful distance ever moving slowly within him: like as in the track of the remorseless monster, Death!
>
> Through the hollow, on the height, by the heath, by the orchard, by the park, by the garden, over the canal, across the river, where the sheep are feeding, where the mill is going, where the barge is floating, where the dead are lying, where the factory is smoking, where the stream is running, where the village clusters, where the great cathedral rises, where the bleak moor lies, and the wild breeze smooths or ruffles it at its inconstant will;

> away, with a shriek, and a roar, and a rattle, and no trace to leave behind but dust and vapour: like as in the track of the remorseless monster, Death!
>
> Charles Dickens, *Dombey and Son*

In all good writing, even of a non-fictional kind, the structure of sentences underpins and intensifies their meaning. In this extract from a piece of journalism, for example, the dreary length of the concrete walkways on a council estate and the time it takes to reach the haven of your own front door are reflected in the deliberate piling up of subordinate clauses and phrases before the main statement:

> In through the concrete passage with its close-set black iron railings, past the battered grey lift which seldom works, up two flights of concrete stairs which smell of urine and drink, past graffiti saying, 'Where can we go for a hit, honey?' and along a concrete walkway, partly blocked by the remains of a brown moquette armchair, you'll find number 86.

The different kinds of effects that writers can achieve through the use of different kinds of sentence structures are illustrated below.

The simple sentence

It is possible to write well using mainly simple and compound sentences. Hemingway, for example, did so. In his opinion, the lengthy complex sentences and ornate diction of writers such as Henry James distracted attention from what was being said, focusing it instead on the writer's style. Hemingway chose to write in simple sentences, using few adverbs or adjectives, so that the truth of a situation could speak for itself. These characteristic features of his style can be seen in the extract below from *A Farewell to Arms*:

> I sat down on the chair in front of the table where there were nurse's reports hung on clips at the side and looked out of the window. I could see nothing but the dark and the rain falling across the lights from the window. So that was it. The baby was dead. That was why the doctor looked so tired. But why had they acted the way they had in the room with him? They supposed he would come round and start breathing probably. I had no religion but I knew he ought to have been baptized. But what if he never breathed at all? He hadn't. He had never been alive. Except in Catherine. I'd felt him kick there often enough. But I hadn't for a week. Maybe he was choked all the time. Poor little kid. I wished the hell I'd been choked like that. No I didn't. Still there would not be all this dying to go through. Now Catherine would die. That was what you did. You died. You did not know what it was about. You never had time to learn. They threw you in and told you the rules and the first time they caught you off base they killed you. Or they killed you gratuitously like Aymo. Or gave you the syphilis like Rinaldi. But they

killed you in the end. You could count on that. Stay around and they would kill you.

The varied rhythm and intonation here are created through the skilful alternation of

a sentence lengths, and
b questions and statements.

The same apparently simple technique puts us inside the character's mind as he asks his anguished questions and comes to equally painful conclusions: *But what if he never breathed at all? He hadn't. He had never been alive. Except in Catherine. I'd felt him kick there often enough. But I hadn't for a week. Maybe he was choked all the time. Poor little kid.* The short, often abrupt sentences suit both the context (the situation the character finds himself in) and the prevailing mood of bewildered grief.

Ian Fleming, on the other hand, chose the simple/compound sentence style for its ability to create tension and move a story along at speed – something else that lengthy complex sentences full of dependent clauses cannot do. In the extract from his *Dr No* that follows, seventy-nine of the eighty-nine sentences are simple, four compound, and only six complex; yet Fleming varies their structure so well that they never become monotonous or dull.

Activity

Read the passage to see how well Fleming manages this style, then carry out the activities suggested below.
(007 has been woken in the night by something crawling up his leg. His instincts tell him it is a tropical centipede.)

The centipede had reached his knee. It was starting up his thigh. Whatever happened he mustn't move, mustn't even tremble. Bond's whole consciousness had drained down to the two rows of softly creeping feet. Now they had reached his flank. God, it was turning down towards his groin! Bond set his teeth. Supposing it liked the warmth there! Supposing it tried to crawl into the crevices! Could he stand it? Supposing it chose that place to bite? Bond could feel it questing among the first hairs. It tickled. The skin on Bond's belly fluttered. There was nothing he could do to control it. But now the thing was turning up and along his stomach. Its feet were gripping tighter to prevent it falling. Now it was at his heart. If it bit there, surely it would kill him. The centipede trampled steadily on through the thin hairs on Bond's right breast up to his collar bone. It stopped. What was it doing? Bond could feel the blunt head questing slowly to and fro. What was it looking for? Was there room between his skin and the sheet for it to get through? Dare he lift the sheet an inch to help it? No. Never! The animal was at the base of his jugular. Perhaps it was intrigued by the heavy pulse there. Christ, if only he could control the pumping of his blood. Damn you! Bond tried to communicate with the centipede. It's nothing. It's not dangerous, that pulse. It means you no harm. Get on out into the fresh air!

As if the beast had heard, it moved on up the column of the neck and into the stubble on Bond's chin. Now it was at the corner of his mouth, tickling madly. On it went, up along the nose. Now he could feel its whole weight and length. Softly Bond closed his eyes. Two by two the pairs of feet, moving alternately, tramped across his right eyelid. When it got off his eye, should he take a chance and shake it off – rely on its feet slipping in his sweat? No, for God's sake! The grip of the feet was endless. He might shake one lot off, but not the rest.

With incredible deliberation the huge insect rambled across Bond's forehead. It stopped below the hair. What the hell was it doing now? Bond could feel it nuzzling at his skin. It was drinking! Drinking the beads of salt sweat. Bond was sure of it. For minutes it hardly moved. Bond felt weak with the tension. He could feel the sweat pouring off the rest of his body on to the sheet. In a second his limbs would start to tremble. He could feel it coming on. He would start to shake with an ague of fear. Could he control it, could he? Bond lay and waited, the breath coming softly through his open, snarling mouth . . .

The centipede stirred. Slowly it walked out of his hair on to the pillow. Bond waited a second. Now he could hear the rows of feet picking softly at the cotton. It was a tiny scraping noise like soft fingernails.

With a crash that shook the room Bond's body jack-knifed out of bed and on to the floor.

At once Bond was on his feet and at the door. He turned on the light. He found he was shaking uncontrollably. He staggered to the bed. There it was crawling out of sight over the edge of the pillow. Bond's first instinct was to twitch the pillow on the floor. He controlled himself, waiting for his nerves to quieten. Then softly, deliberately, he picked up the pillow by one corner and walked into the middle of the room and dropped it. The centipede came out from under the pillow. It started to snake quickly away across the matting. Now Bond was uninterested. He looked round for something to kill it with. Slowly he went and picked up a shoe and came back. The danger was past. His mind was wondering now how the centipede had got into his bed. He lifted the shoe and slowly, almost carelessly, smashed it down. He heard the crack of the hard carapace.

Bond lifted the shoe.

The centipede was whipping from side to side in its agony – five inches of grey-brown, shiny death. Bond hit it again. It burst open, yellowly.

Bond dropped the shoe and ran for the bathroom and was violently sick.

1 How does Fleming manage to vary the pace and movement of his writing here, while working almost exclusively with simple sentences? (Are they all statements, for instance? Does the subject always come at the beginning of the sentence, or at the same place in the sentence? What other parts of speech does he use to begin sentences? Are there any phrases? If so, how do they help to keep things moving?)

2 There are three compound sentences in the paragraph beginning at line 43 (*At once Bond was on his feet and at the door*) and a further compound sentence closes the extract. Do they all move at the same speed, in the same rhythm?

How does he manage to vary their movement to suit the physical actions they describe?

3 Fleming uses very little punctuation other than full stops. Why do you suppose he placed a comma after *It burst . . .* in line 57?

4 How far do you consider Fleming's style a simple one?

The simple sentence style can of course be over-done by less skilful writers. One literary critic wrote this gentle parody to call Gerald Seymour to task for doing so:

> He writes like old *Daily Express* leaders.
> He likes short sentences.
> Often he uses one sentence paragraphs.
> When his man is in bed with a girl, some of the sentences become longer, sometimes even a bit soppy. But not very soppy.
> He has written an exciting book.

Even writers like Hemingway and Fleming however were forced to use complex sentences at times, simply because they offered a wider range of stylistic effects. These will be illustrated below.

The complex sentence

Traditional textbooks tell us that there are three distinct varieties of complex sentence:

- the **periodic**, in which the independent main clause comes last and is preceded by dependent clauses and phrases;
- the **balanced**, which is made up of two independent main clauses that are closely similar in structure;
- the **loose**, in which the independent main clause comes first and is followed by dependent clauses and phrases.

It is true that sentences answering to these descriptions can be found in English writing. Here are three:

Periodic

'That learning belongs not to the female character, and that the female mind is not capable of a degree of improvement equal to that of the other sex, are narrow and unphilosophical prejudices.'

Balanced

'All days march towards death; only the last one reaches it.'

Loose

'I was born in the year 1632, in the city of York, of a good family, though not of that country, my father being a foreigner of Bremen, who settled first at Hull; he got a good estate by merchandise, and leaving off his trade, lived afterward at York, from whence he had married my mother, whose relations were named Robinson, a very good family in that country, and from whom I was called Robinson Kreutznaer; but by the usual corruption of words in England, we are now called, nay, we call ourselves, and write our name, Crusoe.'

Talking point Why is the loose sentence a good structure to use to depict a man telling a story in this rambling kind of way?

To say that a writer has used a balanced, loose, or periodic sentence to express an idea, however, is not very useful. What really matters is to see *why* the writer has constructed his sentence in that particular way – in other words, to understand how the structure of a sentence helps in conveying its meaning.

The uses of the periodic sentence

Periodic sentences can emphasize ideas of length or weight or abundance, as in the example below. The abundant minor clauses are used to intensify an impression of luxuriance and ease and beauty, and therefore to bring out more strongly the hint of menace lurking at the end:

> Even in May, when the lilacs frothed into purple, paved the lawns with shadows, steeped the air with scent; when soft leaves lipped one another consolingly, when blackbirds sang, fell in their effortless way from the green height to the green depth, and sang again still, something that haunted the place set the heart fluttering.
>
> Mary Webb, *Gone to Earth*

They can intensify the idea of delay before achievement:

A last swell of snow, the wind gusting hard, threatening to blow us from our perch, and we were on the South Summit.

They may perhaps be used to spring a surprise if a piece of startling information is saved for the sentence end; but perhaps their main purpose is to build up the importance of a subject by giving a long list of all the qualities it has before actually mentioning it by name:

> [At the beginning, to French-Norman blood was added Scots-Irish blood.] And when you add to these the Indian strain supplying the mystery, and the Jewish strain supplying spectacular showmanship, and you overlay all this with his circumstances, social conditioning, and religious upbringing . . . you have the enigma that was Elvis.

The uses of the balanced sentence

Balanced sentences are also of rather limited use, though very effective in creating effects of contrast:

Children begin by loving their parents; after a time they judge them; rarely, if ever, do they forgive them.
The country is so lovely; the man-made England is so vile.

In balanced sentences such as these the nouns, the adjectives, and the verbs all match each other in form and contrast with each other in ideas. Such sentences have an air of incontrovertible authority, of giving the last word to be said on a subject. This is achieved partly by the symmetrical balance and neatness of the structure, partly by the reflective pause introduced by the intermediate semi-colon, and partly by the falling intonation in the final clause.

The last example is typical of balanced sentences with contrasting ideas, the structure of the second clause being a mirror image of the structure of the first:

Subject noun	**Verb**	**Adjective**
The country	is	so lovely;
the man-made England	is	so vile.

Because the two clauses are so similar in construction and so close together, the contrast between their ideas reveals itself more strikingly.

The uses of the loose sentence

The loose sentence has an enormously wide range, from the bland through the lively to the pleasantly balanced and the rhythmically beautiful. Consider this fast-moving passage from James Agee's *A Death in the Family*:

> They walked downtown in the light of mother-of-pearl, to the Majestic, and found their way to seats by the light of the screen, in the exhilarating smell of stale tobacco, rank sweat, and dirty drawers, while the piano played fast music and galloping horses raised a grandiose flag of dust.

The opening sentence of Jane Austen's *Pride and Prejudice* is more dignified and controlled:

It is a truth universally acknowledged that a single man in possession of a fortune must be in need of a wife.

Turn this into a periodic sentence and its elegant balance and rhythm would be lost:

That a single man in possession of a large fortune must be in need of a wife is a truth universally acknowledged.

So would the air of clinching finality that comes from the falling intonation on 'must be in need of a wife.' In one of the most famous examples of the loose sentence in English, Gibbon creates a mood of gentle melancholy and nostalgia – for his own, as well as Rome's, vanished past:

> It was at Rome, on the 15th of October 1764, as I sat musing amidst the ruins of the Capitol, while the bare-foot friars were singing Vespers in the Temple of Jupiter, that the idea of writing the decline and fall of the city first started to my mind.

Read sensitively, this sentence moves downwards in a series of descending steps, clause by clause, to a final falling intonation on *first started to my mind*. Rearrange the clauses in any other way and the graceful rhythm and falling intonation would be lost:

> It was at Rome, on the 15th of October 1764, that the idea of writing the decline and fall of the city first started to my mind, as I sat musing amidst the ruins of the Capitol, while the bare-foot friars were singing Vespers in the Temple of Jupiter.

The following sentence by Conrad is different again. It also has superb rhythm and sensuous appeal, but this time what is evoked is physical – the last moments of a sinking ship:

> The scuppers of the brig gurgled softly all together when the waters rising against her sides subsided sleepily with a slow wash, as if playing about an immovable rock.

It makes us feel in its rise and fall the rise and fall of the waves; it echoes in the softness of its repeated *s* sounds (*subsided sleepily with a slow wash*) what Auden called the 'swaying sound of the sea'.

Between these two extremes there are all kinds of loose sentences that make no special appeal yet please us with their elegance and clarity.

Evelyn Waugh is a master of the loose sentence, using it to create a series of visual images that unroll in the mind like scenes from a film:

> It is thus I like to remember Sebastian, as he was that summer, when we wandered alone together through that enchanted palace; Sebastian in his wheelchair spinning down the box-edged walks of the kitchen gardens in search of alpine strawberries and warm figs, propelling himself through the succession of hothouses, from scent to scent and climate to climate, to cut the muscat grapes and choose orchids for our buttonholes; Sebastian hobbling with a pantomime of difficulty to the old nurseries, sitting beside me on the threadbare, flowered carpet with the toy-cupboard empty about us and Nanny Hawkins stitching complacently in the corner, saying 'You're one as bad as the other; a pair of children the two of you . . . '
>
> The autumnal mood possessed us both as though the riotous exuberance of June had died with the gillyflowers, whose scent at my windows now yielded to the damp leaves, smouldering in a corner of the quad.
>
> Evelyn Waugh, *Brideshead Revisited*

Henry James is another frequent user of this form, piling clause upon clause until his sentence is as long as most writers' paragraphs:

> It was the hour at which ladies should come out for an airing and roll past a hedge of pedestrians, holding their parasols askance. Here, however, Eugenia observed no indications of this custom, the absence of which was more anomalous as there was a charming avenue of remarkably graceful arching elms in the most convenient contiguity to a large, cheerful street, in which, evidently, among the more prosperous members of the bourgeoisie, a great deal of pedestrianism went forward.
>
> Henry James, *The Europeans*

Social manners were what interested James – the good or bad behaviour of people constrained by the conventions of polite society – and both his sentence structure and his old-fashioned and formal diction (choice of words and phrases) are suited to his subject. A phrase like 'a great deal of pedestrianism went forward' is stilted to the point of being comical to readers of the present time (Hemingway would have written 'people were walking' – if he'd bothered to mention it at all), and the long, rolling, carefully controlled clauses help to create a general air of remoteness from the chaos and crises of ordinary life.

The working together of sentences in prose

Whatever they are like individually, however, the sentences we read do not exist separately, in a vacuum. They are designed to work with other sentences that precede and follow them, like notes and phrases in a piece of music. In good writing, short clauses and phrases balance longer ones that alternate in turn with others of medium length. In the same way, clauses or phrases with rising intonations are 'answered' by others with intonations that fall. Sometimes paragraphs of such sentences complement one another, working towards the same end, as in the examples below; sometimes they contrast with one another, creating striking effects of mood and atmosphere. Consider the following examples:

> **A** At once she saw that something strange was happening in the sky. She thought it was clouds, moving and trembling under a nervous agitation, but Pantalaimon whispered: 'The Aurora!' The sight filled the northern sky; the immensity of it was scarcely conceivable. As if from Heaven itself, great curtains of delicate light hung and trembled. Pale green and rose-pink, and as transparent as the most fragile fabric, and at the bottom edge a profound and fiery crimson like the fires of Hell, they swung and shimmered loosely with more grace than the most skilful dancer. Lyra thought she could even hear them: a vast distant whispering swish . . .
>
> And as she gazed, the image of a city seemed to form itself behind the

veils and streams of translucent colour: towers and domes, honey-coloured temples and colonnades, broad boulevards and sunlit parkland.

Philip Pullman, *Northern Lights*, Scholastic Ltd, 1998

B 'Now, what I want is, Facts. Teach these boys and girls nothing but Facts. Facts alone are wanted in life. Plant nothing else, and root out everything else. Stick to Facts, sir!'

The scene was a plain, bare, monotonous vault of a schoolroom, and the speaker's square forefinger emphasised his observations by underscoring ever sentence with a line on the schoolmaster's sleeve. The emphasis was helped by the speaker's square wall of a forehead, which had his eyebrows for its base, while his eyes found commodious cellerage in two dark caves, overshadowed by the wall. The emphasis was helped by the speaker's mouth, which was wide, thin, and hard set. The emphasis was helped by the speaker's voice, which was inflexible, dry, and dictatorial. The emphasis was helped by the speaker's hair, which bristled on the skirts of his bald head, a plantation of firs to keep the wind from its shining surface, all covered with knobs, like the crust of a plum pie, as if the head had scarcely warehouse-room for the hard facts stored inside. The speaker's obstinate carriage, square coat, square legs, square shoulders, – nay, his very neckcloth, trained to take him by the throat with an unaccommodating grasp, like a stubborn fact, as it was, – all helped the emphasis.

Charles Dickens, *Hard Times*

Other things than sentence structure are at work here to give these two passages their force. In Passage A:

- **a** sound and intonation – Pullman uses these to convey the immensity of the universe: note the feeling of expanding space gained from the long *a* sound in *vast* (line 9); the sense of rising through space achieved by the succession of lifting intonations in the phrase *vast distant whispering swish*; the suggestion of the white noise emanating from space in the quiet sibilants of *distant whispering swish*;
- **b** symbolism: the unearthly light of the Aurora signifying the existence of another world beyond the one we know.

In Passage B:

- **a** repetition of key words like *square*, *facts*, and *emphasis* to convey the emphatic, dogmatic quality of the expression of the speaker, Gradgrind;
- **b** imagery such as walls, caves, and pie crusts, indicative of things impenetrable, hard and dry;
- **c** sound effects – hard consonants and thin vowels intensify the harsh, unyielding quality of Gradgrind's regimen in words like *dry*, *dictatorial*, *bristled*, *bald*, *knobs*, *crust*, *hard*, *obstinate*, *grasp*, *stubborn*.

Nevertheless, the majority of clauses and phrases in A work towards creating a sense of awe and wonder, just as those in B combine to create an opposite mood and atmosphere. In the sixth sentence of A, for example, beginning *Pale green and rose-pink . . .*, a sense of expansion, of lifting and soaring, is achieved by the placing of several phrases before the main clause:

they swung and shimmered loosely . . .
like the fires of Hell,
at the bottom edge a profound and fiery crimson
as transparent as the most fragile fabric,
Pale green and rose-pink,

Notice how the voice rises on the commas at the end of each phrase, carrying us up onto the plateau of the main clause – *they swung and shimmered loosely* – before descending again to the world of external reality:

with more grace
than the most skilful dancer.

In passage B, the repetitive, unimaginative rote-learning favoured by Gradgrind is mimicked by the sentence structure of the passage. Dickens forces us to learn by the same tedious methods as the unfortunate pupils in Gradgrind's school. Not only is every sentence a plain, straightforward statement of hard fact, but four of them share the same main clause, repeated deliberately to drive home the message:

The emphasis was helped by the speaker's square wall of a forehead . . .
The emphasis was helped by the speaker's mouth . . .
The emphasis was helped by the speaker's voice . . .
The emphasis was helped by the speaker's hair . . .

A note on intonation

Falling intonations are very common in English, simply because of its characteristic stress patterns. Nouns, verbs, adjectives, and adverbs containing two syllables always carry the main stress on the first syllable, followed by a lighter stress (or 'off-beat') on the second. Test this for yourself by pronouncing the following words, taken from the Pullman extract above:

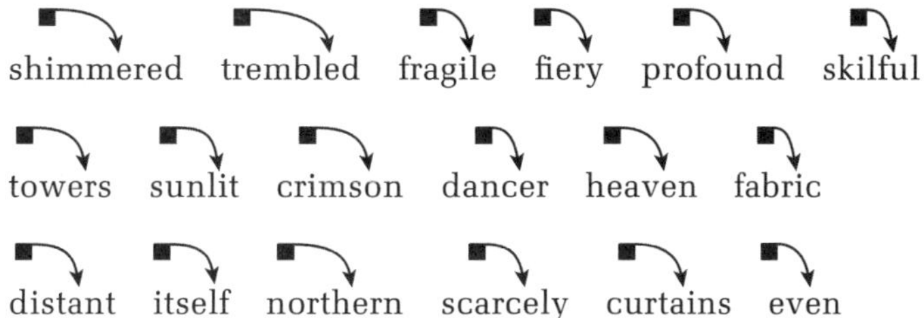

Despite their inbuilt tendency to fall, however, rising intonations can still be created with words like these when

a they are followed by a comma: e.g. *Heaven itself,*

b they are closely linked with a following word or phrase, e.g. *shimmered loosely*; *even hear them*

Monosyllabic words like those in the Dickens extract – *plain*, *bare*, *fact*, *wall*, *wide*, *thin* – on the other hand, have no inbuilt rise and fall, and taken together tend to create an air of flat monotony.

Activity Look at the imagery of the Dickens passage and discuss what it contributes to the overall meaning of the piece.

Stylistic devices

Irony

Key words
Irony: the technique of implying precisely the opposite of what is being said, often in a sarcastic tone (from Greek *eironeia*, simulated ignorance; *eiron*, dissembler).

The word *irony* has three main meanings.

1 It denotes the technique of implying the opposite of what is actually said, e.g. the common use of 'Charming!' as a response to something unpleasant. It is especially effective when the writer pretends to admire and respect someone's behaviour or ideas in order to ridicule them or reveal their vices, e.g. Chaucer's apparently guileless comments on the Wife of Bath:

She was a worthy woman al her lyve.
Husbondes at chirche doore she hadde hadde fyve

where he leaves the tension between the two statements to do the work of casting doubt on her reputation for 'worthiness' or noble behaviour.

2 It reflects some incongruity between what we expect or intend to happen and what actually does occur, or a situation showing such incongruity: e.g. a man who never does anything for his children decides to build a cage for their pet hamster, finishes it to great applause then steps back on to the animal and kills it.

3 It refers to a situation in the theatre in which the audience understands the implications of what is going on better than most of the characters, e.g. Hamlet's calling Polonius a fishmonger: Polonius takes this coded remark as evidence that the prince is mad; the audience understands Hamlet to mean the Polonius is

a a pimp,
b a fisher for secrets.

For our purposes here, the first definition of irony is the important one and we shall concentrate on it.

Dictionaries often confuse irony with sarcasm, or at least make the meanings of the two words overlap to such an extent that it is difficult to tell one from the other. There are similarities between the two, it is true, but there are also differences.

Similarities and differences between sarcasm and irony

1 Both intend to insult, hurt, and ridicule their victims;
2 Both may be uttered or written in a 'sarcastic' tone of voice that makes this intention clear; **but**
3 Irony always works indirectly through pretence, whereas sarcasm (from Greek *sarkazein*, to tear flesh) attacks openly and goes straight for the throat.

Points 1 to 3 can be illustrated on a trivial level.

Scenario: wife and husband wash up and he breaks something:

Sarcasm: 'It's ham-fisted idiots like you that keep John Lewis's profits up. Have you got shares?'

Irony: 'What a deft, light-fingered touch you have, my love. Ever thought of working in a china shop?'

4 Sarcasm works on a lower intellectual level than irony. 'This is stupid – I hate it!' is the gist of its message. It appeals to the emotions rather than the brain, leaving us with negative feelings of anger, dislike and contempt. Irony, in contrast, forces us to think. 'Look at this', the ironist says with tongue in cheek. 'See how good, how fine, how unselfish, how intelligent this is! Don't you love it?' And, because the ideas or behaviour have been exaggerated just enough to bring out their true quality, we realize that

a we do not love it at all;
b we know exactly why we dislike it.

Listening to simulated advocacy or support of things that are bad has clarified our ideas about what is good. We have been pushed into making a moral choice.

Talking point

1 Decide which of the two passages below is an example of irony, which of sarcasm:

A . . . The visitor to London is wonderfully looked after by the benign empire of Sir Charles Forte and need never be out of sight of his modern hotels . . . If he drives out of London he runs still less risk of doing without the uniform standards of Forte. He can stop at a Post House hotel, or at a Little Chef café, in the confidence that the food will always be the same . . . There will be the same kind of steaks – never too tender – the same prawn cocktails, with plenty of lettuce, and the same honest English-style pizzas. And Sir Charles's great system of Portion Control – the secret of so much of his financial success – will ensure that he doesn't eat too much. In at least thirty towns the only hotel is a Forte hotel, which removes any tiresome business of having to choose. What a marvellous change after travelling through France, with all those eccentric little family hotels, where you never know what sort of food will be served, and where it changes from one region to the next!
Anthony Sampson

B . . . Of all the callosities produced in Thatcher's Britain, a majority of our Press has become the most callous . . . Now we are colonized by journalistic muggers with cabbage ears and blocked noses who beat at their typewriters with leaden coshes. Under those indiscriminate blows the keys meld into mere slugs of metal within which there is no decipherable meaning other than hostility. The muggers do not forge words but blunt instruments with which to render those who read insensible, if not permanently brain-damaged. When you actually handle the newspapers for which they commit their acts of aggression, holding them away from you as you might an old sock, you realize that, indeed, time has a warp. Fresh from the presses each issue may be, but it already smells of its near future, the contents of dustbins and the wrapping of fish.
Jill Tweedie

2 Which passage leaves you with a clearer idea of the good qualities that are to be preferred to the ones described?

Irony and style

Irony has different moods for different purposes. When a writer is amused at some minor stupidity, the front he puts on is not a very serious one. The sentence structure is relaxed, the vocabulary is informal, the tone is playful – rhetorical questions may even be asked in a friendly, conversational manner. When writers use irony to attack vice or injustice, however, the style changes to suit the seriousness of the mood. If the technique is to work, we must be lured into believing that the writer means every word of the case that is put forward. Only if we think it is serious will we feel moral indignation and choose to oppose it. The writer, in other words, must pretend to be in love with evil in order to shock us out of indifference and make us choose good. If the tone is too 'knowing', the attitude too relaxed, and the register not quite appropriate, the reader will know and the game will be up.

Activity

Read extracts A to C, then write responses to the following questions:

1 Explain what each writer is attacking.
2 Describe the tone or emotional atmosphere of each passage.
3 Choose
  a the least effective,
  b the most effective
  of these passage of irony. Discuss the qualities of each that led you to make your choice.

A **Dear thingy . . .**
A new and perhaps insurmountable problem now crops up in writing to a commercial firm. The standard form used to be 'Dear Sirs', on the chauvinist assumption (usually correct) that all those in charge would be men. But if that assumption is invalid (or is deemed on liberationist grounds to be invalid) how should the letter begin? 'Dear Sirs or Madams' is obviously inadequate because there might be several sirs and only one madam or several madams and only

one sir. Moreover, it might prove that the madams, if any, were senior to the sirs, in which case 'Dear Madams or Sirs' would be more accurate, though still begging the question of the number of sirs and madams involved. In an extreme case, the top person might be a madam, her immediate deputies sirs, and the third rank another set of madams, so that the appropriate form would have to be 'Dear Madams, Sirs, and other Madams'. Such a form could not be used however unless the hierarchy of the firm were known in intimate detail and it is precisely in cases where the hierarchy is not known that the person wishing to engage in correspondence is at a loss. 'Dear Sirs, including Madams' would raise again the sensitive issue of whether the term 'man' includes both sexes, and if the letter came into the hands of one who felt deeply on this question the reply could well be taken up with a procedural rebuke instead of dealing with the subject of the correspondence. Most letter writers would bridle at the form 'Dear Persons', for to address a member of either sex simply as 'Person' is manifestly less polite than to use the appropriate title (if only one knew what it was). After rejecting frivolous alternatives we have concluded that the correct way of starting a letter to a group of people whose sexual composition is not known is 'Dear Sir or Sirs, Madam or Madams; Madam or Madams, Sir or Sirs'. This can, however, be nothing more than an interim solution, and a highly objectionable one at that, because it puts the sirs before the madams in the opening words, thus perpetuating the assumption of seniority of man over woman which it sets out to avoid. A logician might have to have recourse to the form 'Dear Member or Members of the class of persons designated, if male, by the title Sir and if female by the title Madam'.

But it is doubtful whether the average managing director, let alone his or her secretary, when he or she types the letter, is ready for that yet.

Third leader, *The Guardian*, 16 September 1980

B Jason Prong meets the objectives

Having read *English from 5 to 16*, I wondered how one of my fifth year pupils, Jason Prong, measured up to expectations.

Jason's clenched, tattooed fists demonstrate his mastery of both the abstract noun and antithesis: 'love' on his right knuckles, 'hate' on his left.

On his denim jacket messages show his liking of brevity: he uses both a subject and a predicate in 'Sid Lives', while in his local bus shelter he has scrawled his favourite metaphor: 'Carole is a cow'. The alliteration appeals to him, you see.

When he roams the playground, free after a restless morning trapped at a small desk in a dusty classroom, where he has grappled with a faded blue worksheet which obliged him to fill in gaps in a close procedure exercise, he demonstrates his ability to 'give instructions or orders to someone else'. 'Tell Jonesy that I'm off school, or I'll knack yer.' In influencing a weaker member of his class he has 'chosen an appropriate register'.

He is also 'sensitive to the language limitations of others', kneeing the unfortunate boy in the groin in case he did not understand the verbal threat.

Jason uses 'the resources of the voice expressively'. He leads a raucous chorus of 'Here we go, Here we go, Here we go' as the fifth formers charge into the desk-filled hall for the CSE mockery exams.

When Jason goes to St James's Park he demonstrates 'a range of uses of English'. In the queue outside the ground he 'uses language to speculate' on the outcome of the match: 'Do you think we'll hammer them like we did last year?' He then makes a 'polite request' to the police officer above him. 'Can yer get yer horse's hoof off me Dr Martin's, I've only just bought them?' To the gateman he gives precise information: 'Two please, and that's a fiver I've given you.' Once inside the ground he shows 'a control of emphasis, pause and repetition'. He begins with the effectively repetitious:

'Haway the Lads
Haway the Lads',

while his emphasis in:

'We hate Nottingham Forest,
We hate Liverpool too
We hate Man United
But Newcastle we love you'

is impeccable, bringing out the subtle assonance in 'Not', 'For' and 'pool', 'too'. It is also apparent that his 'accent is intelligible' to the 28,000 listeners in the crowd. Moreover, he is 'sensitive to the non-verbal accompaniments of speech', hoisting 'V' signs and making threatening gestures to the opposition supporters caged in the Leazes End.

When he returns to school on Monday, Jason will 'describe clearly the experiences he has undergone'.

'After the match we chased these Chelsea supporters to the Central Station. There was this kid who fell down in a back lane and about twenty people kicked him in . . .'

As far as reading is concerned, I was surprised to learn that he had 'read whole books of some length requiring some persistence'. He is into both fiction and non-fiction. He has read *Skinhead, I Stamp on Your Face, Nazi War Crimes* and *A History of Motorbikes*. Nor can you pull the wool over his eyes when it comes to distinguishing between 'explicit and implicit meanings'. He much prefers the explicit sexual details of *Rape of the Dusky Virgin* to the implied sexuality of the Mills and Boon book he flicked through in Carole's house while waiting for her to dry her hair.

Writing is not his favourite pastime, but he still meets most of the HMI's objectives. He 'explains processes clearly' in his weekly journal. He tells you precisely how to gut a rabbit or a pigeon and how to break into a house silently. He also writes 'accurate descriptions of people', being particularly observant about the headmaster's less savoury mannerisms. He does not often 'write imaginatively in verse', but there was one poem about Jews being gassed in a concentration camp, which, though frighteningly insensitive, showed 'awareness of structure and stylistic effects'.

Unfortunately, Jason's success is not total. I tried to help him 'experience literature and drama of high quality not limited to the twentieth century, including Shakespeare'. He did manage to make it to the Theatre Royal to see the matinee performance of *Romeo and Juliet* by the Royal Shakespeare Company. Perhaps it was the attraction of an afternoon out of school that drove him to it. Nevertheless he went. His attention began to wander after thirty lines and he began spitting on some poor souls in the stalls below. He was escorted somewhat noisily from the theatre and spent the afternoon doing some Christmas shoplifting in Northumberland Street.

So Jason Prong has met many of the HMI's demanding objectives. Unfortunately he is leaving school at Easter and refuses to have anything to do with profiles.

John Price

C Are cans constitutionally iffy? Once put, the question is not the sort to be ignored. It is not, to be sure, a poser that occupies us in the normal way of business. It does not weigh heavily as we shave in the mornings. It does not get in the way of the breakfast toast. The Common Market and that squeak in the car demand answers that seem for the moment more insistent. But this is just because our minds are muddied by the dross of material things. Then once in a while there comes a question that hammers at the ramparts of intellectual man. Are *cans* constitutionally iffy? There is one. It is quoted from the philosophical papers of the late Professor Austin reviewed this week on another page.

Second leader, *The Times Educational Supplement*, 15 December 1961

Metaphor and metonymy

Key words

Metaphor: 'Application of name or descriptive term to an object to which it is not literally applicable'. (*Concise Oxford Dictionary*)

The word derives from Greek *meta* 'change', and *phero* 'I bear', and has come to mean a change or transfer of significance from one object to another. A ship, for example, is literally a vessel that sails on the sea; a desert can be thought of as a 'sea' of sand: the camel that travels across this metaphorical ocean as the ship sails across the real one can therefore be called a 'ship of the desert'.

Essentially, metaphor depends upon similarity. However dissimilar the two components of the metaphor may be in other ways (is a ship anything like a camel?), they share some particular property that throws light on the thing being described.

Talking point Discuss the metaphor in the preceding sentence.

Metaphors do not belong exclusively to poets and writers. Ordinary conversation is riddled with them:

I see, light dawns, I've got the picture (I understand);
he broke down (likening the mind to a machine), *her heart melted*;

it left me with a nasty taste in my mouth, he tried to feed me the usual routine but I wouldn't swallow it, it gave food for thought, students shouldn't be spoonfed, she needs some work she can really get her teeth into;
this is a seminal book (it has given birth to many others);
you've painted yourself into a corner, your back's up against the wall, you're on the skids/going to the dogs/down the drain/the tubes;
I'm going to disappear in a minute.

In the sentence that introduced this list, 'riddled' itself is a metaphor (from *to pierce* or *perforate with holes*).

The fact that we use metaphor spontaneously and naturally like this shows us the way in which we mentally organize the world by looking for correspondences and patterns in our experience. In fact, extending the meaning of words by using them metaphorically may be one of the ways in which language developed more sophisticated, abstract concepts: the Arab word for 'justice', for example, apparently derives from another word denoting the even distribution of weight on either side of a camel's back; the Hebrew word for 'sin' derives from a word meaning 'to miss the target'. It is easy to see how the metaphysical meaning might grow naturally out of the physical by metaphorical extension. (See also the extract from Randolph Quirk's *The Use of English* in the section on English vocabulary, pages 93–4.)

All good metaphors seem fresh and vivid when they first enter the language, but their shelf-life is short and they soon pass their sell-by date.

Talking point Discuss the expression of the ideas in the previous sentence.

The more obvious the similarity drawn by the metaphor, the more enthusiastically it will be taken up and used, and the more quickly in consequence it will grow stale and die. Dead metaphors linger on, unrecognizable as images any more, in the guise either of ordinary nouns (*river mouth* for instance), or of clichés (*the iron fist in the velvet glove, the dead hand of the law*). Most of the ones quoted above would also qualify as clichés now, in that they spring into our minds ready-made for use whether we want them to or not.

The greater the leap the imagination has to make between the two things brought together in the metaphor, the stronger that metaphor's chance of outliving its time. It will not grow stale through over-use. It will continue to surprise and amuse and interest because it engages the imaginative power of the mind. For metaphor at its best, therefore, we have to turn to literature.

Metaphor in literature

Metaphor is used in exactly the same way in literature as in common speech: to bring out some point of similarity between things otherwise unlike. The purpose is twofold:

1 to reveal as exactly as possible what the thing described is like;
2 to please readers with originality, wit, and strength of style.

The difference between the literary and common use of metaphor lies in the degree of dissimilarity between the two objects involved.

Marvell's 'vegetable love' in *To His Coy Mistress*, and Donne's paired lovers, seen as the twin legs of a pair of compasses in *A Valediction, Forbidding Mourning*, work so well precisely because the thread of thought connecting them is so tenuous. We have to stretch our minds to follow where the poet's imagination leads. We are surprised and amused and delighted by his audacity and wit.

Consider for example the metaphor in the following verse:

> . . . wind wielded
> Blade-light, luminous black and emerald,
> Flexing like the lens of a mad eye.

Properties that belong to one thing – the sharpness and gleam of a knife blade, say – remind the poet of something similar in another – the quality of the light on a stormy day, perhaps, when light flashes out from behind wind-driven clouds – and the two are brought together in the metaphor *blade-light*.

Metaphors are more condensed and allusive than similes, as these lines show. Both are based on similarity, but while similes signal that a comparison is being made by using *as* and *like*, metaphors give us the thing direct and leave us to work out the connections for ourselves. In this respect, the metaphor is a stronger, more concentrated version of the simile. A simile would say that the light was as clear and sharp as the blade of a knife; the metaphor calls it *blade-light*.

Metaphors of a similarly condensed nature are found in the first verse of the poem from which the blade metaphor was taken – *Wind*, by Ted Hughes:

> This house has been far out at sea all night,
> The woods crashing through darkness, the booming hills,
> Winds stampeding the fields under the window
> Floundering black astride and blinding wet . . .

The first metaphor turns landscape into seascape: the house and woods are vessels helplessly adrift, the hills are booming waves. The second turns the fields into panic-stricken cattle stampeded by the wind, itself a rider on some cosmic range. But we have to work to see the qualities that these disparate things have in common. Metaphor often demands closer reading and more imaginative input than the simile.

Talking point Discuss the quality of the metaphors in the following lines:

A Cows are going home in the lane there, looping the hedges with their warm wreaths of breath –
A dark river of blood, many boulders,
Balancing unspilled milk.

B There is the laburnum, its blond colonnades,
And the petticoats of the cherry.

C Over us the planes build
The shifting rafters
Of that new world
We have sworn by.

D . . . the departed lodger, innocence.

Sometimes poets work out the similarity between two apparently dissimilar things in greater detail, carrying the comparison on through several verses or even throughout the whole poem. Hughes uses extended metaphor in this way in *Thought-Fox*:

I imagine this midnight moment's forest:
Something else is alive
Beside the clock's loneliness
And this blank page where my fingers move.

Through the window I see no star:
Something more near
Though deeper within darkness
Is entering the loneliness:

Cold, delicately as the dark snow,
A fox's nose touches twig, leaf;
Two eyes serve a movement, that now
And again now, and now, and now

Sets neat prints into the snow
Between trees, and warily a lame
Shadow lags by stump and in hollow
Of a body that is bold to come

Across clearings, an eye,
A widening deepening greenness,
Brilliantly, concentratedly,
Coming about its own business

Till, with a sudden sharp hot stink of fox
It enters the dark hole of the head.
The window is starless still; the clock ticks,
The page is printed.

Metonymy

 **Key words**

Metonymy: 'Substitution of the name of an attribute or adjunct for that of the thing meant' (*Concise Oxford Dictionary*)
e.g. *bottle* for *alcohol*;
From Greek *meta* indicating 'change', and *onoma*, 'name'.
Metaphor is based on similarity, metonymy on contiguity (from Latin *contingere*, to touch).

Metaphor makes imaginative leaps to connect things that are physically dissimilar. Metonymy uses the name of one physical thing – the Crown or the White House, say – to refer to another entity of which it is a part, or to which it is closely related – the Queen or the President. Like metaphor, metonymy is also part of everyday speech. 'Do you like Shakespeare?' we say (meaning his plays). 'She's in insurance' (meaning the profession). 'The steak is ready for table number four'; 'I'd love a jar' (glass of beer); 'Hollywood is finished'; 'I can always recognize a Bonnard' (meaning the style of the painter); 'Would you take the Chair at the next meeting?'

Metonymy overlaps with **synecdoche** – a term derived from the Greek 'understand along with'. This is the technique of using the name of the part for the whole – 'She's not just a pretty face'; 'Who's the suit?' (formally dressed man); 'That's a nice set of wheels' (car); 'Don't stick your nose in here'. Alternatively, it can use the name of the whole to signify the part(s): 'England did well to beat New Zealand' (for the cricket or rugby teams); 'The Croatians are short of bread as well as weapons' (where *bread* equals food in general). It is often difficult to sort out whether metonymy or synecdoche is being used in expressions like 'Hollywood is finished' and 'Wall Street closed early today': is Hollywood the part here, being used to refer to the film industry as a whole – directors, actors, technicians, and so on – in which case it's synecdoche, or is it a case of one attribute or entity – the physical region called Hollywood – being used to refer to another – the film industry – that is related to it (metonymy)? The sensible solution would seem to be to subsume synecdoche under the umbrella of metonymy and not to worry about the difference.

Talking point Discuss which of the following are metaphors, which examples of metonymy:

The Smoke The Great Wen	terms used to describe the city of London in the eighteenth century (a wen was a kind of cyst)
smokes coffin-nails cancer-sticks the pernicious weed	terms used to describe cigarettes

Activity 1 Read the following extract from *Nice Work*, by David Lodge. (Robyn Penrose, a lecturer at Rummidge University, is talking to Vic Wilcox, Managing Director of J. Pringle and Sons Casting and General Engineering. She has been assigned to 'shadow' him as the University's contribution to Industry Year.)

'One of the fundamental tools of semiotics is the distinction between metaphor and metonymy. D'you want me to explain it to you?'

'It'll pass the time,' he said.

'Metaphor is a figure of speech based on similarity, whereas metonymy is contiguity. In metaphor you substitute something *like* the thing you mean for the thing itself, whereas in metonymy you substitute some attribute or cause or effect of the thing for the thing itself.'

'I don't understand a word you're saying.'

'Well, take one of your moulds. The bottom bit is called the drag because it's dragged across the floor and the top bit is called the cope because it covers the bottom bit.'

'I told *you* that.'

'Yes, I know. What you didn't tell me was that "drag" is a metonymy and "cope" is a metaphor.'

Vic grunted. 'What difference does it make?'

'It's just a question of understanding how language works. I thought you were interested in how things work.'

'I don't see what it's got to do with cigarettes.'

'In the case of the Silk Cut poster, the picture signifies the female body metaphorically: the slit in the silk is *like* a vagina –'

Vic flinched at the word. 'So you say.'

'All holes, hollow spaces, fissures and folds represent the female genitals.'

'Prove it.'

'Freud proved it, by his successful analysis of dreams,' said Robyn. 'But the Marlboro ads don't use any metaphors. That's probably why you smoke them, actually.'

'What d'you mean?' he said suspiciously.

'You don't have any sympathy with the metaphorical way of looking at things. A cigarette is a cigarette as far as you're concerned.'

'Right.'

'The Marlboro ad doesn't disturb that naïve faith in the stability of the signified. It establishes a metonymic connection – completely spurious of course, but realistically plausible – between smoking that particular brand and the healthy, heroic, outdoor life of the cowboy. Buy the cigarette and you buy the life-style, or the fantasy of living it.'

'Rubbish!' said Wilcox. 'I hate the country and the open air. I'm scared to go into a field with a cow in it.'

'Well then, maybe it's the solitariness of the cowboy in the ads that appeals to you. Self-reliant, independent, very macho.'

'I've never heard such a lot of balls in all my life,' said Vic Wilcox, which was strong language coming from him.

'Balls – now that's an interesting expression . . .' Robyn mused.

'Oh no!' he groaned.

'When you say a man "has balls", approvingly, it's a metonymy, whereas if you say something is a "lot of balls", or "a balls-up", it's a sort of metaphor. The metonymy attributes value to the testicles whereas the metaphor uses them to degrade something else.'

'I can't take any more of this,' said Vic. 'D'you mind if I smoke? Just a plain, ordinary cigarette?'

'If I can have Radio Three on,' said Robyn.

2 How does this discussion of metaphor and metonymy bring out the difference between

a Robyn and Vic's characteristic ways of thinking,

b the essential nature of the different kinds of work they do?

4 Language Development

Historical change in language use

At the beginning of Modern English, generally put at around 1500, language was still in a state of flux. The standardization of spelling had not got very far, the only guide being the practice of the clerks employed on government business in the Westminster Chancery – an early branch of the Civil Service – from 1150 onwards. As Freeborn illustrates (*From Old English to Standard English*, Macmillan), their preferred spellings are the ones we know today.

Preferred Chancery spellings	Other spellings less frequently used
such(e)	sich, sych, seche, swich, sweche
much(e)	moch(e), mych(e)
which(e), whych(e)	wich, wech
not/noght	nat
many	meny
any	eny, ony
but	bot
and	ond, ant
if/yf	yif, yef

Since Freeborn also records 17 spellings of *poor*, 21 of *people*, and 46 of *receive* that were current at the time, the need for guidance is clear. Spoken English of course had no such stabilizing influence: everyone spoke with the accent and dialect of their own locality (Sir Walter Raleigh shocked some people by doing so even at Court, a century later).

The fifteenth century

The first exponent of printing in England, William Caxton, was driven by the need to do something about both these problems, which he outlines below.

Caxton on the diversity of English, 1490

And also my lorde abbot of westmynster ded do shewe to me late, certayn euydences wryton on olde englysshe, for to reduce it in-to our englysshe now vsid / And certaynly it was wreton is suche wyse that it was more lyke to dutche than englysshe; I coude not reduce ne brynge it to be vnderstonden / And certaynly our langage now vsed varyeth ferre from that whiche was vsed and spoken when I was borne / For we englysshe men / ben borne vnder the domynacyon of the mone, whiche is neuer stedfaste / but euer wauerynge / wexynge one season / and waneth and dyscreaseth another season / And that comyn englysshe that is spoken in one shyre varyeth from a nother. In so moche that in my dayes happened that certayn marchauntes were in a shippe in tamsyse (*the river Thames*), for to haue sayled ouer the see into zelande (*Holland*) / and for lacke of wynde, thei taryed atte forlond (*Foreland*), and wente to lande for to refreshe them; And one of theym named sheffelde (*Sheffield*), a mercer, cam in-to an hows and exed for mete (*food*); and specyally he axed after eggys; And the goode wyf answerde, that she coude speke no frenshe. And the marchaunt was angry, for he also coude speke no frenshe, but wolde haue hadde egges / and she vnderstode hym not / And thenne at laste a nother sayd that he wolde haue eyren / then the good wyf sayd that she vnderstod hym wel / Loo, what sholde a man in thyse dayes now wryte, egges or eyren / certaynly it is harde to playse euery man / by cause of dyuersite & chaunge of langage .... but in my Iudgemente / the comyn termes that be dayli vsed, ben lyghter (*easier*) to be vnderstonde than the olde and auncyent englysshe /

Freeborn, *From Old English to Standard English*

Points to notice

Spelling

Note how Caxton's spelling varies within the same piece, even though he was influenced to some degree by Chancery practice – one reason why printing did not succeed in standardizing English spelling for some time.

- *v* and *u* were interchangeable at this time, and could be used either as consonant or vowel; *v* initially and *u* elsewhere gradually became the practice.
- *i* and *y* were also interchangeable, although *y* was preferred next to minims like *m* and *n*, for clarity's sake; *y* was also used for the *j* sound at the beginning of words like *yow* and *your.*
- The *e* at the end of words like *olde, mone, lande*, and *wynde* is a redundant inflection left over from Middle English. Since it was no longer pronounced, as it was in Chaucer's day, people weren't sure whether to use it or not, and it gradually faded away. When it came before *s* in plural endings it added to the confusion by being spelled in a variety of different ways: e.g. *goodes, goodis, goodus, goodys.*

Grammar

Note how Caxton uses the strike or virgule, what we would call a *slash* – it did duty for later punctuation marks like the comma and full-stop.

Caxton uses the old Middle English third-person singular inflection of the verb,

> *-(e)th*, e.g. the *mone waneth*, line 8. This was already beginning to be phased out and replaced by the *-es* ending we use today, but *doth* persisted for many more years, and *hath* even longer.

Extract from a Letter from John Paston to his Mother Margaret c1483

And modyr, it pleasyd yow to haue serteyn woords to my wyff at hyr depertyng towchyng your remembraunce of the shortness that ye thynk your dayes of, and also of the mynd that ye have towardys my brethryn and systyr, your chyldyr, and also of your seruauntys, wherein ye wyllyd hyr to be a meane to me that I wold tendyr and favore the same. Modyr, savying your pleasure, ther nedyth non enbasatours nor meanys betwyx yow and me; for ther is neyther wyff nor other frend shall make me to do that that your commandment shall make me to do, if I may have knowlage of it . . . And well remembred, I wot well ye ought not to haue me in jelusye for on thyng nor other that ye wold haue me to accomplyshe if I overleve (outlive) yow, for I wot well non oo (one) man alyve hathe callyd so oft upon yow as I to make your wylle and put iche thyng in serteynte that ye wold have don for your sylff and to your chyldre and seruauntes . . .

Martyn Wakelin, *The Archaeology of English*, Batsford, 1988

Points to notice

Spelling

Paston uses *u* and *v* and *i* and *y* interchangeably as Caxton does, with the same pattern of *v* initially and *u* elsewhere. Spelling as a whole shows less of the Chancery influence, however, probably because the Pastons were Norfolk land-owners without much exposure to London influence.

- Note the *y* where Chancery clerks would have written *e* in the endings of many words: e.g. *seruauntys*.
- The spelling of *modyr* comes direct from O.E. *modor*. The *th* was not substituted for the *d* until the early 1500s.
- *non* (line 11) derives from O.E. *nan*, and is frequently used at this period for *no* or *not*.
- *oo* is derived from the O.E. *an*, meaning *one*. One was also spelled *on* at this time, making it readily confused with the preposition *on*.

Grammar

As a respectful son, Paston uses the polite second-person singular pronouns *ye*, *yow* and *your* when addressing his mother. *Thee*, *thou* and *thy* were the terms to use when you were addressing an intimate or an inferior, followed by the verb ending *-(e)st*; Hamlet, for instance, addresses both Horatio and the gravedigger in these terms:

> If thou didst ever hold me in thy heart,
> Absent thee from felicity awhile,
> And in this harsh world draw thy breath in pain,
> To tell my story . . .
>
> How long hast thou been grave-maker?

or when you wanted to express contempt:

Thou wretched, rash, intruding fool, farewell!

Talking point French still retains the ability to signal close and distant relationships through its *tu* and *vous* pronouns.
Is English the poorer for having only the general-purpose *you*?

Although the form of most nouns was fixed by this period, some older forms persist and survive with modified spellings today. Children and brethren (*Chyldyr* and *brethryn)* are the main examples, along with *geese*, *mice* and *swine*.

Paston also uses the old form of the third-person singular: *nedyth*, line 6.

Vocabulary

Paston's letter shows the lasting influence of the French language on English: *depertyng, embasatours* and *serteynte* are all direct borrowings. He also uses archaic words like *betwyx* and *wot*, used these days only in quaint or deliberately humorous contexts.

The sixteenth and seventeenth centuries

By the end of the sixteenth century spelling and syntax had become largely stabilized.

Older forms lingered on – the *-est* and *-eth* endings; *thee* and *thou*; irregular verb forms like *chode* for *chided, bote* for *bit, stale* for *stole, spake* for *spoke, brake* for *broke*, for instance – but they were gradually dying out, and being replaced by the forms we know today. The following letter from George Bassett to his parents in 1539 has a much more modern look than John Paston's, if one ignores the use of the *long s* (ʃ):

Ryht honorable and my moʃt dere and ʃingler goode lorde and ladye / in my moʃt humble manner I recomaunde me unto yow beʃechynge to have yor dailye bleʃʃinge / and to here of yor goode and proʃprus helth / fore the conʃervatione of whiche / I praye dailye unto almyghty godde. I certifye youe by theys my rude lettres that my Maiʃter and my Ladye be in goode helthe / to whome I am myche bounde. ffurthermore I beʃeche yor lordeʃhipe and ladiʃhipe to have me hertilye recomedyde unto my Brother and Syʃters . . .

(adapted from Freeborn, *From Old English to Standard English*, Macmillan, 1992)

Probably because George was only 14 at the time, his syntax is simple and straightforward and much like ours, apart from the placing of the relative *to whom*, which modern writers would put directly after 'Maiſter and my Ladye'. In other texts of this period the connections between clauses are far from plain, as in the example below:

> **Sir Francis Bryan to Lord Lisle, 11 May 1534**
>
> My good lord, in my most heartiest wise I commend me unto you, and so desire you that I may be to my good lady your bedfellow. And where your servant is here, attending in the Court in divers your business, in those and all other wherein I may do you pleasure ye shall be as well assured of me as of your next friend. And as concerning the King's coming to Calais, this day the King told me in my ear that it should be before August next. Wherefore for making of your provisions ye may do as ye shall think good therein. I have not at this time any other writings worth writing. And for the said time of the King's coming, I would not upon this my writing ye should take this for a precise knowledge, whereby ye might take hindrance in your provisions, for ye know the minds of princes sometimes change and times appointed deferred . . .
>
> *The Lisle Letters*, ed. Muriel St Clare Byrne, Secker & Warburg, 1983

And where your servant is here (lines 2–3) starts a construction that is not completed by anything in the rest of the sentence; the object comes before the verb in the sentence beginning *Wherefore* (line 7); and the order of the sentence beginning *And for the said time* is impossible to resolve for modern readers.

Points to notice

16th century grammar	Modern grammar
wherein	in which
in divers your business	in various business of yours
as concerning	concerning
wherefore	for which reason, therefore
and for	and as for
I would not . . . ye should	I would not wish you to

Would was still a verb in its own right at this period, meaning *to wish* or *desire*: see Falstaff's words to Hal in *Henry IV Part 1*: '[I] Would it were bedtime, Hal, and all well.'

But if the language itself was gradually becoming stable, pronunciation (unfortunately) was not. At the very time when printing was pinning spelling down for good, the sounds it represented began to change. We do not know why the Great Vowel Shift began, but its consequences have made learning to spell a nightmare for generations of English schoolchildren. Martyn Wakelin outlines the problem:

To name just one or two important sound-changes, during this period the Present English Standard English vowel sound in *some, butter*, etc. (/ʌ/) developed from M.E. /u/ and spread from the East Midlands thoughout the south (but not to the north and Midlands); M.E. short *a* /a/ in words like *grass, chaff* and *path* was lengthened to /a:/ in Standard English (with variants in the dialects); /r/ began to fade out before consonants and at the ends of words (e.g. in *cart* and *pear*); M.E. ȝ /gh/ also ceased to be pronounced (as in *bough, daughter, light, weight*) or became /f/ (*laugh, cough*); after /w/, /a/ became /ɔ/ (*what, was, wash*, etc.).

Spelling never caught up with these changes in pronunciation, so that, e.g., the 'new' sound in *brown* still has a medieval spelling, and so do *what, was* and *wash*; and – more noticeably – the *bough, laugh* group still have the medieval spelling indicative of earlier /x/.

Once spelling and syntax were stabilized, educated men turned their attention to the expressive qualities of their language. Debate about acceptable usage raged, centring mainly on the Latin and other foreign terms that were flooding into the language at this period. Then, as now, there were people who used Latin words to impress others, rather than express an idea. Thomas Wilson pins them down in his 'Arte of Rhetorique', 1553, quoted in *The History of the English Language*, David Burnley, Longman, 1992:

The unlearned or foolishe phantasticall, that smelles but of learning . . .will so latine their tongues, that the simple cannot but wonder at their talke, and thynke surely thei speake by some Revelacion . . .

Some seke so farre for outlandishe Englishe, that thei forget altogether their mothers language.

Points to notice

Spelling

Unstressed final e persists: e.g. *latine, talke, foolishe*; and spelling is still somewhat idiosyncratic: e.g. *seke, farre, thei.*

Paston's *modyr* has changed into the modern form *mother.*

Grammar

The modern rule for the possessive marker is not yet established, for although *mothers* has dropped the unstressed *e* inflection of Middle English and is written with an *s*, it lacks an apostrophe.

The third-person singular present tense verb *smelles* has the modern *-es* ending rather than the older *-eth. But* has the meaning *only* at this period: 'only smells of learning', i.e. hasn't much of it; *cannot but* has the force of 'cannot help but'.

Vocabulary

Wilson uses the expression *ynkhorne terme* to denote this affected use of language, because it smacks of the scholar's study rather than of real life. Shakespeare does the same in *Love's Labours Lost*, through the characters of Holofernes the Pedant and Nathaniel:

Nathaniel: I prayse God for you sir, your reasons (phrases) at Dinner have been sharpe and sententious: pleasant without scurillitie, wittie without affection, audatious without impudence, learned without opinion, and strange without heresie: I did converse this day with a companion of the kings, who is intituled, nominated, or called, Don Adriano de Armatho.

Pedant: Nooui hominum tanquam te, His humour is loftie, his discourse peremptorie: his tongue fyled, his eye ambitious, his gate maiesticall, and his generall behauiour vaine, rediculous, and thrasonicall. He is too picked, too spruce, too affected, too od as it were, too peregrinat as I may call it.

Mock as he might, Shakespeare wrote some of his best lines using Latin loan words – could *Absent thee from felicity awhile* be better expressed in purely English terms? – and for the next two centuries at least, Latinate expression was king.

The eighteenth century

The extract from Samuel Johnson's reflections on his *Dictionary*, below, is full of the weighty abstract nouns he favoured. Johnson, you may remember, is the critic who castigated Shakespeare for using the metaphor 'the blanket of the dark' in a tragedy – in Johnson's eyes *blanket* lacked the dignity proper to high poetry.

When we see men grow old and die at a certain time one after another, from century to century, we laugh at the elixir that promises to prolong life to a thousand years; and with equal justice may the lexicographer be derided, who/ being able to produce no example of a nation/ that has preserved their words and phrases from mutability/, shall imagine /that his dictionary can embalm his language/, and secure it from corruption and decay/, that it is in his power to change sublunary nature/, or clear the world at once/ from folly, vanity, and affectation.

The Preface to Johnson's *Dictionary*, quoted in *The History of the English Language*, David Burnley

Points to notice

Johnson's style has several characteristic features.

- The use of weighty abstract nouns, conveying the impression of learned authority: e.g. *mutability* for *change*.
- The use of single verbs where modern writers might use phrasal verbs, i.e. expressions which consist of more than just the verb itself. *Prolong life* might have been replaced by *make life last*; *derided* by *laughed at*; *preserved* by *kept safe*.
- The use of lengthy sentences with embedded clauses and phrases. Johnson could have used a full-stop after *a thousand years* (line 3), since the semi-colon marks the end of a periodic sentence. Instead, he opts for another main clause, *may the lexicographer be derided*, on to which he strings a further eight clauses and phrases (*who shall imagine* is one clause, interrupted by the phrase *being able to produce no example of a nation . . .*).
- The use of the passive voice: *may the lexicographer be derided*, instead of the active, *may we deride the lexicographer*.

The heaviness of the style makes it difficult for readers used to the lightness and flexibility of modern prose.

Non-literary language, fortunately, was more simple. The expression in this article from the *Daily Post* of 1741 will be familiar to modern readers, as will the behaviour described. The English, it seems, do not alter much.

> On Wednesday there was a sharp Engagement between a Preſs Gang and a Mobb, near the May-pole in St Olave's, Southwark, where a Lieutenant, going into a Publick Houſe to search for skulking Seamen was opposed and inſulted by the Company that were drinking there; at which his Men being exasperated began to exercise their Oaken Towels, and laid about them very briskly: The People in return had recourſe to Paring shovels, Broomsticks, Pokers, Tongs, or any thing they could lay hold of. In a Word, the Battle was preſently general, and very bloody; here lay a Taylor, and there a Sailor, and ſo on; and Victory was a long time doubtful, 'till at length ſhe inclined to the Jack Tars side, who drove the Enemy from the Field of Battle, and carried off five Priſoners, ſorely wounded, on board their Tender. In the Heat of the Action the Landlord of the Houſe where it began, 'tis said, receiv'd no leſs than 15 wounds; and on the other Side, one of the Tars had a large Shovel full of burning Coals thrown into his boſem, the Torture whereof drove him into the Street, ſtorming and ſtamping like a Madman . . .

Activity Comment on anything you find interesting in the spelling, phonology, or syntax of this article.

Since the eighteenth century, writing has become generally lighter and more flexible. Vocabulary, except in the swiftly expanding area of specialisms, has become less ponderous; sentences are generally shorter and their punctuation less fussy and obtrusive. There are exceptions to every rule, of course, as certain Victorian writers can show.

The Victorian era

The Victorian era is famous for snobbery, pomposity and hypocrisy. Literary writers were forbidden to be open in their descriptions of behaviour to the point where, when Dickens wanted to have his characters kiss, he had to make them retire behind a door 'from whence issued osculatory noises'. Such attitudes have a bad effect on the language, as the following passage from *The Times* of 14 July 1837, quoted in *The Times* of 14 July 2000, shows:

The Queen moves to Buckingham Palace
Greatly to the regret of the inhabitants of Kensington, Her Majesty and her illustrious mother, the Duchess of Kent, took their departure from Kensington Palace this afternoon for the purpose of taking up their residence at Buckingham Palace.

Shortly after 1 o'clock an escort of Lancers took up the position on the Palace-green, long previous to which an immense concourse of respectable persons had thronged the avenue and every open space near the Palace, from whence a view of the departure of the august personages from a neighbourhood to which from their active benevolence and estimable virtues they have become so endeared could be obtained.

About half-past 1 o'clock an open landau, drawn by four grey horses, preceded by two outriders, and followed by an open barouche, drawn by four bay horses, the servants in the Royal Livery, arrived from the Queen's-mews at Pimlico, and about 10 minutes afterwards they drew up at the grand entrance to the Duchess of Kent's apartments. The Queen, accompanied by the Duchess of Kent and Baroness Lebzen, almost immediately got into the first carriage, amid the deafening salutations of the numerous crowd, which Her Majesty acknowledged with the greatest kindness and condescension.

Below is a passage of recent reporting on a royal theme, from the same newspaper:

St Paul's Cathedral has hosted many great acts of national commemoration since Queen Anne, prematurely aged and worn down by disappointment and ill-health, struggled up the aisle to celebrate the Duke of Marlborough's victories at Blenheim and Malplaquet. The abiding image from yesterday's service of thanksgiving for the one hundredth birthday of Queen Elizabeth the Queen Mother was altogether different. The trappings of pomp and circumstance were on show – trumpeters in the Whispering gallery, a glistening honour guard standing to attention – but the substance of the occasion could not have been less formal. The hymns were familiar to any parish church and the sentiments expressed applicable to loving families

> the world over. Most important of all, the centre of the fuss radiated the characteristics for which she is famous: spontaneity and happiness.
>
> Editorial, *The Times*, 12 July 2000

Activity Discuss any differences in attitude, tone, and written expression you notice in the articles above.

The spread of Standard English

In the nineteenth century, more children went to school than ever before. The first schools were charitable institutions founded by religious bodies, but the Elementary Education Act of 1870 brought education for all under the control of local authorities. As David Burnley shows in *The History of the English Language*, further social change made the strengthening of standardization inevitable.

> As awareness of a correct form of the written language was promoted by increased literacy, the breakdown of old dialect distributions was hastened by easier communication and the mixing of population. The Industrial Revolution created great new cities – Leeds, Sheffield, Birmingham, Manchester, Glasgow – which developed their own urban dialects from the mixture of immigrants attracted to them . . . The rapid development in public broadcasting after about 1920 led in England and abroad to the establishment of BBC English as a *de facto* spoken standard. This standard, alternatively known as Received Pronunciation, is that of a social and educational elite, originally developed from the manner of speech approved by the nineteenth-century public schools, and concurrently by the universities of Oxford and Cambridge.
>
> . . . [This] . . . ensured that *non*-standard or dialect variants would henceforth by considered *sub*-standard – that is, not simply different, but inferior. The tendency to assess the social status of a speaker from the accidentals of his speech is universal in linguistic history, but becomes oriented in Modern English into an opposition between dialect speech and the use of the standard. Although still current, in very recent times this opposition has been mitigated by a change in political sentiment on the one hand, and by the development of the objective study of language on the other.

Summary

Four major changes affected English in the period between 1500 and the present:

1 the continuing loss of inflections;
2 the standardization of spelling and syntax;

3 the acquisition of thousands of Latin, Greek and other foreign terms, to the great enrichment of the language;
4 a movement towards simplicity, clarity, and flexibility of expression.

Checklist of points for examining language change

Spelling

- the spelling of the same word in different ways in the same text
- interchangeable *u* and *v*, *i* and *y*
- redundant final *e* in singulars
- variant spellings of final *e* in plural endings (*es*, *us*, *is*, *ys*)
- the variant spellings *non* for *no* or *not*; *oo* or *on* for *one*
- abbreviation of *the*, *that* and *them* to *ye*, *yt* and *ym* – these are purely spelling conventions and the words were never pronounced with a *y* sound.

Grammar

- *thou* and *thee* used to signal intimacy, superiority, or contempt
- *ye* used to signal respect
- *ye* preserved for use in high styles of writing, e.g. the Bible, the pronouncements of kings and nobles or their messengers
- irregular forms of verbs whose past tense now takes the regular ending: e.g. *spake* for *spoke*
- interrogatives formed by reversing the subject–verb order, e.g. *Know you that my lady is dead?*; the practice of forming questions with the help of the auxiliary verb *do* came into general use after the fifteenth century
- the marker for possession: early forms have *-es*, as in *kinges, mannes*; since variant spellings often used *y* for *e* in such places, the resulting *kingys, mannys* forms misled people into believing the *ys* to be an abbreviation of the possessive pronoun *his*; some later forms therefore mark possession by placing *his* after the noun, as in *the king his men; the man his house*; later still, *s* is used alone, without an apostrophe, until finally we arrive at modern usage
- constructions like *he is come to town; they are gone to the country* are often found in eighteenth-century texts, but have faded out since then; where earlier writers used the verb *to be* with the past participle of intransitive verbs of motion (*come, gone*), modern writers prefer *to have*: *he has come to town*; *they have gone to the country*
- double negatives, e.g. *I do nobody no harm nor never wolde*
- the use of both *which* and *that* to refer to people, e.g. *Our Father, which art in heaven*
- heavy use of commas; they were placed after each short phrase so that the eye is always being distracted by a stop, e.g. *But where I say, that I would have our Language, after it is duly correct, always to last I do not mean that it should never be enlarged: provided, that no Word which a Society shall give a Sanction to, be afterwards antiquated and exploded, they may have liberty to receive whatever new ones they shall find occasion for*
- the use of capitals for important words, as above, or for emphasis.

Vocabulary

- loan words from French and Latin or Greek, the latter two distinguished by their polysyllabic nature, foreign appearance and often esoteric meaning (*esoteric* is an example)
- archaic words, e.g. *wot* for *know.*

Current trends in language use

Language updates itself all the time and is doing so more quickly now than ever, thanks to the spread of new technologies. Visual media distract us from the written word; advertising bombards us with disjunctive grammar; e-mails threaten the death of spelling and punctuation as we know it; and influenced by media personalities like Jamie Oliver, we are all (even those who live in Glasgow and Newcastle) learning to say *pukka, malarkey, clobber, geezer, sorted, chuffed,* and *over the moon* in the accent known as **estuary English.**

Diction

Words acquire new meanings in several ways:

a by metaphorical extension, as in *window, interface, wet* (noun and adjective)
b by the confusion of shape and sound as in *uninterested/disinterested, prevaricate/procrastinate;*
c in the pursuit of originality, as in *wicked* and *anorak;*
d in the attempt to avoid unpleasant associations with the help of neutral words, as in *lavatory / toilet / bathroom / cloakroom / restroom / comfort station;*
e under the influence of social and political ideologies, as in *liberal.*

Of the above processes, (d) and (e) are the ones most noticeably influencing our lives today, and both are discussed below.

Activity

1. To see how words change their meaning over the course of time, look up the following in the microprint or online edition of the *Oxford English Dictionary*: *sex luxury tedious disgusting nice awful appalling presently let*
2. Discuss the meaning attributed to the phrase *so many horrid ghosts* by **a** a sixteenth-century, **b** a twentieth-century audience.
3. Write an explanation of the movement of thought from the physical to the metaphorical in (a) above.

The cult of political correctness

Political correctness evolved from the desire to protect the feelings of vulnerable individuals and groups. Like most radical cults, it originated in the United States. 'If we change language,' wrote the American poet Betsy Warland, 'we change everything.'

The basic idea was to avoid language that would degrade individuals or groups or discriminate against them on the grounds of race, colour, gender, sexual orientation, and so on. The use of pejorative terms like *nigger* and *Pakki* were outlawed and new terms – *Afro-Caribbeans* and *people of Asian descent* – were brought in in their place. *Mongols* became known as *Down's syndrome children*; *cripples* became *the disabled*, then *people with a disability*; the *mentally retarded* became *people with learning difficulties*. Women's professional status was brought into line with men's (theoretically) by the demand for *women* to replace the patronizing *girls* and by the rejection of the *-ess* suffix in words like *poetess, waitress and manageress*. Derogatory terms like *bimbo* and *tart* were also discouraged as threats to women's dignity, though *babe* seems to have slipped through the net so far, as in *Blair's babes*. On a recent edition of Radio 4's discussion programme *Start the Week*, a male author apologized for using male terms of reference for people in general throughout his book, and the editor of this book made a stand for female equality by requesting a change in the usual wording of part of the wedding ceremony: from *I now pronounce you man and wife* to *I now pronounce you husband and wife*.

So far, so good. The new vocabulary encouraged empathy and understanding among the majority and a new sense of dignity amongst those formerly discriminated against. The best of the new terms were not simply patronizing euphemisms: *Down's syndrome children*, for example, promoted understanding and acceptance by drawing attention away from a set of characteristic physical features to their underlying cause. Using *disabled* instead of *crippled* achieved much the same effect, and few would quarrel with the replacement of the blunt *mentally retarded* with the more empathetic *people with learning difficulties*. The question now is whether political correctness has been pushed to the point where it becomes not only absurd but even sometimes counter-productive, insulting and disadvantaging those whom it set out to protect.

Talking point 'People may laugh at it, but PC has made them much more careful in the way they talk about other people.' Discuss.

Their success in protecting victimized minority groups led PC campaigners to widen the scope of their attack. By harnessing a series of adverbial premodifiers to the past participle *challenged*, they created whole new categories of victims who had never been seen before – or at least, not in that light:

Definite article	**Adverbial premodifier**	**Past participle acting as noun**
The	vertically	challenged
"	horizontally	"
"	follicularly	"
"	chronologically	"

With the help of the suffix *-ism*, PC campaigners attacked society as a whole, accusing it of malevolent attitudes like *sexism, lookism, sizism, speciesism, smellism, rectocentrism, phallocentrism, gradualism, colourism*, and so on.

Activity

1 Give the pre-PC terms for each group of people described above.

2 Explain the meaning of the abstract nouns ending in *-ism* above.

3 Examine the list of words and their preferred PC alternatives below, and assess how far you think each is helpful in the quest for social harmony and understanding. Are there any you would like to see banned? If so, why?

women/*womyn*; manhole cover/*personnel access structure*; always late/*temporally challenged*; manslaughter/*personslaughter*; firemen/*firefighters*; ugly/*cosmetically different*; spendthrift/*negative saver*; idle/*motivationally deficient*; dishonest/*ethically disoriented*; chairman/*chairperson*; spokesman/*spokesperson*; black coffee/*milkless coffee*; stupid/*intellectually challenged*

4 Read the material below, then write an article or letter giving your opinions on political correctness to be published in either a tabloid or broadsheet newspaper. Name the type of paper you have chosen.

An advertisement seeking 'enthusiastic and hardworking employees' left two businessmen facing prosecution for discriminating against the idle.

Jason Pitt and Bill Wood, seeking workers for their Midlands Media publishing operation, were told by Wallsall Job Centre that the advertisement could contravene measures to protect disabled job-seekers. (*The Times*, June 2000)

Today is the start of National Marriage Week, yet, thanks to lack of publicity, few people know it. Ignored by both broadcasting and the press, it arrives and departs each year without a trace.

Why should the media ignore an event with such potentially wide appeal? In many people's eyes, the reason lies in the fashionable cult of political correctness. 'Marriage smacks of tradition and the Establishment, which a lot of broadcasters dislike,' says Richard Kane, director of the charity Marriage Resource. 'As you can see from most soaps, there has been increasing emphasis in recent years on relationships as opposed to marriage, and relationships which are disposable, which you can leave if you get tired of them.'

Just how pernicious such attitudes can be was discovered recently by long-standing Labour supporter and BBC stalwart John Mortimer. When plans for a radio serialization of *Rumpole* were rejected on the grounds of possible offence to feminists, Mortimer was moved to attack. Those who work in the media have the responsibility to reflect opinions of every kind – a responsibility they are currently being denied the chance to discharge.

Princess Michael of Kent is planning a lavish costumed birthday party for her two children in the style of Marie Antoinette, the French Queen who went to the guillotine. Guests will dine alfresco on a hog roast at Kensington Palace's roofless orangerie.

But after a short exchange, the dwarfs are off. Plans for a group of diminutive circus performers to entertain the 500 young guests with juggling and acrobatics have been vetoed by palace officials as politically incorrect . . . The idea of dwarfs had been dropped as 'too insensitive'.

Britain's 25,000-strong community of dwarfs are divided on whether they should have been excluded . . . (*Sunday Times*, 18 June 2000)

Advocate of PC: 'Political correctness is necessary because discrimination exists, and when you dig beneath some of the silliness, there are some serious issues.'

PC advocates also like to legislate on the technical side of language use. Grammar is frowned upon by US extremists as simply 'the arbitrary rules of literary procedure subservient to a sexist political agenda'.

The influence of social and political ideologies

As social and political attitudes change, words change to reflect them. Mary Ann Sieghart shows us the process at work:

It was on a trip to Washington, in the early 1980s, that I first heard the word 'liberal' used as a derogatory term. In Britain, 'liberal' meant tolerant, fair-minded and centrist; you could hardly be too liberal in the same way that you can hardly be too moderate. In Reaganite America, however, it had come to mean 'ultra left-wing' . . .

Has this use of language come to cross the Atlantic? William Hague's new phrase, 'the liberal elite', is hardly intended to be complimentary. If liberalism is no longer to mean belief in the value of individual liberty . . . then it will be a sad day not just for the English language, but for British politics too.

In America, 'liberal' used to carry the same connotations as it still does in Britain . . . The rot seems to have begun in the late 1960s. Research in Lyndon B. Johnson's archives has turned up memos from White House staff urging everyone to avoid the word 'liberal' because it was starting to take on a bad odour.

By the 1980s . . . it was being used as a shorthand for discredited positions on crime, the economy and defence. Now . . . it simply means wrong.

When Americans describe Mr Clinton as a 'closet liberal', you begin to realise what a dirty word it has become . . . Democrats will call themselves progressive, moderate, even populist, anything but the L-word. 'Liberal' has come to mean 'unelectable'.

The Times, 16 June 2000

The increasing trend towards abstraction

Most of us work with ideas now, rather than with our hands. As our lives move increasingly from the physical world towards virtual reality, language grows increasingly abstract in response. Every specialism and every profession today has its own characteristic set of **jargon**, impenetrable to outsiders. For people inside the profession, such words and phrases are an acceptable shorthand. Their meaning can be ascertained because every word can be traced back to a known referent. *Deictic language*, for example, can be hunted back to the use of items like *there, this, you*, or *then.*

When the only referents are concepts enshrined in abstract nouns, however, a writer's meaning may become problematic. What does Sir Nicholas Serota mean exactly when he describes an artist's work (carefully arranged piles of rubbish on a couple of tennis courts) as 'exploring the tension [abstract noun] between order [abstract noun] and chaos [abstract noun]'? What does a report on fox-hunting mean precisely when it claims that 'the experience [of being hunted] seriously compromises the welfare of the fox'? We get a vague idea, but it would be hard to re-express it in simpler terms.

Activity

1. Assess the following passage for clarity of expression.
2. Re-express it as far as possible in your own words.

What is Writing?

We know that a language is a corpus of prescriptions and habits common to all the writers of a period. Which means that a language is a kind of natural ambience wholly pervading the writer's expression, yet without endowing it with form or content: it is, as it were, an abstract circle of truths, outside of which alone the solid residue of an individual *logos* begins to settle. It enfolds the whole of literary creation much as the earth, the sky, and the line where they meet outline a familiar habitat for mankind. It is not so much a stack of materials as a horizon, which implies both a boundary and a perspective; in short, it is the comfortable area of an ordered space. The writer literally takes nothing from it; a language is for him rather a frontier, to overstep which alone might lead to the linguistically supernatural; it is a field of action, the definition of, and hope for, a possibility.

(Roland Barthes, in *Barthes: Selected Writings*, ed. Susan Sontag)

Euphemisms

The use of euphemisms in many circles also encourages the growth of abstract language. Everyone, it seems, is frightened of expressing themselves in plain, staightforward language, presumably because it might commit them to something or lay them open to attack. Thus, as we saw above, those who have to decide on issues like fox-hunting shrink from declaring it to be cruel and pronounce instead that it 'severely compromises the well-being of the fox'. Doctors and sports reporters have caught the bug, talking of patients being in 'a mortality situation' and footballers in 'goal-scoring situations' – *dying*, and *with a chance to score.* Where political correctness uses euphemisms to avoid being judgemental, those in authority use it to disguise unpleasant truths and motives, nowhere more commonly than in the field of employment. *De-recruiting, letting go* and *downsizing* are all euphemisms for *sacking*, for instance. Faced with sacking 5,000 people at Chrysler's Wisconsin plant, the management came up with the face-saving formula that it was offering *a career alternative enhancement programme*.

Neologisms

New technologies, new immigrants, new ways of working, shopping, socializing, and worshipping, increased foreign travel, and new eating habits have all brought new words flooding into English at a rate unprecedented since the Renaissance. The Internet and World Wide Web alone have generated an expansive new vocabulary with its own website dictionary; hardly a day goes by without some new word or phrase appearing in the media. Some, like *eco-warrior, nerd, stiffed, steep learning curve*, and *happy-clappies* may not last, but many will stick and pass into the general store of words.

The ever-increasing stock of new words makes the dictionaries that list them a vital tool. Dermot Purgavie keeps us up to date with progress:

> Cyberslang, the geek word for the jargon of the Internet, has grown so dense and baffling that there is now an on-line dictionary to guide us through its mysteries. If you can't tell an Annie (an 'orphaned' Website that needs updating) from an Archie (a piece of software for finding files), you need to check in with the dialect trackers at Netlingo.
>
> There is now an on-line dictionary for almost everything, from Standard English to the quirky vernacular of skateboard dudes . . . and now . . . the grand old dowager of the word business, the Oxford English Dictionary . . .
>
> Dictionaries are one more thing to have profited from the Net's ability to expose the esoteric to a big and curious universe. There's the Dictionary of Mountain Bike Slang (mothers will be relieved to find that 'to bonk' is to run out of energy on the pedals) and the Magician's Dictionary, which tells us there are 13 types of magic, none of them to do with sawing a lady in half or fishing a dove out of your trousers . . .
>
> Students of the truly arcane won't want to miss Forthright's Phrontistery ('a thinking place'), where, among other linguistic labours, thousands of 'rare and obsolete' words are being lovingly warehoused. Such things as decaudate (cutting off the tail), floccilation (plucking fitfully at the bedclothes) and pandiculation (stretching and yawning) will be preserved in electronic eternity.
>
> Unfortunately, [there is] no British-American dictionary, but the famous transatlantic language gap is well catered for at an American-run site called Britspeak. It provides links to a dozen dictionaries that uphold the idea that English is a second language for Americans, and vice versa, among them one devoted entirely to the vocabulary of *Men Behaving Badly*, and an exploration of Cockney rhyming slang.

> Many feature a daily word to increase your linguistic skills. A Word a Day e-mails you a new word – grok, bleb, bander-snatch, disembogue – each morning. So now, more than a quarter of a million people in 184 countries are bounding out of bed and giving their vocabulary a vigorous workout while the rest of us are still pandiculating.
>
> *Night & Day*, in The *Daily Mail*, 16 April 2000

Activity List five new words you have noticed and explain their meanings and origins.

Grammar

As talk takes over from writing, language becomes freer, looser, and less bound by rules. In writing, the trend is towards shorter, less elaborately structured sentences, with fewer embedded minor clauses.

> There's probably no such thing as the perfect family. Not anywhere. Not in the USA. Not even this close to the movie capital of the world. We should know that. I mean, we've all seen American Beauty, right? But life with the Bacherachs . . . It looks so seductive and sexy and safe. You'd pay to see the movie. And the best thing about it? You could be sure the soundtrack would be just great.
>
> *The Times* Magazine, 17 June 2000

Speech, influenced by American films and television, shows a similar paring down. Words with a purely grammatical function – mainly prepositions, conjunctions like *if*, the relatives *who* and *that* and parts of the auxiliary verb *to have* – are either left out or abbreviated:

This morning I found I had to be [in] two places at the same time.
I can't sleep on that side of my head, [that] is all.
I [had] better go back to LA.

Minor clauses are shortened by the omission of the usual introductory conjunctions and relative pronouns:

What's the name of the guy [who] stole the car?
[If] You do that, you're in trouble.

Language itself, it seems, like dress and manners, is falling under the spell of 'cool': the hard man gives nothing away, not even words.

The obsolescence (gradual dying away) of the adverb in favour of the adjective is another aspect of the paring down of grammar. *Really* has become *real* for most Americans: *real soon, real good, real neat*, while *good* does duty for *well* both here and in the US – 'My husband would say I'd done good', remarked a 60-year-old member of the Women's Institute – and *great* is any modern sportsperson's version of *very well:* 'Yeah, I played great out there today.'

Other adverbs with the normal *-ly* ending are also disappearing fast. *He played excellent* is Keegan-speak for *He played excellently*, and even the most educated people today are more likely to use the comparative form of the adjective *quicker* than its adverbial equivalent *more quickly* in sentences like *Mechanization helped the work to be done more quickly* – even in writing.

Two further examples of this move towards simplicity in grammar are worth mentioning. One is the dropping of the conjunction *as if* in favour of the adjective *like*: *It was like they couldn't wait to go.* (Old-fashioned textbooks claim that *like* should be used only when comparing a noun with another noun or pronoun, e.g. *Prince William is like his mother*, while *as if* should be used only with verbs.)

Finally, confusion between the past tense and the past participle of verbs has led to the dropping of the conventional past tense form in certain circles. *I seen* (for *I saw*) and *I done* (for *I did*) are standard outside the middle and upper classes in both America and England, and others such as *I've took* and *I've wrote* are becoming more frequent. As a general rule, the more remote an irregular verb is from ordinary conversation, the more likely it is that people will forget its past tense and participle forms. Does the grammar book advocate *she strove*, for instance, or *she strived*? *Eve span*, or *Eve spun*? *He sprang*, or *he sprung?*

Prescriptivists fume at solecisms like the above, but as Stephen Pinker points out (*Words and Rules*, Weidenfeld and Nicolson, 1999), they're on the losing side. Since all distinctions in English inflection have been declining for the past thousand years, it's the people prescriptivists call illiterate who are at the cutting edge of language, not the old fogies clinging grimly on to their books of rules.

Talking point Look up the distinction between *less* and *fewer* and *between* and *among*. Why do you think most people today ignore these distinctions? Is it a good or a bad thing?

Random language change

Certain changes in language use, however, like those affecting prepositions, appear to be random. The following usages have all appeared recently in the quality press. The established usage is given in square brackets:

attachment for	[to]	his old school
infatuated by	[with]	his new girlfriend
pregnant with	[by]	her boyfriend – the traditional use of *pregnant with* [a child] means carrying [a child]
bored of	[by / with]	studying
the secret to	[of]	success
the cure to	[for]	baldness
convenient to	[for]	shops and transport

the reputation as	[of]	a flirt
make a point to	[of]	be [being] punctual
travellers were hit with	[by]	a breakdown in the computer

Winds used to *ease up:* they now *ease down* or *ease away.* We used to fill forms *in;* today we fill them *out.* All are influenced by American usage. Writing follows speech, so the media are merely reflecting what people are saying. One prepositional change does seem valuable, however: the introduction of *down to*, expressing responsibility, as in *It's down to you to tell him*, as the antithesis of *up to*, expressing choice*: I don't mind: it's up to you*. A move towards greater precision and greater force, perhaps.

Phonological change

Professor John Wells of University College, London, has identified three phases of change in Received Pronunciation this century:

> In the early part of the century people made a series of vowel shifts. The vowel in words such as 'cloth' and 'cross' switched from that of 'thought' to that of 'lot', and people stopped making a distinction between 'flaw' and 'floor'. People also stopped using a tapped r-sound between vowels, as in 'very sorry'. [Professor Wells] said: 'Nowadays we listen with amazement to British films of the Thirties and Forties, made before these changes took place.'
>
> In the mid-twentieth century, words such as 'sure', 'poor', and 'tour' started to sound identical to 'shore', 'pour', and 'tore'. People started to insert a t-sound into words such as 'prince', making it sound like 'prints', a ch-sound became respectable in words such as 'perpetual', and a j-sound in words like 'graduate'. The glottal stop began to replace the t-sound in phrases such as 'quite nice', 'it seems'. In the recent period, since the 1970s, the glottal stop is extending into ever more phonetic environments, such as 'not only, but also', while the l in words such as 'milk', 'myself' and 'middle', is turning into a w. Words such as 'Tuesday' and 'reduce' have acquired ch- and j-sounds, making them 'chooseday' and 'rejuice'. Professor Wells . . . now plans a new survey and is inviting people to give their preferences for about 100 words, such as a shopping mall, the plural of youth, and the month February.
>
> *The Times*, 10 October 1998

Other linguists are finding that non-standard southern English features are appearing amongst the working-class population of Glasgow: traditional consonant sounds such as the *-ch* in *loch* are declining, as is the usual Glaswegian pronunciation of *milk*, 'mulk', while sounds such as the *-th* of *tooth* are being spoken as 'toof'. Since working-class Glaswegians have little contact with people in the south, linguists suspect the influence of *East-Enders*. The same phenomenon is being experienced among Liverpudlians, whose characteristic nasal twang is being replaced by the tones of the London area. Young people under 30 have started to say 'fink' instead of Irish-influenced 'tink', and 'bruvver' instead of 'brudder'. Here again, *EastEnders* is suspected of involvement in the change.

Influential though the London soap may be, however, other factors are at work as well. The uprooting of settled communities in the south-east of England and their resettlement in overspill sites such as the new town of Milton Keynes has led to what linguists call a 'levelling down of accents'. Children brought together from different areas no longer speak like their parents and grandparents but like their peers, evolving a new accent of their own that may well conquer the south and east of England in future as Received Pronunciation did in the past.

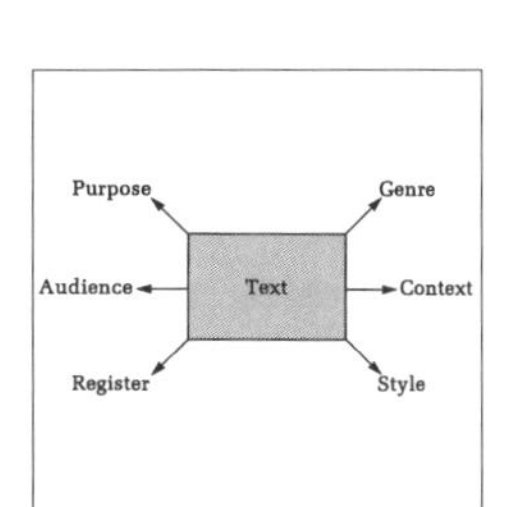

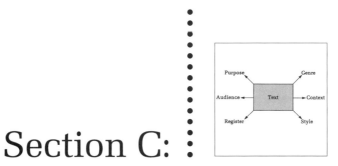

Section C:
Analysis and Evaluation of Prose

5 Frameworks: Guidelines for the Analysis and Evaluation of Prose

For the purpose of English language studies, every spoken utterance, every piece of writing, is a text. Novels, films, plays, poems, advertisements, conversations – all are texts to be studied with the guidance of the **frameworks** set out below.

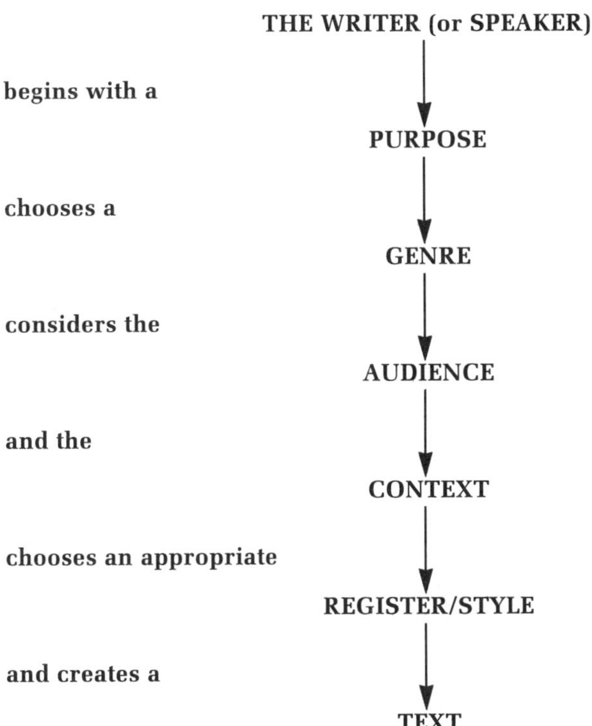

Purpose

1 General

Most people who write (or speak) for a public audience are driven by one of the following intentions:

1 to make money;
2 to spread ideas and information;
3 to persuade others to share their particular philosophy – social, political, sexual or religious – of life.

The motives overlap, of course, but one of them will always have greater force than the others for the individual writer concerned. The style generally reveals which one it is.

2 Specific

Writers or speakers have more specific purposes in mind, however, when they start their work. For the most part, they want to do one of the following:

1. express their own feelings, attitudes, wishes, and intentions, to *condemn, approve, praise, rebuke,* or *celebrate*: the **expressive function** of language
2. influence other people's actions, emotions, beliefs, and attitudes, to *persuade, advise, order, threaten, warn, encourage,* or *exhort*: the **directive function**
3. convey information, to *inform, report, describe, assert, declare, announce, confirm,* or *refute*: the **informative function**
4. connect directly with the readers' emotions by the use of devices such as intonation, sound, rhythm, imagery, and so on in order to communicate meaning that could not be otherwise conveyed: the **poetic function** of language.

Activity

Assign each of the following passages to one of the categories above, pointing out the characteristic features of each.

a [The old Northmen] understood in their heart it was indispensable to be brave; that Odin would have no favour for them, but despise and thrust them out, if they were not brave. Consider too whether there is not something in this! It is an everlasting duty, valid in our day as in that, the duty of being brave . . . We must get rid of Fear: we cannot act at all till then.
(Thomas Carlyle, *Odin*, in *An Anthology of English Prose*, Dent, 1948)

b Who bends not his ear to any bell which upon any occasion rings? But who can remove it from that bell which is passing a piece of himself out of this world? No man is an island, entire of itself; every man is a piece of the continent, a part of the main. If a clod be washed away by the sea, Europe is the less, as well as if a promontory were, as well as if a manor of thy friend's or of thine own were: any man's death diminishes me, because I am involved in mankind, and therefore never send to know for whom the bell tolls; it tolls for thee.
(John Donne, *Devotions,* University of Michigan Press, 1959)

c The Gestalt movement of the early and mid-twentieth century emphasised that the whole is different from the sum of the parts. The major theorists realised that an understanding of all of the parts within any given structure will not provide a complete understanding of the total structure. Instead, meaning derives from the inter-relationships of those parts, and of each part of the whole. For example . . . we tend to hear speech rather than isolated utterances when listening to conversation.
(*Key Concepts in Communication*, ed. John Fiske, Methuen, 1983)

Genre

A **genre** is a category to which a given text may be said to belong. To qualify for inclusion in a particular genre, a text must have some readily distinguishable features that clearly mark it off from texts in other genres. Fairy tales, romantic novels, lyric poetry, textbook writing, and literary criticism are all genres of writing. Another characteristic of a genre is its historical stability: it can be found to have existed over a considerable period of time.

Audience

If writers and speakers want to be heard – and of course they do – they must design their material and their style to suit their targeted audience. Since they cannot know the individual tastes of every member of that audience, they create a general idea of what they may be like – a stereotyped image, in fact. Those to whom writing is an end in itself, however, ignore audience design; readers are expected to rise to the level demanded by their work or be disappointed.

Context

Context is the term used to describe (a) the set of physical and social circumstances in which a speech utterance or communicative interchange (jargon for *conversation*) takes place; (b) the wider social, political and historical circumstances which constitute the speakers' cultural background.

Where writing is concerned, the immediate context is the medium in which the piece appears (in a book, a magazine, on TV, etc.), and the physical environment in which it may be read or heard (a library, a commuter train, a sitting room, etc.).

The wider context is the social, educational, political and historical circumstances which constitute the speakers' cultural background.

Context is an important consideration for both writers and speakers, since it helps determine which style and register are appropriate to use.

Register and style

Register

This is the term generally used to describe a form of language associated with a particular kind of subject matter. Law, for example, has a terminology of its own (*legalese*), as do the many branches of science and religion. The following are all examples of different registers:

1 In the event of accidental fatal injury to the Insured, or, if more than one Insured, to any of them, and/or the spouse of an Insured, occurring in the Buildings and due to outward and visible violence caused by thieves or fire the Company will pay the sum of £1,000.

2 Looking back to the graphic formula recently given for sulphuric acid, it will be seen that some atoms are connected by a single tie, some by two, and the sulphur atom by no fewer than six. These ties are intended to show the combining power or valency of the elements, and it will be observed that here also hydrogen is taken as the unit, since an atom of hydrogen has the lowest combining power of any element.

3 Almighty and most merciful Father: we have erred and strayed from Thy ways like lost sheep. We have followed too much the devices and desires of our own hearts. We have offended against Thy holy laws. We have left undone those things which we ought to have done: and we have done those things which we ought not to have done: and there is no health in us.

The above extracts reveal most of the characteristics of the individual registers chosen, which are outlined below.

Extract 1

a an impersonal use of language: *the Insured, the spouse*;
b the awkward-sounding repetition of specific terms like *the Insured*: this is to avoid any possible ambiguity;
c the convoluted sentence structure making the meaning hard to grasp: this is caused by the need to insert five qualifying phrases between the beginning of the sentence, *In the event of accidental fatal injury to the Insured*, and its completion, *the Company will pay the sum of £1,000,* again to avoid possible loop-holes.

Extract 2

a an impersonal use of language achieved by use of the passive voice, cutting out human observers: *it will be seen that, it will be observed that*;
b use of terms belonging exclusively to science: *atom, tie, valency*;
c the use of clear, precise language;
d the use of well-structured sentences in which the main clause is followed by dependent clauses and phrases in a clear and logical progression.

Extract 3

a use of the vocative (literally *calling on,* i.e. direct address to): *Almighty and most merciful Father*;
b use of archaic (out-of-date) language to distance us from everyday life: *Thy, erred and strayed, lost sheep* (sheep mean only meat to us these days);

- **c** use of archaic phraseology also: *there is no health in us* rather than *we are unhealthy*;
- **d** the creation of an emotional, almost hypnotic, mood by the use of repetition and parallel phrasing:
  We have erred . . . We have followed . . . We have offended . . . We have left . . . undone . . . done . . . done . . . not to have done.

Certain kinds of social situations have their characteristic registers, too: the **phatic communication** of strangers thrown together by accident, for example (*Do you come here often?*), or the cooing talk of adults addressing small babies.

Since register clearly overlaps with **jargon**, it seems best to limit it to describing the set of terms used by a particular trade, vocation, or profession. The broader term **style** can be used for everything else.

Talking point Do (a) red-top tabloids (b) advertising have registers of their own?

Style

We can distinguish five main language styles (or registers, if you prefer to use the older term) in English speech and writing:

1. the high, ultra-formal style used for important public ceremonies
2. the formal style used for all public communications of a serious nature
3. the modified formal style used for general-purpose public communication
4. the colloquial style of ordinary, everyday communication
5. the ultra-colloquial style based on slang; used largely by the radical, innovative young who are bored with the old ways of speech and want to show their 'cool'. It is led by Afro-American street-talk in the US and Afro-Caribbean street-talk here.
   (We may soon need to add a sixth: the abbreviated style of the electronic media.)

1 The ultra-formal style

This is the style used by toastmasters, by clergymen addressing members of congregations or praying to God on our behalf, by Black Rod at the opening of Parliament, and so on.

It is marked by the use of:

- **a** **vocatives** (direct forms of address: *O God (we call upon Thee); My Lords, Ladies and Gentlemen*;
- **b** the use of **archaic language**: *I beg to move . . .*; *pray silence for His Excellency*; *the Right Honourable Member*; *without let or hindrance*; *those whom God hath joined*;
- **c** the use of **the subjunctive mood**: *let no man put asunder*; *let the word go forth*; *be it known that*, etc.

2 The formal style

The formal style is characterized by:

a a considerable number of **abstract nouns** denoting concepts, largely derived from Latin and Greek: *integration, hegemony, ideology, signification*, etc.;
b the use of **single transitive verbs** rather than phrasal verbs: *discover* rather than *find out*; *contact* rather than *get in touch with*, etc.;
c the use of **complex sentences** with embedded clauses and phrases, e.g. *The large corporate organizations, with interests spread across media and other sectors of the British and international economies, that are the logical result of the process of concentration, are known as multi-media conglomerates, of which Thorn/EMI and ACC are good examples*;
d the retention of the conjunction *that* at the head of dependent clauses: *The Prime Minister said* ***that*** *the matter was being investigated*;
e frequent use of the passive voice: *The matter* ***was being investigated***;
f the absence of colloquial language and slang.

3 The modified formal style

This style is characterized by:

a a greater number of plain English words;
b the use of phrasal as well as single verbs;
c a preference for the active voice – for people doing things rather than for action expressed by abstract nouns, e.g. *Political Correctness encourages people to avoid using terms that may discriminate against others*, rather than *Political Correctness encourages the avoidance of any terms that may lead to social discrimination*;
d the frequent omission of *that* at the head of dependent clauses: *The Prime Minister said the matter was being investigated*;
e the use of abbreviated verb forms, particularly in speech: *wouldn't, can't, isn't*, etc.

Overall, it is less stiff than the formal style and flows more easily, especially in speech.

4 The colloquial style

This style is characterized by its use of:

a familiar, homely words that belong to the private rather than the public arena;
b shorter, more assertive sentences: *This is rubbish*;
c rhetorical questions and exclamations: *Two grand for a dress? Blimey!*;
d the narrative formula *turned round*: *He turned round and said . . .*;
e fillers such as *like, know what I mean, sort of thing, I mean*, etc.

5 The ultra-colloquial style

This is a largely spoken style, written down mainly by authors creating street-wise, often criminal, always hard-edged characters. The most interesting because most radical slang comes from Afro-Caribbean and Afro-American English users: a form called Ebonics almost constitutes a second language in Black high schools in America, where teachers can hardly understand what pupils say.

Slang is characterized by the use of:

- **a** newly coined words: *dumbing down, anorak, yo, man, my man, chick, cool, wicked*;
- **b** the omission of letters from the middle or end of words: *gonna, doin', ain't*;
- **c** the use of disjunctive grammar: the omission of conjunctions and relative pronouns from the head of dependent clauses: *[If] you do that, you're dead*; *Who's the guy [who] got done for speeding?*
- **d** the omission of the main verb: *They [there are] some details missing*; the omission of auxiliaries like *have, would,* and *is*: *I gotta* [I have got to]; *he [would] like to go but he can't*; *He say he [is] going to shank you*;
- **e** the omission of little function words like *a, of,* and *to*: *[A] Man like him, he don't even know how to brush his teeth*; *You take care [of] yourself, now*;
- **f** the complete absence of abstract nouns.

Activity

Assign each of the extracts below to one of the categories above, taking care to list the characteristics that distinguish it.

a The arguments about the exploitation of this great discovery have, however, barely begun. The human genome is destined to provoke secular controversies, both scientific and ethical, as intense as the charges of heresy that followed Galileo's discovery that the Earth revolves round the Sun. Recognising its potential is one thing, and even that is a matter of scientific dispute; realising it is another. The hope is, that within a couple of decades, it will enable science to probe into the genetic roots of illness and find new cures. It should enable greatly improved diagnostic tests and better understanding of the side-effects – on each individual – of drugs.
Editorial, *The Times*, 23 June 2000

b The mapping of the human genome raises ethical dilemmas most of us have not begun to contemplate, but for Venter speed is of the essence; to sit back and ponder while people suffer from diseases that might be cured is positively inhumane. His company name itself [Celera] reflects his belief that delay, given the immense stakes for humanity, is ethically unacceptable.
Ben Macintyre, *The Times*, 23 June 2000

c The pub laws treat drinkers like they're kids.They tell you when you can drink and when you've got to stop. That's not the way to treat adults or get them to act responsibly. You couldn't even get a drink in the afternoon a few years back. Now at least you can pop into the pub and have a pint or a cuppa. But at 11 pm we're still told we've got to stop drinking and go home. The government ought to let pubs and councils fix opening times to suit themselves – that would give us something to say Cheers! about.

d Stick was careful. He said he was doing his time for a grocery store in Oakland County, not any homicide or robbery in downtown Detroit. DeJohn said, 'I know that. It's cool.' He said, 'Believe me, my man. You my man and it's cool. But it don't change you did Sportree and the dude was with him.' Stick said, to DeJohn only, okay, but it was unavoidable. DeJohn said, 'They all unavoidable when you have to do it. Like the two brothers in the shopping mall, in the parking lot, I believe was Northland.'
Stick, Elmore Leonard, Penguin, 1984

6 Directed Writing

The directed writing component of your exam will ask you to do two things:

1 use a passage of stimulus material as the basis for a new piece of writing of your own;
2 write a commentary on the changes you have had to make to the original in order to carry out the task.

Approaching the tasks

One method of coping with both these tasks is to approach them through the frameworks for language study that you have already met, namely:

1 **Purpose:** to inform; instruct; explain; argue a case; persuade; write discursively; entertain;
2 **Genre:** newspaper writing; spoken English; diary; novel; play; short story; advertisement, etc;
3 **Audience:** age; gender; social class; interests, etc.;
4 **Context:** what your common sense and general knowledge tell you about your readers;
5 **Style:** the kind of writing chosen as appropriate for the audience – this includes:
Lexis – Anglo-Saxon or Latinate? abstract or concrete? formal or informal? denotive and factual or connotative and emotive?
Grammar – address to audience: personal, using personal deixis, *I, you*? impersonal, using collective nouns such as *people,* third-person pronouns, *he, she, it, one,* or *they?*
– short, simple and compound sentences? lengthy ones with embedded phrases and clauses? mainly assertions? questions? commands, direct and indirect?
– single verbs? phrasal verbs? a mixture?
– heavy use of adjectives and/or adverbs? (jargon: *pre-* and *post-modifiers*)
– disjunctive grammar?
Stylistic devices – hyperbole, imagery, irony, etc.
Phonology – deliberate use of sound patterning – alliteration, assonance
Graphology – presentational devices such as bullet markers, block capitals for headlines, etc.

Suppose your brief were to turn a passage of modified formal prose into an advertisement for a women's magazine. Run your eye down the list of framework categories and select the language uses that are most appropriate for what you have to do, as follows:

1 Purpose: *persuade* is the obvious category.
2 Genre: *advertising*.
3 Audience: *women* in general.
4 Context: your media savvy tells you that you are addressing women who like reading smart ads in the glossy pages of women's magazines, and who have money to spend on new products.
5 Style: *lexis* – generally short words, apart from those with technical content, and largely emotive;
grammar – some disjunctive grammar; short sentences; direct and indirect commands; compound sentences rather than complex ones; single verbs; personal address; heavy use of adjectives and adverbs;
phonology – use of patterned sound;
graphology – key words in larger letters, positioned to catch the eye.

Example

Task: read the following information and use it as the basis for an advertisement for a new moisturizing cream.

> **What's the main benefit of the new skincare?**
> Many new plant extracts have anti-aging properties. Clarins uses Plant Auxins – molecules from sunflowers that help them withstand harsh environmental conditions – in its new anti-aging line Extra-Firming. Primordiale Intense, £26, Lancôme's latest anti-aging face cream, contains two newly captured extracts – Honey of Acacia, with hydrating properties, and Helianthus, which protects sunflowers from drying out in the sun.
>
> The biggest developments are in the way plant extracts are delivered to your skin. Many plant elements are naturally unstable when extracted, so ensuring they work with maximum efficiency is a high-tech business. Howard Murad, product creator at botanical skincare company Murad, develops skin-penetrating liposomes that stop unstable ingredients from evaporating on the skin's surface.
>
> (Nicola Moulton, *She*, June 2000)

Step 1: Analysis of the given material

1 Purpose: to inform women of the development of new beauty aids, preparatory to their becoming established on the market.
2 Genre: advertising.
3 Audience: women who care about their appearance.
4 Context: women's magazines.
5 Style: *lexis* – technical words such as *molecules, unstable, delivered, liposomes*;
grammar – mainly simple and compound sentences, kept as short as possible for easy reading; most take the form of

statements of fact; one use of the personal pronoun *your*, but the address is largely impersonal, concentrating on the new products and the processes of developing them; the style overall is formal, without any stylistic devices to detract from the pseudo-scientific approach; there are no emotive words: *harsh* is used in a purely factual, objective sense to describe the difficult conditions met in the physical environment;
graphology – apart from a sub-heading in larger print to break up a long column of reading, there are no presentational devices.

Step 2: The new piece of writing

You can now proceed to the second half of your task, the writing of a new text. The analysis you have just completed will help you greatly in this, because the stylistic features you need for your new piece will be very different. In a sense, they select themselves.

My ad would be headed by a picture of an attractive model with beautiful skin, and would read:

Soft, gentle, soothing.

If only the British climate were more like Helianthus.

The ideal climate may not be easy to come by, but at least your ideal skincare is. Helianthus from Lancôme has natural plant extracts to guard against the drying effects of sun and weather.

It penetrates deep into your skin, smoothing away dry patches and protecting against further damage with its gentle, moisturizing softness. Nothing is more natural. Nothing is more effective. Let's face it, if it's good enough for plants, it's good enough for you.

Helianthus, guarding you against the sun and wind.

Step 3: The commentary

Having written your ad, your next task is to write a commentary describing the changes you have made to the original. If you need a checklist to guide you, go back to the frameworks like this:

1 **Purpose:** my purpose was to persuade people to buy Helianthus rather than to simply inform them which products are available.

2 **Audience:** my audience is the same as that for the original piece, so no change is necessary from this point of view; however, since women are always striving for perfection, prefer pure and natural ingredients to harsh chemical ones, and respond readily to words with a sensuous appeal, I have tried to gear my writing accordingly.

3 Context: the context again is unchanged.

4 Style: *[this of course is the framework to concentrate on]*

Lexis – I have changed this considerably, replacing technical terms like *molecules, unstable, delivered, liposomes* with words of a more familiar kind, e.g. *moisturizing,* and selecting other words for their emotive appeal: e.g. *ideal, guard, smooth, protect, gentle, softness, natural, good;* I have used the familiar colloquial expressions, *easy to come by* and *Let's face it* to give the effect of ordinary speech.

Grammar – I have made the address more personal, with repeated use of *your* and *you,* and the inclusive pronoun *us* in *Let's face it*; this gives the impression of direct address, of someone speaking personally to other people out of shared experience. I have used disjunctive grammar to some extent, once at the beginning of the ad in the subjectless, verbless phrase *soft, gentle, soothing,* and again at the end, where the phrase *guarding you against the sun and wind* lacks a main verb. My intention was to give the piece a livelier feel and quicker pace than the original. I have used various cohesive devices to tie the piece together, e.g. the conjunction *if only* in line 2, pointing up the difference between climate and product; the juxtaposition of ideal skincare and Helianthus in line 4; the back reference to the product achieved by the use of *it* at the start of the third sentence and in the middle of the sixth; and the repetition of the product name at the beginning of the final phrase. I have used the classic advertising ploy of creating expectation in the claims *Nothing is more natural. Nothing is more effective.* This leads readers to suppose that Helianthus is more natural and more effective than anything else on the market, although it actually claims only that it is as good as other products with these qualities. The original piece made no such claims.

Stylistic devices – I have used parallel phrasing in order to give the message more impact, e.g. *the ideal climate . . . come by/ ideal skincare is*; *Nothing is more natural/Nothing is more effective*; *good enough for plants/good enough for you.* I have also tried to pattern the sound with the repetition of the letter *s*, to give a *more sensuous appeal: e.g.* **s**kin . . . **s**oothing . . . *moi***s**turi**z**ing . . . **s**oftne**ss**. The original piece made no attempt to use such devices.

Graphology – I have opened the ad with key words in larger print, to catch the reader's eye: the choice of lower-case letters rather than block capitals is in keeping with the softness and intimacy of the approach. The first three words are calculated to play on the audience's emotions, while the second line introduces the product and places stress on its name: *If only the British climate were more like Helianthus.*

Once you have got used to using the frameworks in this way, you can turn the category headings into the key words of topic sentences:

> *I have had to make significant changes to the original material in order to make it appropriate for a different* ***purpose****,* ***audience*** and ***context****.* [The nature of these will emerge in the course of your commentary, which you could then begin as outlined below.]
>
> *I have changed the* ***lexis*** of the original considerably, choosing words . . . [Explain the nature of these new words, why you've chosen them, and what effect you intend them to have.]
>
> *The* ***grammar*** of my piece differs from that of Text A in several ways . . . [Explain the nature of these new constructions, why you've chosen them, and what effect you intend them to have.]
>
> *I have used various* ***stylistic devices*** to add force to my expression. These include . . . [Explain the different effects you hope to achieve with each of these devices. **Phonology** can be dealt with under this heading if you prefer, since giving it a category of its own may make it seem unduly important.]
>
> *I have taken* ***graphology*** into account in creating my text . . . [Explain how the changes you have made to the presentation of the material make it more appropriate to purpose, audience and context.]

This may seem a rather stilted and awkward approach, but it does have the virtue of showing the examiners that you have met all their requirements.

Summary

1. Examine the expression of the original piece and form an impression of its **style**.
2. Make analytical notes for yourself under the category headings **lexis**, **grammar**, **stylistic devices**, **phonology**, **graphology**.
3. Use the same category headings to develop an appropriate style for the new piece you have been asked to write; it will usually differ markedly from the original.
4. Write your text.
5. Write a commentary on the changes you have had to make to the style of the original text in order to make it appropriate to its new **purpose**, **genre**, **audience**, and **context.**

Practice material

In the examples below, marginal comments show you the kind of points you need to consider in directed writing tasks. The original texts are followed by new pieces of writing derived from them. Write a commentary discussing (a) the changes that have been made; (b) the reasons for them.

You should note that you may be asked to write rather longer pieces than the sample texts given below.

Example 1

The question asked for the following material to be used as the basis for an article about women's attitudes to their bodies, in a broadsheet such as *The Guardian.*

Text A

Sunday 15 January
9st (excellent), alcohol units 0, cigarettes 29 (v.v. bad, esp. in 2 hours), calories 3879 (repulsive), negative thoughts 942 (approx. based on av. per minute), minutes spent counting negative thoughts 127 (approx.).

6 p.m. Completely exhausted by entire day of date-preparation. Being a woman is worse than being a farmer – there is so much harvesting and crop spraying to be done: legs to be waxed, underarms shaved, eyebrows plucked, feet pumiced, skin exfoliated and moisturised, spots cleansed, roots dyed, eyelashes tinted, nails filed, cellulite massaged, stomach muscles exercised. The whole performance is so finely tuned you only have to neglect it for a few days for the whole thing to go to seed. Sometimes I wonder what it would be like if I left it to revert to nature – with a full beard and handlebar moustache on each shin, Dennis Healey eyebrows, face a graveyard of dead skin, spots erupting, long curly finger-nails like Struwelpeter, blind as bat and stupid runt of species as no contact lenses, flabby body flobbering around. Ugh, ugh. Is it any wonder girls have no confidence?

7 p.m. Cannot believe this has happened. On the way to the bathroom, to complete final farming touches, I noticed the answerphone light was flashing: Daniel. 'Look, Jones. I'm really sorry. I think I'm going to have to give tonight a miss. I've got a presentation at ten in the morning and a pile of forty-five spread sheets to get through.' Cannot believe it. Am stood up . . . However, one must not live one's life through men but must be complete in oneself as a woman of substance.

9 p.m. Still, he is on top-level job. Maybe he didn't want to ruin first date with underlying work-panic.

Annotations (left margin):

- running metaphor
- piling of participle phrases – effect of overwhelming busy-ness
- humour through grotesque imagery & exaggeration
- paralinguistic expressions of emotion
- disjunctive grammar to reveal shock
- pious echo of feminist philosophy

Annotations (right margin):

- use of highly emotive adjectives sets tone for whole piece
- disjunctive language – effect of rush & exhaustion
- hyperbole
- disjunctive grammar, this time to create effect of stumbling around in distress
- alliteration to strengthen sense of disgust

colloquial language appropriate to expression of private thoughts

11 p.m. Humph. He might have bloody well rung again, though. Is probably out with someone thinner.

5. a.m. What's wrong with me? I'm completely alone. Hate Daniel Cleaver. Am going to have nothing more to do with him. Am going to get weighed.

Bridget Jones's diary, Helen Fielding, Picador, 1996

disjunctive grammar to express tight-lipped anger

Text B

detached tone & analytical stance

For the greater part of human existence the ideal body image of women has been the same: one of rounded curves. In the early Stone Age, fatness was a symbol of fertility; centuries later, Rubens celebrated the prosperity of his patrons through the plumpness of their women. Cellulite was something to be praised rather than feared.

Today, all that has changed. As Mrs Simpson remarked, no woman today can be too rich or too thin. Fat is now a cause for disgust or concern; the unfortunate result of greed or faulty nutrition. Magazines publish endless articles about diets, and an apparently endless stream of Bridget Joneses chronicle their futile struggle with their weight.

To some, this obsession with body image is harmless vanity. To others, it is the outward sign of an inner neurosis: the Bridget Joneses of this world diet to punish themselves for not being perfect in every way; when dieting fails they turn to cigarettes and drink, increasing both weight and guilt and setting up an endless cycle of punishment, self-disgust, and failure. This unfortunate phase in our history will end only when women learn to value themselves for something other than appearance, and in our current media-dominated society, the portents for that are not good.

total absence of humour

balanced sentences

complex sentence structure with several clauses & phrases

formal lexis: abstract nouns e.g. existence, nutrition, vanity, neurosis

understated expression of attitude contrasting with emotion of previous text

Example 2

The information in the *Mirror* editorial below was used as the basis for a letter to *The Independent*.

Text A

It is hard for any of us to completely understand what it means to crack the genetic code.

Other brilliant scientific advances, such as landing on the moon, could be seen.

Yet discovering the book of life is the greatest advance of all. The world is a different place today – and soon will be a better place thanks to it.

The possibilities are endless. For the first time humans will be able to be more than nature made them.

Of course there are dangers. Scientific advances never come without risks – look at atomic power and GM foods.

But the genome project offers so much hope it shouldn't be held back by worries.

There must be proper monitoring of what is done. There must be ways to prevent dangerous people abusing it. But discovering the book of life offers so many advantages they far outweigh the problems.

It will be possible to overcome terrible diseases. We will be able to live longer and in better health.

Cancer and heart disease will disappear. We will no longer pass on hereditary illnesses to our children.

There have been many fantastic medical breakthroughs in the past century. But the genome project is like all of them rolled together and much more besides.

It is also an incredible tool for learning about the history of mankind and tracing its future.

The speed of scientific advance nowadays is breathtaking. But after yesterday, you ain't seen nothing yet.

We can hardly begin to imagine what wonders it will lead to.

The *Daily Mirror*, 27 June 2000

use of personal pronoun appeals to readers' shared experience & attitudes

simple, weak expression avoids Latinisms e.g. 'were tangible achievements'

graphological devices: italic print & underline emphasize importance of point made – graphological variation throughout appeals to eye & sustains interest

conjunction used to begin a sentence rather than tie two together – a concession to readers, to feed them one thought per sentence; also has effect of driving point home

parallel structures, but flat, brusque, no attempt at balance & harmony – 'pile-driving' effect

colloquial lexis

simple, short sentences

simple phrasal verb rather than single, more sophisticated one, e.g. surpass

use of large areas of 'white space' helps poor readers, enables each point to be assimilated before next one is made; makes sure each point is given max. impact

slang, to anchor this abstract scientific brilliance to real life, express emotion in macho, populist way (echo of hard-boiled US films)

sits oddly with connotations of previous slang – impression of open-eyed wonder more suitable to children's encyclopaedia

Text B

inversion of normal imc-dc order, to emphasize point about danger

more sophisticated cohesive device than 'but' or 'yet'

compare this formal expression with 'cracking'

more organized conclusion, logically developed, than in previous text

> Sir,
>
> That deciphering the genetic code brings dangers in its wake few would deny; the consequences of earlier scientific discoveries such as nuclear fission haunt us still.
>
> Nevertheless, though still too theoretical for most of us to grasp, the Human Genome Project promises greater things than all earlier medical advances put together. It will revolutionize the diagnosis, prevention and treatment of most genetic disease, eliminating cancer and heart disease and freeing our children from the threat of inherited ills.
>
> Nor will its influence be confined to the field of medicine alone. Deciphering the code will teach us the secrets of our evolutionary past, which in turn may help to shape our vision of the future of our human race.
>
> If abuse of this massive advance in scientific knowledge can be avoided, its potential has no limit. Wisdom in dealing with the information derived from the Code of Life will be just as important as learning to read it in the first place.

formal lexis, highly Latinate, compressing the expression of several ideas into a short space, largely through use of abstract nouns

expresses more than 'the history of mankind'

Directed writing practice

The activities below offer you the opportunity to practise the skills you need for directed writing tasks.

Activity

1 Read the following newspaper article and write a letter to your MP setting out arguments against the advertising practices described. Write a commentary on your letter, explaining the way you have adapted the original material for your own use.

2 Write a leaflet based on the following newspaper article, warning smokers of the dangers of their habit and the advertising pressures that make those dangers greater.

3 Write a commentary on the changes you have made in the subject matter and your writing style in the course of adapting it for a different purpose, audience and context.

It was once said that you could tell where an Englishman came from whenever he opened his mouth. Now you can size him up just as easily by observing what he, or she, shoves in it. For the cigarettes Britons smoke say as much about their place, both social and geographic, as does the cut of their clothes or the lilt of their voice.

Cigarette companies, unable to advertise on television and anticipating further restrictions on marketing, have developed a new strategy to sell cancer sticks. They are targeting their myriad brands at very specific groups, often by running highly localised campaigns and point-of-sale promotions. So successful is this proving that a forthcoming report will show that 66% of 15 and 16 year-old boy smokers in Newcastle use the same brand, Lambert and Butler.

The usually secretive cigarette industry has taken the unusual step of explaining its tactics to *The Times*. Gallaher, responsible for such celebrated – or notorious – names as Benson & Hedges and Silk Cut, admits: 'Companies will target different types of people.' Its spokesman reveals that while Silk Cut sells heavily in the South East, elsewhere 'in certain parts it doesn't sell at all'. In contrast, Kensitas Club – which he admits he had never heard of before working for the firm – sells phenomenally well in Glasgow, yet outside the city 'it has practically no presence at all'.

All this might not matter to anyone other than marketing boffins, except that health workers warn that, broadly speaking, the cheaper cigarettes tend to be even worse for you, and they are being targeted at the impressionable – the poorly educated and the young.

Amanda Sandford, research manager at ASH, the anti-smoking pressure group, says that an attempt by Imperial Tobacco to sell its downmarket Regal brand to young men in the North and Midlands was phenomenally successful – with alarming consequences. A study by the Health Development Agency showed that the witty advertising campaign, relying on word play about a slob called Reg, resulted in a sharp increase in sales to teenage boys. 'Another study looked at two areas, one poor, the other affluent, and the poorer one was subject to a lot of advertising with a large amount of cigarettes sold. In the wealthier bit, there was hardly any advertising and not many sales,' she says.

The cigarette companies claim that they are merely strengthening the resolve of existing smokers rather than attempting to find new puffers, and that the advertising follows the smokers. Whatever the truth, the middle classes seem far more wary. While only 15% of professionals smoke, for manual workers the figure is as high as 40%. This is reflected in sales of Lambert & Butler. Londoners might be surprised to learn that it is Britain's best seller. Rarely seen in the capital, it is ubiquitous in Wales and the West Country.

'It used to be premium brands such as Bensons and Silk Cut that you saw advertised,' says Sandford. 'Now there has been a subtle shift. It's the cheaper brands that are advertised. Their sales are increasing and these cigarettes are even more damaging.'

On the other side of the social ashtray is Marlboro Light, proving that it is not just the poor who puff. At any gathering of Sloane Rangers, particularly women, you will see them all drawing on Marlboro Light. Once such creatures were distinguishable by their Alice bands, now it is by their smokes.

Prof Gerald Hastings of the University of Strathclyde, who conducted the Newcastle study with teenage boys, says brands such as Marlboro Lights are aspirational, popular with 18 to 24 year-old college students who have graduated from what he terms 'scummier brands'.

'It is the wrong question to ask whether companies target different types of people,' he says. 'Look at the results. There is incredible brand loyalty, particularly among the young, and very distinct groups smoke different cigarettes. The name Marlboro would be worth millions on its own, because it is seen as exciting and sexy. We are growing ever more image conscious – and the cigarette companies are aware of it.'

Jasper Gerard, *The Times*, 20 June 2000

Activity

Read the main part of a letter from John Paston to his mother Margaret, below. (Its spelling and grammar were discussed in Chapter 4, on pages 221–222.) Use it as the basis of a conversation John had with his wife about his mother, before he wrote the letter. The conversation should include John explaining to his wife what he is going to say to his mother. Describe your methods in adapting the form of the original, and use the frameworks to help you describe any changes you have made to the style.

And modyr, it pleasyd yow to haue serteyn woordys to my wyff at hyr depertyng towchyng your remembraunce of the shortness that ye thynk your dayes of, and also of the mynd that ye have towardys my brethryn and systyr, your childyr, and also of your seruauntys, wherein ye wyllyd hyr to to be a meane[1] to me that I wold tendyr and favore the same. Modyr, savying your pleasure, ther nedeth non embasatours nor meanys betwyx yow and me; for ther is neyther wyff nor other frend shall make me to do that that your comandment shall make me to do, if I may have knowlage of it. And if I haue no knowlage, in good feyth I am excuseabyll bothe to God and yow. And well remembred, I wot well ye ought not to haue me in jelusye[2] for on thyng nor other that ye wold haue me to accomplyshe if I overleve[3] yow, for I wot well non oo[4] man alyve hathe callyd so oft vpon yow as I to make your wylle and put iche thyng in serteynte that ye wold have don for your sylff and to your chyldre and seruauntys. Also, at the makyng of your wylle, and at every comunycacyon that I haue ben at wyth yow towchyng the same, I nevyr contraryed thing that ye wold have doon and parformyd, but alweys offyrd my sylff to be bownde to the same.

[1] meane = means of influencing; go-between.
[2] jelusye = mistrust, suspicion
[3] overleve = outlive
[4] oo = one

Activity

1 Use texts A, B, C, and D below as source material for *either* an attack on, or a defence of, the trends in the handling of the English language that they describe. Present your argument in the form of:

a an article for a broadsheet newspaper;

b a speech in a Student Union debate;

c a script for a talk on an arts programme on Radio 4. (If you're stuck for a title, try 'English in the Firing-Line'.)

2 Write a commentary on the style you have adopted for each piece.

Text A

The other day, I found myself, unexpectedly, in animated discussion with a lively and intelligent group of [Scottish] 19-year-olds. . . . It was not, however, the accent that was striking. It was the words, or, to be more precise, the absence of words, that made me feel my age.

A discussion about a mutual acquaintance ran something like this: 'He was, like, such a geek – I just went, get me out of this. It was so, you know, I can't believe this is happening.' An account of some misunderstanding or failure to communicate would be transmitted as: 'I'm like, hello? Excuse me?' And if the person involved was more than usually obtuse, there would be some simple way of conveying it, such as: 'It was, like, d'oh!'

Gradually, as we talked, I found that the word 'like' . . . was coming in extremely handy. I even began to pick it up myself. Instead of pedantically completing a sentence, as in 'I told him that I was amazed to hear what he had done', Lou could produce a neat piece of conversational shorthand such as: 'I was, like, what is going on here?' It was very catching.

. . . In other ways, however, the language, such as it is, is curiously old-fashioned. The over-use of the word 'like' can be traced back to the Beat Generation of the 1950s – Jack Kerouac or Allan Ginsburg would have been perfectly at home with its laid-back imprecision. Another favourite, 'cool', goes back even further, and has been in the vocabulary for longer than any street-wise word I can think of. Television has undoubtedly speeded the development of this vernacular.

. . . On Radio 1, Sara Cox . . . speaks little else. And in teenage magazines it is given literary form, as in: 'Where can find your fave luminary this month? Which sassy stud is criss-crossing the planet in order to mingle with his adoring fans?'

The result has been labelled 'slop English' by Philip Norman, suggesting something lazy and ill-considered. In some ways, however, it is remarkably well-defined – forbidden territory for those of an older generation who think they can pick it up.

. . . This is more than just a form of communication. It is a defence against adulthood. . . . It is hard to attack it without sounding stuffy.

In the end, I was struck more by the use of exaggeration than by the syntax or vocabulary, and there is, surely, nothing new about that. . . . I have only one answer to those who complain that all this spells the death of the English language. It is, like, excuse me?

(Magnus Linklater, *The Times*, 3 August 2000.)

Text B

In an attempt to make the Bible accessible to her black Sunday School students, preacher's daughter P. K. McCarey has come up with her own version of the Good Book: *The Black Bible Chronicles*.

The result is startling: where the King James Bible commands: 'Thou shalt not take the name of the Lord thy God in vain; for the Lord will not hold him guiltless that taketh his name in vain', McCarey's version warns: 'You shouldn't diss the Almighty's name, using it in cuss words or rapping with one another. It ain't cool, and payback's a monster.'

The Black Bible Chronicles depict the serpent as 'a bad dude' who speaks a language Eve can understand: 'Nah, sister he's feeding you a line of bull. You won't die. The Almighty just knows that if you eat from this tree you'll be hipped to what's going down.' Does it work? Apparently so. According to Ms McCarey, the effect on one student was to make him conclude that the snake was like a drug dealer reassuring a potential user that crack cocaine was harmless. Whether the account of the first day of Creation is as successful is perhaps more dubious: 'Now when the Almighty was first down with his programme, He made the heavens and the Earth. The Earth was a fashion misfit, being so uncool and dark, but the Spirit of the Almighty came down real tough, so that He simply said, "Lighten up!" And that light was right on time.'

The book covers Genesis to Deuteronomy, describing Noah as 'one cool brother', and telling how Cain 'wasted' Abel.

Undeterred by critics, Ms McCarey is now hard at work on her version of the Gospels, bringing Jesus to young Blacks by making him speak like them: 'Don't sweat me, man', he tells the Pharisees.

Whatever charges worried theologians may bring against her, inconsistency can't be one. A declared feminist, she insists she is simply telling the Bible like it is – hence God's politically incorrect admonition to Eve on the marital state: 'Your ol' man is your boss.'

Text C

A publicity handout arrives, passed on by my distinguished colleague Nicholas Bagnall, the *Sunday Telegraph's* Literary Editor.

It tells of the British launch of the 'New American Shakespeare', 'An exciting new range of up-dated Shakespearean texts,' using 'the language of the inner city and speaking the way today's kids speak.' Subtle alterations, it goes on, have been made to reflect the attitudes and aspirations of 'the kids'.

Excerpts are enclosed, taken from 'Romeo and Juliet'. I shall give you a flavour. [AV stands for 'authorised version'; NA for 'new American' version.]

AV: Benvolio: Here comes the furious Tybalt back again.
NA: Benvolio: Yo! Head up, man! It's Tybalt and he's lookin' bad.
AV: Romeo: Alive in triumph and Mercutio slain! Away to heaven respective lenity, and fire-eyed fury be my conduct now!
NA: Romeo: You live, Jack – And my main man done gone been wasted. The gloves are off, y'hear, 'cos I'm feelin' mean.

Wonderful stuff. Eat your heart out, A. L. Rowse. The authors are Mike Lepine ('Sixties beat poet, Seventies radical') and Mark Leigh ('One of New York's premier underground artists, this is his first venture in high culture.')

. . . But then I read on, with growing unease. 'To fully appreciate [sic] the vibrancy of the new text, it has to be experienced in performance,' write the publishers, *Verbal Books*.

. . . I see what Bagnall's up to. He, noble man, wants to give up the personal demonstration and have it transferred to my office. No way. No one lays that kind of cheap jive on the main man Mandrake.

(*Mandrake* column, the *Sunday Telegraph*, 14 July 1985)

Text D

If you don't use, or don't understand, terms like 'large salads', 'pants', 'bunch of arse' or 'your mum', you're probably on the wrong side of 25 and therefore 'sad'. Get real, you doughnut.

The young latch on to the new idioms from America, using them as previous generations used back-slang, to keep the older generation at bay. Parents hate the new forms of expression for the same reasons their offspring love them: they have nothing to do with the norms and values of ordinary conventional respectable life. 'Innit' is a particular source of annoyance to middle-class parents. As Alex Spillius remarks in his article 'Can you talk britspeak?' (*Independent on Sunday*, 24 March 1996), 'Though a bastardisation of "isn't it?", "innit" is an invariable, that is, it can be used as a reflection on any statement, as in: "Ruud Gullit's a boss player, innit." Middle-class kids use it as they use Cockney rhyming slang and expressions like "pukka" and "sound" – to make them merge with the crowd.'

Activity The texts below are taken from seventeenth- and eighteenth-century newspapers. Rewrite them as they might appear in a modern tabloid, then write a commentary detailing the changes you have had to make to the originals.

Text A

WORCESTERSHIRE – FEB. 26

A riot lately took place at Dudley, amongst the Colliers, on account of wages. – In consequence of similar demands, their wages had been several times raised to a great height, which induced Lord Dudley to obtain a fresh set of hands out of Staffordshire at lower wages. The former gang, enraged at this, threatened to pull down Lord Dudley's house; but as troops were immediately called in, all mischief, we understand, was prevented.

Text B

ENGLAND AND IRELAND

New Roſs, May 15. Of late we have been much troubled with Tories* who have robbed ſeveral perſons, and amongst the reſt, as we are informed, the Bishop of *Killaloe* of a very conſiderable ſum; they are now ſomewhat thinner than 2 months ſince, the hand of Justice having ſeiſed ſeveral of them and puniſhed them according to demerit.

* *Tories* = outlaws

Text C

Oxford, Sept. 4. This Morning, a hopeful young Gentleman of this City Shot himſelf, upon a diſcontent he conceived at the Death of a Virgin, to whom he was Contracted.

Text D

Windſor, Sept. 6. His Majeſty and his Royal Highneſs ſince their return from *Wincheſter*, have been to divertiſe themſelves in the Park, where 'tis ſaid a Buck Hunting is intended next Week, though others report that his Majeſty intends for *White-Hall* on the 8th Inſtant.

Text E

London, Auguʃt 23. This day a Perʃon being a Lodger in *White Fryers,* intending 'tis ʃuppoʃed to Murther his Child, (which is an Infant of three Months old) ʃtuck Pins into the Fleʃh of it, in feveral places ʃo far that the heads could hardly be diʃcerned, upon the diʃcovery of ʃuch his Barbarous cruelty, to prevent the Punniʃhment due to his demerits he is Fled and not as yet apprehended though moʃt imagine the Child will not Live.

Text F

ADVERTISEMENTS

In *Kerby-Street* in *Hatton-Garden,* at the Sign of the *Phyʃitian, Chirurgeon,* and *Golden-Anchor.*

L*iveth an eminent and Learned Phyʃitian, who hath Travelled through moʃt parts of the known World, and ʃpeaks theʃe Languages following, viz.* Turkiʃh, Mooriʃh, Sweediʃh, Daniʃh, Spaniʃh, Portugues, Italian, French, Dutch, *and ʃome others, who, by reaʃon of his great Travels, and general Converʃation in moʃt of the Eminent Hoʃpitals, hath attained to many rare Secrets in Phyʃick and Chirurgery, and for a Teʃtimony of his many eminent Cures performed in other Kingdoms and Countries he hath Certificates to produce, which will be ʃatisfactory to any Ingenious Perʃon; and ʃince his Arrival in London, after 20 Years Travel, and 12 Years at Sea in quality of Doctor Chirurgion hath in the ʃeveral Pariʃhes where he Lived, Certificates to ʃhew of the great Cures he hath performed; and doth now undertake to engage his Life in the Curing of the* Morbus Gallicus, *or French Diʃeaʃe.*

Text G

The Castle-Inn *in* West-Smithfield, *near the Barrs, being a Houʃe of conʃiderable Trade, accommodated with Ware-Houses, Stables, Out-Houʃes, Sheads, Hay-Lofts, Dove Houʃes, convenient Drinking-Rooms, good Cellerage, and all things elʃe neceʃʃary for an Inne, is to be let by Leaʃe or yearly Rent, as like wiʃe the Furniture now ʃtanding to be ʃold at a Reaʃonable Rate. Inquire at the ʃaid Inn and you may be further ʃatisfied.*

Activity

Imagine you are a literary agent specializing in children's books. Using the article below (Text A) as source material, write a short guide entitled *Writing for Dyslexic Children*, to be sent to all the authors on your list.

Passages taken from the work of several writers are also included (Texts B, C, D, and E), and you should use these where appropriate to illustrate the points you make.

Write a commentary detailing any changes you have had to make to the original to fit it for its new purpose.

Text A

Just what makes it possible for a dyslexic individual to read a text easily, and what inspires him to do so?

It is a recurring phenomenon that dyslexic children who have apparently been bibliophobics will suddenly take off with a particular author. . . .
I had noticed that this happened with such writers as Dahl, Tolkien and Enid Blyton, and had put together part of the jigsaw. But it was a long, hard look at J. K. Rowling's books and their instant popularity that finally confirmed what I had suspected: these authors have not one, but many factors in common, and it is the combination of all of them that makes their books so successful with reluctant readers.

Those who find reading difficult are not going to browse through text as an idle distraction. What they read must be worth the trouble and effort. An action-packed tale, with interesting characters and an exciting plot, is essential. That sounds pretty obvious. But dyslexics need rather more than this.

Dyslexic children and adults have problems with both concentration and memory functions. Difficulties with auditory memory and information processing are common symptoms. It therefore comes as no surprise that many dyslexics can remain engaged in a story only if they can visualise clearly what is going on.

[Besides being very descriptive], episodes must be in a logical sequence. Again and again, dyslexic readers describe the experience as making a personal video in their minds of the characters and plot.

Writers such as Rowling facilitate this approach, [unlike, for example, Helen Forrester, whose popular book *Tuppence to Cross the Mersey* is inaccessible to most dyslexics by virtue of its style:

My widowed grandmother lived in the Wirral, and here, while visiting her, I spent the happiest days of my childhood, on sandy beaches or in wind-swept gardens. I remember with love the rain-soaked hills looking out onto stormy seas and the turbulent estuary of the Mersey.]

I tried this on an 11-year-old dyslexic. 'I'm sorry, Miss,' he said. 'I can't read books about "turbulent estuaries".'

Rich and stimulating vocabulary is enjoyed by dyslexics, as long as it is concrete. Anything abstract or nebulous can be a real stumbling block.

Moreover, it is often not individual words, but a complicated sentence structure that stops such a reader dead in his tracks, distracting and confusing him . . .

Finally, I learnt from the successful professional authors involved in our survey [of what turns dyslexic adults and children on to reading] the importance of rhythm and cadence in prose, as in poetry. These are to the writer what tone is to the artist. The effect is hypnotic, carrying the dyslexic reader along and adding infinitely to his or her satisfaction.

(Adapted from Patience Thompson's article *Harry Potter and the Dyslexics, Daily Telegraph*, 22 September 1999)

Text B

Jack led them to the back of the hall, and looked at the floor. There was no hole to be seen at all. It had gone completely. The children looked about for a trap-door in the floor, but there was none. Philip began to wonder if Jack had dreamt it all.

Then his sharp eyes saw a spike made of iron set deeply in the wall at the back of the hall. It shone as if it had been much handled. Philip took hold of it.

'Here's something strange!' he began, and pulled hard. The spike moved smoothly in some sort of groove, and suddenly there was a grating noise at Lucy-Ann's feet. She leapt back with a startled cry.

The ground was opening at her feet!

(Enid Blyton)

Text C

Mr Wonka opened the door. Five children and nine grown-ups pushed their ways in – and *oh*, what an amazing sight it was that now met their eyes!

They were looking down upon a lovely valley. There were green meadows on either side of the valley, and along the bottom of it there flowed a great brown river . . .

'*There*!' cried Mr Wonka, dancing up and down and pointing his gold-topped cane at the great brown river. 'It's *all* chocolate!' . . .

The children and their parents were too flabbergasted to speak. They were staggered. They were dumbfounded. They were bewildered and dazzled. They were completely bowled over by the hugeness of the whole thing. They simply stood and stared.

(Roald Dahl)

Text D

Most like a spider she was, but huger than the great hunting beasts, and more terrible than they because of the evil purpose in her remorseless eyes. Those same eyes that he had thought daunted and defeated, there they were lit with a fell light again, clustering in her out-thrust head. Great horns she had, and behind her short stalk-like neck was her huge swollen body, a vast bloated bag, swaying and sagging between her legs; its great bulk was black, blotched with livid marks, but the belly underneath was pale and luminous and gave forth a stench. Her legs were bent, with great knobbed joints high above her back, and hairs that stuck out like steel spines, and at each leg's end there was a claw.

(J. R. Tolkien)

Text E

He could feel them watching him, hear their rattling breath like an evil wind around him.

The nearest Dementor seemed to be considering him. Then it raised both its rotting hands – and lowered its hood.

Where there should have been eyes, there was only thin, grey, scabbed skin, stretched blankly over empty sockets. But there was a mouth . . . a gaping, shapeless hole, sucking the air with the sound of a death-rattle.

A paralysing terror filled Harry so that he couldn't move or speak. His Patronus flickered and died.

White fog was blinding him. He had to fight . . . *expecto patronum* . . . he couldn't see . . . and in the distance, he heard the familiar screaming . . . *expecto patronum* . . . he groped in the mist for Sirius, and found his arm . . . they weren't going to take him . . .

But a pair of strong, clammy hands suddenly wrapped themselves around Harry's neck. They were forcing his face upwards . . . he could feel its breath . . . it was going to get rid of him first . . . he could feel its putrid breath . . . his mother was screaming in his ears . . . she was going to be the last thing he ever heard –

And then, through the fog that was drowning him, he thought he saw a silvery light, growing brighter and brighter . . . he felt himself fall forwards onto the grass –

Face down, too weak to move, sick and shaking, Harry opened his eyes. The blinding light was illuminating the grass around him . . . The screaming had stopped, the cold was ebbing away . . .

Something was driving the Dementors back . . . it was circling around him and Sirius and Hermione . . . the rattling, sucking sounds of the Dementors were fading. They were leaving . . . the air was warm again . . .

(J. K. Rowling)

Activity Read the following article on Spelling Reform and write an impassioned letter to the Education Secretary, either advocating the idea of simplifying English spelling, or strongly rejecting it.

Write a commentary on changes you have made to the original.

Should we simplify spelling?

People have been calling for simpler spelling of English words since at least the sixteenth century. In 1876 a Spelling Reform Association was founded in the United States, and in 1908 the Simplified Spelling Society was founded in Britain to campaign for a revision of spelling.

The Society's first attempts at revised spelling look almost more difficult than the real thing. In 1948 it proposed a system of 'nue speling' in which the sentence 'the language would be improved by the adoption of new spelling for words' should be written: 'dhe langgwej wood be impruuvd bie dhe adopshon of nue speling for wurdz.'

. . . Only this year the Simplified Spelling Society launched another system called 'cut spelng', or CS, which removes all unnecessary letters from words. Silent letters like the 'g' in gnaw or the 'b' in debt are automatically dropped as are letters whose sounds are only pronounced by careful speakers. So *teacher* becomes *teachr* and *doctor* becomes *doctr.*

'Normal written English' in CS is spelled 'norml ritn english'. Critics of the system have described it as an appalling mutilation of the English language.

One problem in English is the large number of different vowel sounds made by only five vowels, a e i o and u. For example, in 'bun', 'thunder', 'mother', 'one' and 'wonder', 'u' and 'o' are both used for the same vowel sound. The Simplified Spelling Society would spell them all with a 'u': 'bun', 'thunder', 'muther', 'wun' and 'wunder'.

Spelling reform has been achieved in other countries. In the United States, Noah Webster deliberately chose American spellings in preference to English ones when he compiled his famous dictionary of American English in the 19th century. More recently, in Ireland, wholesale changes to the way in which Irish Gaelic is spelled have been introduced.

So what are the main arguments for and against changing the spelling of English?

In favour

- It would be easier to learn. Far fewer people would make mistakes. This would help people whose difficulties in reading or writing turn them off education early in life.
- Less time and effort would be spent learning spelling. More time could be given to the creative or practical uses of language.
- The many people for whom English is a second language would find it much easier to learn.

Against

- A sense of our linguistic heritage would be lost. It would be difficult to see patterns of 'root' words and how English had developed.
- Much literature would need to be translated into the new spelling.
- The changeover period with both systems being used at the same time would be completely chaotic.
- Some people, whose educations were finished, might not be able to adapt. They would experience all the problems that poor spellers now face.
- Signposts, guides and maps would all have to be replaced at a very considerable expense.
- Many new systems have been proposed. One would have to be chosen.

[The writer does not mention a further objection based on the constantly changing nature of pronunciation. Add this for yourself.]

Those who argue in favour of reform point to decimal coinage as an example of how problems of transition can be overcome. Those who argue against it point out that English is already the world's leading language spoken by at least 750 million people. English is arguably the richest language in the world in terms of vocabulary. The Oxford English Dictionary lists 500,000 words. By comparison, German is said to have a vocabulary of 185,000 words and French fewer than 100,000. That is a lot of words to change – but the argument will go on as to whether it is worth doing so.

(Brian Keaney & Bill Lucas, *Guardian* Education, 20 October 1992)

Activity

Turn the following extracts from Samuel Pepys's Diary into the opening paragraphs of a novel about life in London during the plague years. Write in the first or third person as you wish, and introduce dialogue as appropriate.

Write a commentary on the changes you find it necessary to make.

10 June – In the evening home to supper; and there, to my great trouble, hear that the plague is come into the City, though it hath, these three or four weeks since its beginning, been wholly out of the City; but where should it begin but in my good friend and neighbour's, Dr Burnett, in Fenchurch Street: which, in both points, troubles me mightily.

11 June – (Lord's Day) Up, and expected long a new suit; but, coming not, dressed myself in my new black silk camelot suit; and, when fully ready, comes my new one of coloured ferrandine, which my wife puts me out of love with, which vexes me . . . I out of doors a little, to show, forsooth, my new suit. I saw poor Dr Burnett's door shut; but he hath, I hear, gained great goodwill among his neighbours for he discovered it himself first, and caused himself to be shut up of his own accord: which was very handsome.

17 June – It struck me very deep this afternoon going with a hackney coach from my Lord Treasurer's down Holborn, the coachman I found to drive easily and easily, at last stood still, and come down hardly able to

stand, and told me that he was suddenly struck very sick and almost blind – he could not see; so I 'light, and went into another coach, with a sad heart for the poor man and for myself also, lest he should have been struck with the plague.
15 August – It was dark before I could get home, and so land at Churchyard stairs, where, to my great trouble, I met a dead corpse of the plague, in the narrow alley, just bringing down a little pair of stairs. But I thank God I was not much disturbed at it. However, I shall beware of being late abroad again.
16 August – To the Exchange, where I have not been a great while. But Lord! how sad a sight it is to see the streets empty of people, and very few upon the 'Change! Jealous of every door that one sees shut up, lest it should be the plague; and about us two shops in three, if not more, generally shut up.

Activity

Read the material below, then write the dialogue of a three-way discussion broadcast on Radio 4's *Front Row* arts programme. Your topic is the function of a cinema critic: should his or her brief be a purely aesthetic one, confined to the discussion of style, or should it concern itself also with questions of morality? Give two of your participants diametrically opposite views, and allow the third to waver with the arguments.

Write a commentary on changes made to the form and style of the original.

Text A

There is a sequence of violence in *Gangster No 1* – a revenge killing inflicted on a rival boss – that is so ghastly, out-of-control and brilliantly filmed it made me dizzy with adrenalin and nausea.

To inspire one of those sensations is worrying enough. To inspire both at the same time requires a sort of genius. The power of this chilling scene is that it is witnessed entirely through the eyes of the victim. As the film blinks in and out of consciousness, we see Paul Bettany, stripped to his blood-spattered underwear, smashing a carriage clock ('Here. Have a clock.' Thump), a bottle of vodka and a fruit bowl into the victim's face. Glass splashes everywhere.

Somewhere, just below eye-level, but not out of earshot, Bettany noisily disembowels his luckless, helpless victim with tools that vary from hatchets to carving knives. The blackouts grow fractionally longer. The fade-ins become blurry, short and remote. Finally, there is just a succession of surreal shots of Bettany's contorted visage screaming, laughing or snivelling before the screen is snuffed out.

This is not thoughtless carnage. It's an explosion of rage that is worked up to as carefully and rigorously as an old-fashioned Greek tragedy.

Bettany is scary mostly because he is so morally bankrupt, emotionally stunted and finally meaningless. Every single one of those reasons will be used to damn and vilify a film that stands head and shoulders above the current crop of British gangster movies precisely because it takes itself very seriously indeed.

. . . McGuigan directs this bleak game of musical chairs with period perfection. The slightly deranged incidental music, interrupted by blasts of Sacha Distel, is a masterpiece of mood setting.

Inevitably, it's the gangland argot that bends the ear. There are more expletives in the film than you can fire asterisks at. But there's a juicy raw poetry about the writing that wouldn't sound out of place in a Berkoff play.

(James Christopher, *The Times*, 8 June 2000)

Text B

This week *Gangster No 1* opened. The latest in a wave of British gangster films, it contains, among other things, a scene of a man being shot in the leg and then hacked to pieces while still alive, all filmed from the point of view of the victim. Meanwhile, Channel 4 is running a television series based on the film *Lock, Stock and Two Smoking Barrels*, the success of which has helped inspire this wave of violent movies.

. . . Before the scene I described above, the psychotic hero of *Gangster No 1* fastidiously undresses so as not to soil his clothes with the blood he is about to spill.

. . . The style is best captured by the concept of 'cool', the supreme aspirational quality of all youth culture. In its most harmless sense, 'cool' means being on top of things, looking good and generally knowing how to behave. But in the context of these movies, 'cool' is a clinically psychotic condition. It means not caring about anything but your own survival and success and being unable to identify with the suffering of others.

. . . The enforcer in *Lock, Stock* is being 'cool' when he comes out with this much admired piece of comic dialogue: 'If you hold anything back, I'll kill ya. If you bend the truth or I think you're bending the truth, I'll kill ya. If you forget anything, I'll kill ya. In fact, you're gonna have to work very hard to stay alive, Nick. Now do you understand everything I've said? Because if you don't, I'll kill ya.'

This is funny because it expresses something horrible with mathematical precision in a Cockney accent. But what, exactly, are we laughing at? There is a fine line between ordinary street cool and gangster cool. The first is an adolescent neurosis, the second a criminal psychosis. These films exploit the first by celebrating the second. Some would say that, in doing so, they offer catharsis; rather than encouraging violence, they release it in harmless fantasy. Furthermore, they would argue, the films are like cartoons, they are not 'realistic'.

This ironic, distanced violence comes directly from the films of Quentin Tarantino, who, in *Reservoir Dogs* and *Pulp Fiction*, used violence structurally rather than morally. Death and injury were, in effect, the terms of the characters' lives; they were not aberrant incidents, they were normality.

. . . But, as Leigh has astutely pointed out, this ironic violence is a moral cop-out. Of this wave of films he writes: 'Yet what capsizes the new British gangster films more than anything is their attempt to reconcile thuggery with broad, crowd-pleasing comedy, to play the Tarantino cool card, wherein black humour removes the need to engage fully with what's going on.'

Even before this becomes a social point, this is an aesthetic one. Funny, sharp and well-crafted as Ritchie's film is, it is almost impossible to watch twice for the simple reason that it is devoid of any psychological or moral tension.

. . . Then comes the social point. The argument about whether screen violence results in real violence goes on, with both sides taking positions for less than objective reasons. . . . We know that children learn by imitation and cannot necessarily distinguish between cartoons and reality.

What we forget is that some children are aged between 18 to 25, the primary target audience for all film-makers. There is, in the end, something irredeemably nasty about new British gangster films. . . . The formalism they derive from Tarantino has become, in the hands of these directors, an oppressive wallowing in amorality, as if the only way they can find to entertain their audiences is to transport them to a world where nothing matters and anything can be done.

. . . Meanwhile, the real violence on London's streets rises inexorably. A connection? Up to you. All I would say is that the hypothesis that there is absolutely no connection is, from a cultural perspective, not credible. For what better validation could the people without hearts and minds have than the revelation that the makers of films and television programmes like nothing better than to pretend that they also have neither?

(Brian Appleyard, *Culture, The Sunday Times*, 11 June 2000)

Activity

In Channel 4's experimental programme *Big Brother,* ten contestants were made to live together under 24-hour surveillance. Members of the public voted each week to evict one of the contestants and the idea was to see who could survive both voting and the conditions longest and win a prize of £70,000.

One contestant, Nick Bateman, was evicted when his housemates discovered he had systematically deceived and manipulated them as well as broken the rules.

Below is his parting speech and the response of Nichola, the Bolton textile artist that viewers voted to evict rather than Nick.

Use these to make assessments of the character and feelings of the two people involved, then write a short story revealing what happens when the two housemates meet again 'in real life', outside the house.

[Nick sits back in his chair, arms extended, and speaks in a flat monotone throughout apart from a slight rise–fall on the word 'horrible'. Nichola's body language is much freer, with sweeping movements of the arms at times.]

Nick: Um (1.0) I (.) shall (.) be leaving the house (1.0) in (.) about (.) 15 minutes (1.0) time (.) at 5 o'clock (2.0) um (1.0) I've broken a rule about speaking about nominations and therefore (1.0) I should have to face the consequences of that (2.0) I'm truly sorry and I wish all of you (1.0) the very best (2.0) in the future (3.0) I've made a mistake (1.0) I have to live by that mistake (1.0) and again I'm very sorry for what I did (3.0) it's made a nice stay here (1.0) horrible.

[Embarrassed and visibly moved, his housemates embrace him one by one and wish him good luck. Nichola, the next to be nominated for eviction after Nick, is asked by the programme presenter how she feels after Nick's public humiliation.]

Nichola: Em (1.0) it was horrible (.) it was horrible because none of us in the house (1.0) we all find (.) being in the house (1.0) is such like a har- it's like a traumatizing situation to be there anyway (.) so actually to throw one out by the back door was like this is really significant and like the 'eavens hopened and . . .

Presenter: Were you worried about him?

Nichola: Yeah (1.0) of course I was (1.0) it's like a human being (1.0) like the rest of us (1.0) it doesn't matter what goes on in people's lives (1.0) things happen for a reason (2.0) he did that for a reason maybe because under pressure from like being in boarding schools and that other . . .

Presenter: So you can sympath- you know – understand him a little bit?

Nichola: Of course (1.0) we can all sympathize (.) of course.

Presenter: Would you get in touch with him now you're out?

Nichola: Yes of course I will.

Presenter: Would you?

Nichola: Yes of course I will.

Presenter: OK (.) Now . . .

Nichola: He's not committed a crime (.) he 'as like broken rules from Big Brother (1.0) he's not committed . . .

Presenter: Well (.) I think you're a very big-hearted girl.

Nichola: No (.) he's not committed a crime . . .

Index

A

Abstract nouns 105
  derived from Latin 87–88
  in informative prose 139–140
  in literary writing 225
Accent 47, 52–54
  gender and social class 58
  RP as the norm 52
  RP and regional accents 52–54
  social prestige 56
Acquisition of language 30, 32–35
Active voice 108
Adjectival clauses 123
Adjectives 106–107
  inflections in Old English 97
  remaining inflections 101
Adverbial clauses 124–125
Adverbs 108–9
Advertising, language of 186–191
  anchorage 188
  creative use of language 190
  diction 188
  disjunctive grammar 189
  rule-breaking 143–145
  stereotyping 187
Alliteration 190
Anglo-Saxon basis of English 79
  inflections of 95–99
Articles 111–112
Audience 243, 245
Audience design 168
  in broadcasting 181–185
  in newspapers 168–175
Auxiliary verbs 107

B

Babbling 31
Bias see *Connotation*
Black English 69–76
Body language see *Paralinguistic features*

C

Chancery spellings 219
Chomsky's Innatist theory 32
Clause analysis 115–129
  usefulness of 130
Clauses, arrangement within sentences 135–136
  categories of 115–117, 120–125
  length within sentences 133–135

Clichés 171
Colloquial language 248–249
  in newspapers 170
Completers 116
Complex sentences 120
  complex complex sentences 127
  handling of 127
  literary varieties 199–205
  match with complex vocabulary 136
  punctuation of 125
Composite sentences 127
Compound sentences 117
Conjunctions 111–112
Connotation 172
Consonants 63
  phonetic symbols for 60–62
  in RP and regional dialects 66–68
Content words 137–138
Context 243, 245
Conversation 10–20
  children's versus adult 18
  controlling conventions 12
  Grice's rules 11
  Lakoff's rules 11
  male and female 18–20
  repairs 14
  underlying principles of 10–12
Cooing, babies' 31
Creole 69
  age and gender 71
  correctness of 73
  Jamaican 70
  modified 72
  as subversive technique 73–74

D

Declension in Old English 96
Definite article 111–112
Denotation 172
Dependent clause 115, 120
  categories of 122–125
  function of 121
Dialect 47–60
  gender and social class 58–60
  regional variations in 49–51
  social prestige of 56–57
  standardization of 228
Diction, current trends in 230–235
  abstraction 233–234
  euphemisms 234–235
  neologisms 235–236
  political correctness 230–233
Diphthongs, phonetic symbols for 63
Discourse interaction see *Conversation*

Disjunctive grammar 189
Divergence of speech 183

E
Electronic media, language of 192
 e-mail 192–193
 text-messaging 193–194
Emotive language
 in advertising 188
 in newspapers 171
English
 Anglo-Saxon basis of 79
 arrival in Britain of 78
 as world language 89
 Black 69–74
 family background of 77
 heterogeneous nature of 85
 lost grammar of 95
 sounds of 60–65
 spoken and written, relative values of 20
 suprasegmental features of 21, 32
Euphemisms 234–235

F
Fillers, role in speech 9
Flesch Reading Ease Test 133
Fog index 136
Four-letter words 80
Frameworks 243
French see *Loan words*

G
Gender 97
 accent and dialect 58
 language of 161–162
 lost inflections for 100
 male-as-norm syndrome 162–165
 male control through language 166–167
 titles and naming 165
Genre 243, 245
Glottal stop 64
Glue words see *Structure words*
Grammar 104
 appropriate versus correct 142
 current trends in 236–238
 essential points of 132–133
 grammatical characteristics of good writing 133–135
 introduction to 95
Graphology 251
Greek (see also *Loan words*)
 elements in English 89–92
Grice's rules of conversation 11

I
Iambic metre 191
Imagery 211–215
Indefinite article 111–112
Independent main clause 115
Indo-European family of languages 77–78
Infinitives, split 142
Inflections in Old English 95–99
  levelling of 99
  loss of 100
    advantages of 103
    disadvantages of 104
  remaining in modern English 101–102
Insulting terms, male language 166–167
International Phonetic Alphabet 60–64
Intonation, speech 24–28
IPA see *International Phonetic Alphabet*
Irony 206–208
  as stylistic device 208
  distinguished from sarcasm 207

J
Jamaican creole see *Creole*
Jargon 247

L
Language
  acquisition of 30–36
  current trends in 230–239
Latin (see also *Loan words*)
  elements in English 89–92
Layout, newspapers 168
Legalese 245
Loan words
  French 81–82
  Greek 83
  Latin 85–89
  Old Norse 80–81

M
Magazine style 177–178
  gender 178–180
  the youth market 180–181
Male-as-norm syndrome 162–165
Marriage and female identity 165–166
Media, language of 168
Meaning (see also *Semantics*)
  affective 156
  associative 153
  penumbral 155–156
  pragmatic 154
  propositional 154–155
  prosodic 153–154
  sentence 153

words and referents 149–151
words as a closed system 151
Metaphor 211
in conversation 211–212
in literature 212–214
distinguished from simile 213
extended 214
Metonymy 215
distinguished from metaphor 215
overlapping with synecdoche 215
Middle English 82
Modes of address 181–182, 221–222
Multiple complex sentences 126

N
Newspaper writing 168–175
block language 175
buzzwords 170
denotation and connotation 172–173
diction 170–172
exclusive and inclusive reporting 173–174
grammar 174
personalization 172
stereotyping 174
typography 169
white space 258
Noun clauses 122–123
Nouns 105
Anglo-Saxon 79–80
inflections in Old English 96–97
lost inflections 100
parts of speech 105
remaining inflections 101
Nomination 35
Number, Old English verbs 98

O
Old English see *Anglo-Saxon*
Old Norse 80–81
Onset, speech 25

P
Paralinguistic features 15
Parallel phrasing 191
Parsing 104, 114–115
usefulness of 130
Participles 128
misuse in phrases 129
Parts of speech 104–113
prescriptive approach to 113
versatility of 112
Passive voice 108
in informative prose 140–141
Patois see *Creole*

Patronizing terms 166–167
Patterned sound, advertising 190–191
Pidgins 69
Phonetic symbols 60–64
Phonological change in Received Pronunciation 56–57, 64–65, 238–239
Phrases 115, 128–129
  and economy of expression 128–129
  in apposition 128
  misuse with participles 129
Pitch 24
Politeness 11
Political correctness 230–233
Positive feedback 15
Pragmatics 154
Prefixes, Latin and Greek 89–90
Prepositions 110–111
Prescriptivist attitudes
  to creole 73
  to dialect 56
  to grammar 104
  to parts of speech 113
  to vocabulary 93
Prestige, dialect and accent 56
Pronouns 105–106
  inflections in Old English 96–97
  lost inflections 100
  remaining inflections 102
Proto-words 32
Punctuation
  in complex sentences 125–127
  in compound sentences 118–119
  in simple sentences 116–117
Puns 171
Purpose 243–244

R

Received Pronunciation 52–54, 56
  sounds of 64–66
Referee design 184
Referent 149–150
Regional accents 52–53, 65–68
Register 243, 245–247
Repairs, conversational 14
Rhythm 23
Roots, Latin and Greek 90–91
RP see *Received Pronunciation*

S

Sarcasm 206–208
Scientific register 245–246
Semantics 149–157
Semi-colon in compound sentences 118–119
Sensationalism 171
Sentence categories

in informative prose 115, 117, 120, 127
in literature 196, 199–205
Sentence stress 22
Sentence structure (see also *Clause analysis*)
changes over time 224
meaning and style 195–205
peculiar to speech 7
transformation 38
Simile see *Metaphor*
Simple sentence 115
in informative prose 119–120
in literature 196–199
punctuation of 116–117
Skinner's Behaviourist theory 33
Slang 73–74, 247, 249
Social class, accent and dialect 56–58
Social life, titles and naming 166–167
Sound-patterning 191
Sounds
of International Phonetic Alphabet 60–64
of Received Pronunciation 64–65
of regional dialects 65–68
Speech
acquisition of 30–45
characteristic features at different stages 39–41
checklist of features 39–42
children's learning strategies 36
Chomsky's Innatist theory 32
cognitive basis of speech 35
grammar 37–39
Interactionist theories 34
sentence transformation 38
Skinner's Behaviourist theory 33
role of fillers in 9
role in learning foreign language 6
sentence structures peculiar to 7
suprasegmental features of 21, 32
unconscious rules governing 7
value of, relative to writing 20
Standard English 47, 49–51, 228
Standardization of dialects 228
Stream of consciousness technique 145–146
Stress 21–22
in advertising 192
in sentences 22
Strike 220
Strong verbs 108
Structure words 137
constructions creating 138–141
Style (see also *Register*)
categories of 247–250
Subject nouns 138–139
false subjects 138–139
Subordinate clause see *Dependent clause*

Suprasegmental features 21, 32
Synecdoche 215
Syntax 104

T
Talk shows
  radio 183–184
  television 185
Technical register 245–246
Tempo, speech 29
Tenses, Old English verbs 97
Text 243
Tone unit 24
Tonic syllable 24–25
Turn-taking, conversational 13

V
Verbs 107
  inflections in Old English 97–98
  lost inflections 100
  remaining inflections 102
  strong and weak 108
Virgule 220
Vocabulary
  in complex sentences 136
  Latinate 85–88
  prescriptive attitude towards 93
  style 80–81, 82, 85–88
Voices, of verbs 108
Vowels, phonetic symbols for 62

W
Weak verbs 108
Word play 171, 190–191
Word stress 21–22
Work titles 166
Writing
  breaking the rules
    in advertising 143–145
    in literature 145–148
  children's 45
  good, grammatical characteristics of 133–135
  value of, relative to speech 20

Y
Ynkhorne termes 225